W9-ARM-171

Wellington and Waterloo

Wellington and Waterloo

The Duke, The Battle and Posterity

R.E. FOSTER

Cover illustrations
Front: Field Marshal Sir Arthur Wellesley (1769-1852) 1st Duke of Wellington, c.1840 (oil on canvas), Haydon, Benjamin Robert (1786-1846). (National Army Museum, London / The Bridgeman Art Library) *Back:* Front page from a late-Victorian toy theatre game by Benjamin Pollock. (Author's collection)

First Published 2014
by Spellmount, an imprint of The History Press
The Mill, Brimscombe Port
Stroud, Gloucestershire, GL5 2QG
www.thehistorypress.co.uk

British Library Cataloguing in Publication Data.
A catalogue record for this book is available from the British Library.

ISBN 978 0 7524 8877 6

Typesetting and origination by The History Press
Printed in Great Britain

Contents

Abbreviations		7
Preface and Acknowledgements		8
Introduction: Perceptions and Perspectives		11
1	Before Waterloo: Battles for Recognition 1769–1815	23
2	Waterloo: The Battle of Giants	47
3	The Battle of Posterity: Opening Shots 1815–1818	72
4	Heroes and Villains: Wellington, Waterloo and other Battles 1819–1832	103
5	Wellington and Waterloo Despatched 1832–1852?	133
6	Victorians Remember: Wellington and Waterloo Reassessed 1852–1901	164
7	Battling into Posterity: Wellington and Waterloo 1901–2015	194
Select Bibliography		224
Notes		233
Index		253

Abbreviations

Arbuthnot   Francis Bamford & 7th Duke of Wellington (eds.), *The Journal of Mrs Arbuthnot 1820–1832.*

Creevey   Sir Herbert Maxwell (ed.), *The Creevey Papers.*

Chad   7th Duke of Wellington (ed.), *The Conversations of the 1st Duke of Wellington with George William Chad.*

Croker   Louis J. Jennings (ed.), *The Croker Papers.*

Ellesmere   Alice, Countess of Strafford (ed.), *Personal Reminiscences of the 1st Duke of Wellington by Francis, the 1st Earl of Ellesmere.*

Fraser   Sir William Fraser, *Words on Wellington.*

ODNB   H. C. G. Matthew & Brian Harrison (eds.), *Oxford Dictionary of National Biography.*

PD   *Parliamentary Debates.*

Shelley   Richard Edgcumbe (ed.), *The Diary of Frances, Lady Shelley 1818–1873.*

Stanhope   Philip Henry, 5th Earl Stanhope, *Notes of Conversations with the Duke of Wellington 1831–1851.*

WD   J. Gurwood (ed.), *The Despatches of Field-Marshal the Duke of Wellington, KG, during his various campaigns [...] from 1799 to 1818.*

WP   University of Southampton Library, MS 61, Wellington Papers.

WS   2nd Duke of Wellington (ed.), *Supplementary Despatches and Memoranda of Field-Marshal Arthur Duke of Wellington, KG.*

Preface and Acknowledgements

As a young boy, the first serious history book I bought was John Naylor's *Waterloo*. At senior school, in Taunton, I was in Blackdown House, which took its name from the Somerset hills nearby. Surmounting them is a triangular obelisk to the Iron Duke overlooking the town from which he took his title. Unthinkingly, at home, on my parents' farm, I daily donned the footwear indelibly associated with his name. In the early 1980s, having completed my undergraduate degree at Southampton, I was lucky enough to be the recipient of a major state studentship from the British Academy. Serendipitously, the Wellington Papers were then in the process of being deposited in the University's Hartley Library. The resulting doctoral thesis, on the Duke's Lord Lieutenancy of Hampshire, appeared in book form in 1990. By then, I had embarked upon a teaching career, one which included withdrawing an application I had submitted to Wellington College: if you are not careful, you can become obsessive. Twenty years later, however, my wife indulged me, by taking me to Brussels to mark a personal milestone. This allowed me to realise a long-standing ambition in visiting the iconic campaign sites of 1815. It is no exaggeration to say that the present book originated from what I saw and felt that day. I am grateful to Alan Lindsey who guided us with such informed enthusiasm on that occasion.

My day at Waterloo, on 23 October 2011, crystallised thoughts that had been lurking in my mind for some time. I did not want to write an analysis of the battle or a guide to the field. Neither did I aspire to produce a biography of the Duke. Readers will find that my brief account of the campaign occurs in chapter two, whilst the Duke dies at the end of chapter five! Insofar as it is possible with such well-trodden paths, I wanted to take a different tack. Specifically, with the bicentenary of Waterloo imminent, I wanted to discover how the intertwined stories of the battle and its victor had been perceived in the intervening 200 years. The present book is primarily an exploration of reputations and memories. I am grateful to The History Press for having the confidence in me to carry it out, especially Jo de Vries, head of publishing, and Rebecca Newton, my project editor.

Research for those who are not tenured academics is hugely dependent upon the support of others. It is no exaggeration to say that I could not even have contemplated writing the current book without the exponential advance of online resources over the past decade. I have been enormously indebted to Project Gutenberg and the American University Online Library: they have made available in seconds many essential titles which would have been difficult or prohibitively expensive to obtain. No less a debt is due to those who have seen fit to digitise Hansard's *Parliamentary Debates* and a portion of the British Library's newspaper archives for the nineteenth century. The digital archive of *The Times* has proved similarly indispensable.

My obligation to more traditional repositories remains, first and foremost, that to Professor Chris Woolgar and his colleagues in the Hartley Library at Southampton responsible for its Special Collections. I would also like to thank the friendly, helpful staff of the Templer Research Centre at the National Army Museum. Closer to home, I have had full value for my Council Tax payments by making regular use of the reference section in Salisbury City Library and Wiltshire Libraries' online facilities. Helen Cunliffe has endeared herself as an assiduous school librarian in regularly demonstrating to me the truth that one should never discard old volumes.

As the writing has progressed, Phil Badham has tolerated my technophobia with unfailing patience. In like vein, Sam Cox of Wiltshire Graphic Design has been generous with help and advice for the maps, whilst Melanie Jeffery has promptly answered queries relating to sources in French. I am also grateful to those who have read and criticised part or whole of successive chapter drafts: Isabella Dodkins, David Jones (whose sharp eye and sense of grammar and style have saved me from many infelicities of both), Dr Richard A. Gaunt of Nottingham University, and Professor Mike Clark of Southampton University. I am especially indebted to the latter for several stimulating conversations about methodology and the nature of memory.

At a late stage, Dr Rory Muir very generously read the entire text and diplomatically highlighted a number of egregious errors. I regret that the first volume of his monumental biography of Wellington appeared in print too late for me to be able to use.

My children, Susanna and Edmund, have acted as harsh and unrestrained critics, in a way that only one's offspring can. By far my greatest debt, however, in this project as in life, is to my wife, Michaela. She has accepted, with typical generosity, my unreasonable requests for her to be reader, creator of maps and financial support. She may not believe that I am more consumed by her than with the Duke and his battle, but it is true. The errors and faults of the book are mine; any merits, and the dedication, are hers.
Waterloo Day, 2013.

Introduction

Perceptions and Perspectives

In the parish of North Newton with St Michael Church in Somerset where I grew up, there is a memorial to Sir John Slade (1762–1859). Slade joined the 10th Light Dragoons in 1790. By April 1809 he was a Major-General. Briefly, from January–March 1811, he commanded the cavalry in Wellington's army in the Peninsular War. Aficionados of that conflict know him by his sobriquet, 'Black Jack'. Both scholars and writers of historical fiction are agreed that he was 'as incompetent an officer as ever was placed in command of a brigade of cavalry, and a coward, too, by common consent'. The Duke sent him back to England, a prime example of the sort of officers that frightened him more than they did the enemy. Slade's memorial in Norton Fitzwarren church says that he 'descended to the Tomb full of years and universally respected'. The epitaph could only possibly be true because Wellington had predeceased him.[1]

Slade, consequently, was not with the Duke at Waterloo. He thereby missed being part of an action that many immediately hailed as analogous to being with Henry V at Agincourt almost exactly 400 years before. As soon as he heard the news, Lord Stewart was 'deeply mortified that my Lot did not lead me to share a part in the splendid triumph that has added new lustre to the British Name'. The passage of years only served to reinforce such feelings for those under arms but not actually at Mont St Jean on 18 June 1815. Major-General Peter Fyers saw fifty-three years' service in the Royal Artillery and could boast of being known to both Nelson and William IV: when he died in 1845 it was recorded that, 'to his unceasing regret' he had missed Waterloo.[2] By then, memorials to both Wellington and Waterloo were seemingly ubiquitous, but where the national Waterloo memorial stands, is a moot point. The imagination of posterity has been captured no less forcibly. Google, to take one ephemeral example, lists over 14,000 results for The Wellington Arms and over 15,000 for The Waterloo Inn. Given his frustration over the ill-discipline arising from the evils of drink amongst his men, and his subsequent fear that beer houses were breeding grounds for sedition, the Duke would have been appalled. Neither would he have been impressed that the most common Internet search for Waterloo today is for Waterloo Road, since 2006 a television drama about a challenging Scottish comprehensive school. If nothing else, it affords an example of how the name of a small Belgian town has become an integral part of British culture; or, as Robert Southey put it in 1816:

A little lowly place,
Obscure till now, when it hath risen to fame,
And given the victory its English name.[3]

Waterloo also triggered an avalanche of writing: in 1815 alone, there were at least seventy titles relating to it. Sir John Fortescue pointed out a century ago that the many accounts since had been 'more prolific of new conjectures than of new facts'. Despite what he implied, the essence of many of the conjectures too, was in print within two years of the battle having taken place. There was some truth in Wellington's 1817 complaint that 'every creature who could afford it, travelled to the field; and almost everyone who could write, wrote an account'.[4] Nor, surely, is it coincidental that it was Philip Guedalla, biographer of the Duke and historian of the Hundred Days, who coined the aphorism that, 'History repeats itself. Historians repeat each other.' In 1986, Donald Horward's bibliographical study listed over 2,000 books on the campaign and battle. A search of the forty-eight titles comprising the British Library's nineteenth-century newspapers online website yields 150,000 results for the 'Duke of Wellington' and over half a million for 'Waterloo'.

Why so many? Even in 1815 the broad outlines of an answer to this question were clear. A British commander and his army had first withstood, and then repulsed, one of the greatest commanders and armies of any age. In doing so, they had epitomised the supposed national virtues of endurance and tenacity. Waterloo also, in its decisiveness, provided an appropriately dramatic final scene to the great drama that was the generation of struggle that had followed the French Revolution. One participant in the battle was therefore right to suggest that, 'Many a battle had been fought in the Peninsula with as much credit and bravery, but there was a combination of circumstances at Waterloo which gave éclat irresistible.' Victor Hugo memorably called it the hinge of the nineteenth century.[5]

Contemporaries, as Wellington had noted, consequently wanted to visit the scene of the action. Viscount Palmerston, Secretary at War, stopped off at Quatre Bras and Waterloo en route from Namur to Brussels on 29 October 1818. With a dose of characteristic cynicism, he reported to his sister how:

> by the assistance of a good plan and description and some peasants we met on the ground, we satisfied ourselves completely about Waterloo – walked over the position of our army, picked some bullets out of the orchards of La Haie Sainte and Hougoumont, cut a bundle of sticks at the latter enough to beat [c]lothes with during the rest of our lives, bought [a] French sword which probably never [saw] the battle, and came on here b[y] ½ past 8 this evening.[6]

Maps, guides, and mementoes of doubtful provenance were already, as they remain, established ingredients of the Waterloo tourist industry.

One early visitor, James Simpson, rejected the suggestion that he was a tourist. He conceived of himself as a pilgrim, for whom visiting the battlefield was a quasi-religious act: 'The very ground,' he wrote, 'was hallowed and it was trod by us with respect and gratitude.' Even more, however, he insisted he and his fellow travellers were patriots: 'Multitudes, impelled by an interest which would unworthily be called mere curiosity, crowded the packets to Belgium, eager to see a field so near and so recent, to learn the tale on the spot and to breathe the very air of a region shining with their country's glory and resounding with their country's praise.'[7] High-minded in the view of Simpson, such feelings could easily degenerate into a baser national chauvinism. Rees Gronow, in his reminiscences of the battle acknowledged as much, and rather unconvincingly denied 'any share in the vulgar John Bull exultation which glories in having "licked the confounded French."' No British contemporary, however, bettered the surgeon Charles Bell in capturing the contradictory emotions of revulsion and horror that was the reality for so many at Waterloo on the one hand, and the tsunami of relief and exultation that greeted news of the victory at home on the other.

Bell spent eight days tending casualties of the battle before visiting the scene
of it:

> The view of the field [he wrote] the gallant stories, the charges, the individual
> instances of enterprise and valour, recalled me to the sense which the world
> has of 'Victory' and 'Waterloo'. But this was transient: a glooming, uncontrol-
> lable view of human nature is the inevitable consequence of looking upon
> the whole as I did – as I was forced to do. It is a misfortune to have our senti-
> ments so at variance with the universal sentiment. But there must ever be
> associated with the horrors of Waterloo, to my eyes, the most shocking signs
> of woe – to my ear, accents of entreaty, outcry from the manly beast, inter-
> rupted by forcible expressions of the dying – and noisome smells.[8]

Bell, as he recognised, was decidedly untypical of his countrymen in his
balancing of the emotions. Waterloo was, and is, remembered less for the
blood than the victory. As the historian Denis Richards wrote with dismiss-
ive accuracy during a 1952 spat over casualty numbers during the Battle of
Britain: 'Napoleon lost the battle of Waterloo: who remembers the casualties?'[9] The fact does much to explain why the balance in the unending
struggle between those who would see the battlefield as a site of remembrance and those who see it as a tourist attraction (in stark contrast, it might
be noted, to the Great War battlefields), has always lain with the latter.

Waterloo, with the passage of time, would also be remembered as
much for what it began as for what it ended. Late in life, a former pupil
at Kimbolton School recalled that the severe English and boarding master,
George Cole, had ordered a half-holiday when news of the victory reached
him: 'There was no more work that day, and though most of us were too
young fully to appreciate the effects of the victory, the joy on everyone's
countenance [was] [...] sufficient to impress us with the fact that the event
was of great and vital importance to the country.' What that importance
consisted of is a theme of the present study. For Sir Edward Creasy, writing
in 1851, only weeks after the Great Exhibition had opened, the salient fact
was that, 'No equal number of years can be found, during which science,
commerce, and civilisation have advanced so rapidly and so extensively, as
has been the case since 1815.' He judged the peace that Waterloo heralded
as the precondition for what he described. For that reason, he continued, it
'deserves to be regarded by us, not only with peculiar pride, as one of our
greatest national victories, but with peculiar gratitude for the repose which

it secured for us, and for the greater part of the human race'. For various reasons, however, as will be seen, the celebrations of a great national victory were about to end. Two centuries on, the sober conclusion of the best modern guide to the battlefield judges merely that Waterloo 'was a blood-soaked milestone on the long and tortuous road called progress'.[10] But even this is debatable. What Waterloo means has evolved with time; it remains elusive and chameleon-like. Perhaps it is still too soon to tell.

That Waterloo was somehow special, if only for those who were there, can surely be agreed. As Sir William Fraser put it nearly seventy-five years later, 'Waterloo gave a patent of Nobility to all who were present. So long as Britain shall exist, a man who can trace his ancestry to one who fought at Waterloo will have a position of distinction.' Whilst Wellington was alive, the distinction was commemorated each 18 June at Apsley House by the dinner he gave to surviving officers. Whilst many will be aware of that event, the ways in which Britons generally remembered Waterloo and those who fought in the battle have attracted far less attention. It is something the present study attempts to rectify. Suffice for the moment to say that the nation, though it lauded Waterloo men far more than the veterans of earlier conflicts, fell well short of what Fraser claimed. Returning home, Captain Cavalié Mercer remembered, with some bitterness, that he and his men had first had to endure several hours off Dover harbour because of bad weather before being ferried ashore by a pilot-gig whose 'fellows charged us a guinea a-head for thus carrying us about 200 yards'. Many thereafter did, it is true, became local celebrities. Corporal John Dickson, the last survivor of the charge of the Scots Greys who settled in Crail, Fifeshire, spent 18 June 1855 in the coffee room of his local inn, clay pipe in hand, ready to recount his Waterloo story to both habitués and visitors. This was not unique 'for, be it known, "Waterloo Day" was a high day in the village, kept in ripe memory by the flags flying and the procession of school children, decked in summer attire and gay with flowers, to do honour to "mine host", whose deeds of valour were on every tongue'.[11]

Not all, however, could boast as distinguished a service record as Dickson. Growing up in Stow-on-the-Wold in the early 1860s, W. J. Rylance remembered a six-foot dragoon called 'Long Charlie', whose chief memory of the battle was the 'unhorsing and killing of a French officer, but [he] was most proud of the watch and money he took from his pockets'. Rylance remembered that after Waterloo, Charlie was 'hawker or poacher by turns, a regular old reprobate, but to me always a hero'. Waterloo may have set him apart but he hardly lived a life of virtue and, as the following chapters demonstrate, his example was very far from being the worst. Most Waterloo men, however, simply led unremarkable lives, many continuing in the army after 1815. William Thackeray, writing before his novel, *Vanity Fair* (set against the backdrop of Waterloo), brought him lasting fame, had strong views as to how the latter were neglected by their country. He did not:

> know whether to respect them or to wonder at them. They have death, wounds, poverty, hard labour, hard fare, and small thanks [...] if they are heroes, heroes they may be, but they remain privates still, handling the old brown-bess, starving on the old twopence a day. They grow grey in battle and victory, and after thirty years of bloody service, a young gentleman of fifteen [...] calmly takes the command over our veteran, who obeys him as if God and nature had ordained that so throughout time it should be.[12]

The better-known Waterloo veterans today were those who aspired to an audience beyond the alehouse by writing about their experiences of the campaign. Far more wrote letters, many in response to William Siborne, who solicited them from surviving officers for the endeavours that were to make him the unofficial doyen of Waterloo studies during Wellington's lifetime. Such letters reveal an extraordinary range of perceptions about what was going on throughout 18 June. They also exhibit a considerable variation, on the part of those who wrote them, as to how accurate they believed themselves to be. Writing in 1835, for example, Lieutenant-Colonel Dirom said he could remember 1815 'as if it had only occurred yesterday'. A fortnight later, Lieutenant William Fricke of the 1st Light Dragoons, King's German Legion, asked Siborne to 'excuse me if my description is faulty, to which a 20-year gap contributes greatly' – quite apart from the practical difficulties of the day which he spelt out with wry irony: 'An elevation in front of us hindered us completely from taking note of the positions of the French army, because we were unable to see it, except when we charged, but such a moment was not suitable for taking notes.'[13] Fricke's comments are a salutary reminder. The discrepancies and uncertainties in the story of Waterloo have provoked many allegations about personal bias and national posturing: many of them are to be explained by the honest disagreement arising from conflicting testimony.

The latter points can be illustrated by brief reference to the biggest of all Waterloo controversies, the contribution of the Prussians to Wellington's victory. Stationed on the Duke's left for much of the battle, Sir Hussey Vivian witnessed something of the impact they were making upon the French rear, and their arrival on the Anglo-Allied left. He was adamant in 1837 that, 'I care not what any one may say to depreciate the importance of the Prussian aid [...] but for that aid our advance never would have taken place [...] it's not fair not to give it its due weight and the Prussians their due credit.' For 'FM' of the Guards, by contrast, writing on Waterloo Day 1866, the perspective had been very different. Positioned on Wellington's right, he first saw Prussians at about 9 p.m. when the French were in headlong retreat:

> Blücher came up at the time above indicated and took the front – not till then, however, as some would have it. I have been told that the Prussians fought side by side with us on that memorable day. Such, however, was not the case. I never saw the Prussians until we had beaten the Invincible Guards. They came up at that time, and not before.[14]

Then and now, how you see Waterloo depends upon where you stand.

Wellington, the best known British witness, knew where he stood. He said so in his Waterloo Despatch of 19 June. Long experience had made him adept in this most demanding of official forms of communication. As early as June 1809, he had taken strong exception when he heard of alleged remarks made by Samuel Whitbread in Parliament to the effect that he had lied in his accounts of the most recent actions:

> I am not in the habit of sending exaggerated accounts of transactions of this kind. In the first place, I don't see what purpose accounts of that description are to answer; and in the second place, the Army must eventually see them; they are most accurate criticks: I should certainly forfeit their good opinion most justly if I wrote a false account even of their actions, and nothing should induce me to take any step which should with justice deprive me of that advantage.[15]

But Wellington clearly knew, in modern parlance, how to spin. After the indecisive Battle of Albuera in 1811, he instructed Marshal Beresford to 'write me down a victory'. He also conceded that some of his despatches contained omissions; brevity was a means to the end of being the soul of discretion. As he told Lord Hatherton in May 1820:

I never told a falsehood in them, but I never told the whole truth, nor anything like it. Either one or the other would have been contradicted by 5,000 officers in my army in their letters to their mothers, wives, brothers or sisters and cousins, all of whom imagined they as well understood what they saw as I did.[16]

Wellington was clear, however, that those officers' accounts, let alone those of the men they commanded, must be inferior to his own. In a much repeated metaphor, he reflected that:

The history of a battle is not unlike the history of a ball. Some individuals may recollect all the little events of which the great result is the battle won or lost; but no individual can recollect the order in which, nor the exact moment at which, they occurred, which makes all the difference as to their value or importance.[17]

Wellington judged, not without some reason, that if anybody was to attempt such an exercise successfully, it was him. He did, after all, combine experience with the liberty to roam the field, and was served by a staff whose job was to keep him informed as to how events were unfolding.

To pursue the ballroom metaphor, however, the Duke said nothing about the role of his dancing partners. Were not Napoleon and Blücher as entitled as he was to adjudicate on the course of events? Whilst the present study concerns itself primarily with the British perspective on Waterloo, it is important to remember that there are French and Prussian ones, arguably no less valid. French apologists for their defeat were legion: in 1846, the British press published a sardonic piece entitled 'What the French say of the Battle of Waterloo', which adduced no fewer than twelve reasons in mitigation or exculpation, including the militarily-more-than-dubious one that they had not lost! The French, understandably, remain sensitive on the subject: in 1998 a Paris councillor wrote to Tony Blair demanding that Britain rename its Eurostar terminus at Waterloo station. And whilst long-standing Anglo-French rivalries were reinforced by Waterloo, Anglo-German ones over who, precisely, had won the battle were created by it. The marriage of the 8th Duke of Wellington's heir to a great-granddaughter of Kaiser Wilhelm II in 1977 did at last suggest that a belle alliance between the two sides had finally been reached – though only on a personal level.[18]

Aspersions denigrating Wellington's achievement at Waterloo, whether emanating from French or Prussian sources, could be guaranteed to rally

Britons to the defence of their most famous living son.[19] He was the subject of approximately 1,400 titles during the nineteenth century. He also appears in about 5 per cent of the British Museum's collection of caricatures, not to mention over 300 paintings and drawings, and 180 published engravings. The Duke, as has been insufficiently acknowledged, was the creation of the media. It could hardly be otherwise for he became famous in absentia. Wellington could not really be said to be living permanently in mainland Britain until the end of 1818. Before then, the public face of Wellington was the product of a blank canvas on which his character had been imagined or, if the sources were his friends, as they wanted it to appear. The public persona was not, of course, entirely divorced from reality, but the real human being that was the Duke was revealed slowly, at first to an elite inner circle, and only really more completely, as will be seen, through them after his death. In life, the person he most resembles in British public life today is Her Majesty Queen Elizabeth II: forever in the public gaze and at the public service, but hardly a rounded personality: at once both universally known and yet unknown.

The Queen's reputation rests, in part, on her being set above the political fray. Much the same has been said for Wellington; indeed he claimed it for himself. Whilst the notion is not without some substance, it is also, paradoxically, bogus. Uniquely amongst modern Britons, the Duke chose to follow his exalted military career with an even longer one in the higher reaches of public life. Wellington's name, therefore, at least as much as that of his most famous battle, carried political connotations for his contemporaries. His second career, as chapters four and five attempt to show, was bound both to inform and colour perceptions of his earlier one. The British public was far less agreed about what it thought of the political as opposed to the military Duke. He was seen as being on the 'wrong' side of popular opinion, at least during the Reform Bill era. His longevity was such that he survived the resulting unpopularity to pass his last years as father of the nation, something akin to a mid-nineteenth-century Nelson Mandela. But he was, and remains, political. Just prior to elections for the Scottish Parliament in 2003, one SNP candidate called on Edinburgh City Council to remove the Duke's statue and replace it with one of Robert Burns, since Wellington's 'says nothing distinctive or relevant about Edinburgh and Scotland now'. The call was seen as anti-English and rightly attacked as an insult to those Scots who had fought and died under Wellington.[20] Neither side, however, seemed aware that he was Irish.

Another claim made by the Duke, which many modern writers accept, was that he 'had made it a rule never to read any work whatever bearing on his military career'. He went even further in 1847, when he wrote to J. W. Croker that, 'It has always been my practice, and is my invariable habit, to say nothing about myself or my own actions.'[21] The opposite would be nearer the truth. At the very least, there were those around him, for example Colonel Gurwood, Mrs Arbuthnot and Earl Stanhope (formerly Lord Mahon), who informed him about recent publications and opinions, if only to elicit his response. Stanhope noted that the Duke spent an hour and a half with him in 1836 discussing Robert Southey's history of the Peninsular War. In December 1851, the last letter Stanhope ever received from Wellington was one thanking him for recommending that he read volume 11 of Thiers's *History of the French Revolution*. Within hours he had done so – and reported that it 'appears to be very interesting'. The evidence that Wellington was a voracious reader about himself, including at Waterloo, is overwhelming; he even annotated some of the books whose perceived falsehoods irritated him most.[22]

And, contrary to what he wrote to Croker, the Duke was also a great talker. Ellesmere's daughter recalled hearing how Wellington had attended a dinner at Lord Glenelg's 'in company with several young officers, whom after dinner the Duke invited to ask him any questions they pleased as to his old campaigns'. Ellesmere himself was treated to a personal account of Burgos as he drove over from Basingstoke to Stratfield Saye with the Duke in February 1836. Charles Greville, who was one of those at Burghley with the Duke for New Year 1838, recorded that he spoke at length about the Peninsular War when they were out shooting. 'It is impossible to convey an idea of the zest, eagerness, frankness, and abundance with which he talked, and told of his campaigns, or how interesting it was to hear him.'[23]

Wellington was not so much lying when he denied reading and talking about his heroic past as making a distinction between official pronouncements and off-the-record conversations. He never presumed that those listening would be so ungentlemanly as to set down the detail of what they remembered him to have said. The present work endeavours, in showing Wellington as he was, as well as how he was perceived to be, to recognise that distinction. This perforce means returning to original sources of information and anecdotes. Too many lives of Wellington, to vulgarise Guedalla's epigram, simply regurgitate the more familiar tales, citing earlier biographies as their authority. That approach is eschewed here: hence the predominance

of contemporary as opposed to secondary sources in the notes. I trust that
the latter are not overly burdensome, but as I have frequently discovered in
my work on a man who has been the subject of so many stories, there is
nothing more irritating than an unreferenced bon mot. The result is a story
of Wellington and Waterloo that follows familiar broad outlines, but is told
with many less-familiar details.

A striking example of how this approach can yield fresh insights is an
anecdote mentioned in virtually every book on Wellington, his exchange
with the artist, Henry Pickersgill, as the latter was painting his portrait:

> Finding the Duke getting rather drowsy under the operation, he wished
> to excite his attention and thus give some expression to his face. He suc-
> ceeded only too well. Pickersgill said 'I have often wished to ask your Grace
> a question.' The Duke was far too prudent to say 'What is it?' 'Were you really
> surprised at Waterloo or not?' The Duke instantly replied 'No! but I am now.'[24]

Where modern books provide a citation for the story (usually reduced to
the final two sentences), it is invariably to Sir William Fraser's 1889 *Words
on Wellington*. As Fraser tells it, the story was obtained third hand from Lord
Wilton on 'one occasion' with the assurance that 'this version is absolutely
correct'. Something akin to it was indeed circulating in the press in 1844
when it was described as having taken place 'lately'.[25] In fact, Pickersgill had
been at Stratfield Saye working on his portrait a full decade before in the
autumn of 1834. And it was the artist himself who described what had happened only a few months later. It is worth citing *in extenso*:

> availing himself of one of those pauses which invariably succeed the with-
> drawal of the cloth from an English dining table, the worthy R. A. arose and
> assuming that solemnity of manner by which he is so peculiarly distinguished,
> begged leave to propound a query to his grace, obligingly intimating (as a
> merciful recorder will sometimes do to a culprit at the bar of the Old Bailey)
> that 'he need not reply to the question if it was at all disagreeable'. The duke,
> good-humouredly, begged him to proceed. All eyes were of course directed to
> the painter whose form appeared to dilate, and whose countenance became
> pregnant with the mighty secret he expected to fathom.
>
> 'And thrice he cleared his throat and then began.'
>
> 'Pray will your Grace be obliging enough to inform me, if it be really true,
> as has often been reported, that your grace was taken by surprise at Waterloo!'

So far from resenting this somewhat impertinent inquiry, the duke, as soon as he recovered from the fit of laughter into which it threw him, condescended to satisfy Mr Pickersgill, that he had not been guilty of the unsoldierlike neglect imputed to him, and that he might satisfy his inquiring friends, on his grace's authority, that he did not achieve the conquest of Waterloo by mistake.[26]

The earlier account does not alter the substantive point about Waterloo, but it is very different in detail and tone as regards the Duke. There was a Wellington who could be roused to laughter as well as one who could be reduced to fury. Privately, he laughed a lot. The late-Victorian public who read *Words on Wellington* in large numbers were more familiar with the terse iron persona that Fraser's book helped to consummate.

The Pickersgill anecdote demonstrates that Wellington, for all his expressed contempt of the media, was mindful of what we now call 'image' (though he would have preferred to call it 'honour'). He was after all, as he felt his critics often forgot, only human. When painting the Duke in 1824, Sir Thomas Lawrence proposed that his subject be depicted holding a pocket watch to signify his waiting for the Prussians. Wellington objected that this might suggest that he was anxious for their arrival and protested, 'That will never do. I was not waiting for the arrival of the Prussians at Waterloo. Put a telescope in my hand if you please.' Lawrence, like so many others, deferred to the great man, but his idea had clearly touched a sensitive nerve. Moreover, though he did not speak or write officially about the various controversies relating to his military career, the Duke was not above getting others to do so, on his behalf. He told Stanhope, in May 1834, that one reason he had not yet read Napier's *History of the War in the Peninsula* was that 'I might be tempted into contradicting him – into authorizing somebody to answer him for me.'[27] Understandably, nothing was more precious to his honour than Waterloo, which apotheosised both himself and his army. In the thirty-seven years following the battle he would defend his chosen position no less doggedly than the one he had assumed on 18 June 1815 – not least because, in the forty-six years leading up to Waterloo, his personal and political battles for recognition had been particularly hard fought.

1

Before Waterloo: Battles for Recognition 1769–1815

*E*arly in 1785, largely in an attempt to reduce living costs, the widowed Countess of Mornington went to live in Brussels. Accompanying her was her third son, the aimless 16-year-old Arthur Wellesley.[28] He would surely have spent some leisure time in the Forest of Soignes, nearly 30,000 acres of woodland extending over several miles south-east of the city to the village of Waterloo and beyond. Whether Arthur ventured that far, or further, to the hamlet of Mont St Jean, is uncertain. But since one of the major roads south from Brussels ran through the forest it would seem likely. In April 1815, the boy, now sure of his purpose, returned to Brussels as Duke of Wellington. A little over two months later, the army under his command won the decisive victory of Waterloo. One of the charges Napoleon levelled against his nemesis was that he took a great risk deploying his men in front of what Robert Southey described as, 'One gloomy, thick, impenetrable shade.' Wellington denied it. Writing in the 1840s, he claimed that he 'had a perfect knowledge, having seen it frequently, and of which no knowledge could have been had by any other officer in the Army'. This was surely a cryptic allusion to his sojourn in Brussels. But he did not elucidate. Similarly, he had little to say about his heading a brigade in Flanders in 1794–1795. It was, said *The Times* a month before Waterloo, 'a circumstance not generally known', that Wellington's first campaign had taken place in the Netherlands.[29] Like so much else in the Duke's early life, as he battled to win recognition, they were episodes that he chose to forget. Critics would charge that selective memory was a lifelong trait, which manifested itself in his last campaign too.

Wellington had been born in Dublin, probably on 1 May 1769. His parents were the unworldly Garret Wellesley, first Earl of Mornington, and Anne Hill, daughter of Viscount Dungannon. The man Victorians revered as the embodiment of Englishness was consequently Irish. Though the family traced its origins to Somerset, they had migrated to Ireland in the thirteenth century. By the eighteenth century, they were unexceptionable members of the Protestant Ascendancy. Yet Wellington never set foot in Ireland after 1809, and in his will of 1807 expressed the desire that his children neither live nor go there.[30] This conscious downplaying of his Irish, as opposed to his British, ancestry might be seen by critics as being all of a piece with his subsequent failure to afford due credit to the Prussians for the part they played in the triumph of the British Army in 1815.

But Wellington's life before 1815 should not be seen as one long inexorable preparation for the slopes of Mont St Jean. He was well into middle age by then, and had already been hailed as one of Britain's most distinguished warriors by dint of his achievements in the Peninsular War. These too, though, can easily be seen out of context, still more so his earlier years in India. Wellington was not so well known (at least, not so soon or as completely), to his countrymen as the familiar biographical approach might lead us to suppose. Neither were some of his accomplishments universally perceived as victories. This was partly a question of media. Looking back from the vantage point of the early 1860s, Rees Gronow rightly pointed out that:

> If the present generation of Englishmen would take the trouble of looking at the newspapers which fifty years ago informed the British public of passing events both at home and abroad, they would, doubtless, marvel at the very limited and imperfect amount of intelligence which the best journals were enabled to place before their readers. The progress of the Peninsular campaign was very imperfectly chronicled.

But there was also an even more important personal and political dimension to Wellington's story of which contemporaries were only too aware: suspicions lingered as to how far his success was attributable simply to his being the undeserving recipient of favours from his elder brother and a government of which he became a member. The aim of the present chapter is to sketch the broad outlines of that tale, to show when and how the Duke became recognised as a national hero. Without it, the subsequent story of Waterloo is denied its true perspective. It is also, inevitably, the story of the army. An institution which had always had something of an ambivalent standing in the minds of Englishmen, its reputation was not helped by the fact that in Wellington's youth it had been humiliated in the war against the American colonists. When the Duke's formidable mother despaired of her son as 'food for powder and nothing more', she spoke with a deep sense of frustration.[31]

Lady Mornington's frustration suggests that Wellington's reticence when it came to talking about his formative years stemmed from an embarrassing awareness that his childhood had not lived up to his later standards of success and purpose. His parents clearly invested their greatest hopes in their eldest son, Richard (1760–1842), who distinguished himself at Eton and Oxford. Their other surviving children were William (1763–1845), Anne (1768–1847), Gerald (1770–1848) and Henry (1773–1847). Though Arthur followed his elder brothers to Eton in 1781, his younger sibling, Gerald, quickly outshone him there. Henry's entering Eton in 1784 was the cue for the undistinguished Arthur to be withdrawn. Stories about him during these early years are very few; several only entered the public domain after his death. One recalled a school holiday when the Wellesley brothers were invited to stay with their aunt, Lady Dungannon, in Shropshire. En route, in order to shock her, they concocted the story that their sister Anne had eloped with a footman. The brothers' fiction would be echoed later in reality: in March 1809, Henry's wife, Charlotte, was to elope with the future Lord Uxbridge, Wellington's cavalry commander at Waterloo.[32]

Another story circulating widely at the time of the Duke's death, strangely overlooked by most biographers, is more revealing respectively of Arthur and Richard. It concerned an encounter he and his brother Richard had with David Evans and his sister, whilst staying in North Wales. Wellington, then aged about 12, challenged 8-year-old David to a game with the latter's marbles. When Wellington made to steal them, David's 10-year-old sister was enlisted to recover them. Richard, relishing the battle:

> incited the two to fight, and mounting himself upon a heap of dirt upon the roadside, dared the girl, to touch Arthur [...] and laughed at the fun; but when he beheld his brother Arthur drop his colours, and deliver the marbles, and beat a hasty retreat, the tears fell from his eyes.[33]

Whilst he lived, Richard, the generous and dominant elder brother, apparently paid for David Evans to receive a weekly newspaper. No less telling,
Wellington 'never shewed any mark of remembrance' of the episode, except
for one brief meeting with Evans soon after Waterloo.[34]

Richard's aid was of greater importance in the rise of Arthur than the
latter was wont to admit. Following Lord Mornington's death in May 1781,
his embittered widow was left with six children and limited funds. It fell
to Richard to assume the role of patriarch. He decided that Arthur might
benefit from a year at the Royal Academy of Equitation at Angers in Anjou.
The recollections of Alexander Mackenzie, his governor there in 1786, of a
sickly Arthur Wellesley who spent most of the time on a sofa playing with
a white terrier, do not suggest that the investment reaped an immediate
dividend.[35] His mother remained unimpressed, for on his return to England
she saw him for the first time in a year 'at the Haymarket Theatre, saying,
"I do believe there is my ugly boy Arthur."'[36] Angers did at least confirm
that the army would be Arthur's destination. Brother Richard, second Earl
of Mornington, duly smoothed his passage. He spent some £4,000 on
Arthur's behalf, money used to obtain him commissions in seven regiments
between March 1787 and April 1793. Though he did not serve with any of
them, Arthur rapidly rose from ensign in the 73rd Foot to major in the 33rd.

Just what transformed the dilettante Arthur Wellesley into the soldier who took his profession seriously remains something of an enigma.
Undoubtedly the galvanising period was the eighteen months or so that
followed the outbreak of war with Revolutionary France in February 1793.
The best explanation is that the consequent opportunity to prove himself coincided with the need: he had been courting Lady Catherine (Kitty)
Pakenham since autumn 1792 only to have his suit rebuffed in the spring
of 1793 by her brother, Lord Longford, on the grounds that he could not
adequately provide for her.[37] Wellesley responded by taking an active interest in military matters. By September he was the 33rd's commanding officer
with the rank of lieutenant-colonel. A later rare admission was that it was
around this time also that he burnt his violin – the facility for music had
been inherited from his father – both a symbolic rejection of his frivolous
past and a recognition that he must do better. Characteristically, 'he disliked
any mention of the circumstance'.[38]

Wellesley's first active service, however, proved inglorious: in June 1794
he landed with his regiment at Ostend as part of the Duke of York's ill-fated
campaign in the Netherlands. He would later rationalise York's debacle

with the wry observation that, 'I learnt what one ought not to do, and that is always something.'[39] Two years later, the 33rd was posted to India. Newly commissioned as Colonel Wellesley, Arthur left Portsmouth to join it. Whether through an awareness of his lack of theoretical knowledge, or the sharp shock his brief practical experience in the Low Countries had administered him, the time on the journey was not wasted. As well as books on Indian affairs, he took with him several hundred volumes covering the art of war from Caesar to Frederick the Great.

Britain had been the dominant European force in India since Clive's 1757 victory at Plassey. Its affairs there were overseen by the East India Company, in turn supervised by a six-man Board of Control in London. The Company, whose headquarters at Fort William, just outside Calcutta, was generally content to maintain its trading monopoly through a series of alliances and agreements aimed at preserving a rough equilibrium amongst the indigenous peoples. Notionally, the most important were those who comprised the Maratha Confederacy headed by the Peshwa in Poona. Outside the Confederacy, the Nizam of Hyderabad was the most important figure in central India, with Mysore the dominant state in the south. Inevitably, the Company judged that force was sometimes necessary to preserve its position. If he did not already know it, Colonel Wellesley's autodidactic voyage presumably taught him that there had already been three wars against Mysore and one against the Marathas.

Wellesley's first months in India passed quietly enough. Then, unexpectedly in October 1797, it was announced that his brother Richard was to be Governor-General. The latter had put his brains and connections to good use, having been an MP since 1784 and a member of the Board of Control since 1793. At once brilliant, charismatic, vain and condescending, and frustrated in what he believed to be his legitimate political ambitions at home, the new Governor-General believed that a more aggressive policy in India was the way forward both for himself and Britain. Arthur, for good and ill, was destined to have his own reputation tied to, and determined by, that of his elder brother for the foreseeable future.[40]

Mysore, ruled by its Sultan, Tipu, with ambitions to extend his influence in southern India at Britain's expense, was on an obvious collision course with the Governor-General. The outcome was a foregone conclusion: Tipu died during the brief and bloody storming of his capital, Seringapatam, in May 1799. Arthur, commanding a division, played only a limited part in the military operation. Even so, it would prove contentious. Ordered by his

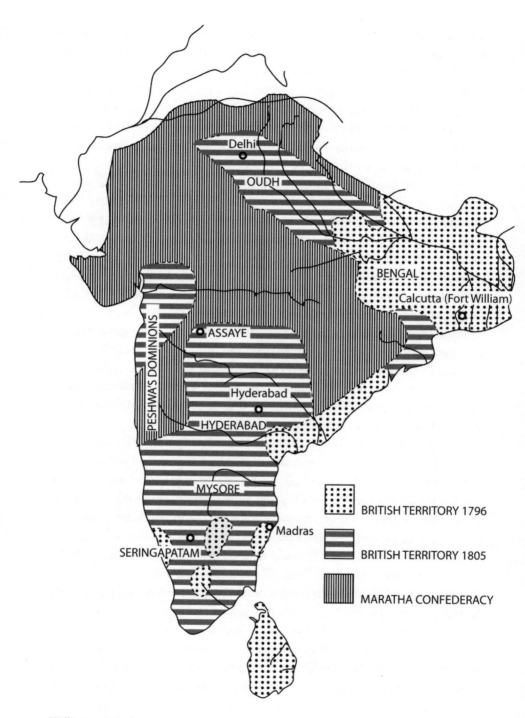

Wellington in India

superior, Lieutenant-General Harris, to take a defensive outpost known as the Sultanpettah Tope, during the night of 5 April, a failure to reconnoitre properly meant that he initially failed. It was surely only the fact that his brother was the Governor-General that saw him advanced, ahead of more senior claimants, to the governorship of Mysore. Sympathetic Wellington biographers tend to draw a veil over the episode, or cite his determination to learn from a rare military reverse. The sequence of events, however, would live long in the memory of Wellington's detractors. Twenty years later, Lady Shelley noted, 'murmurs' persisted that 'his appointment was due to family interest'. A full decade after that, in 1829, when the Duke was Prime Minister, a hostile press reminded readers that 'it required years of victory entirely to wipe away the impressions then received'. Even Wellington himself later had the good grace to admit, in private, that it was a pivotal moment: the less-than-deserved 'command afforded me the opportunities for distinction, and thus opened the road to fame'.[41]

The distinction to which Wellington referred came in the Second Maratha War. The Peshwa of the Maratha Confederacy, rightly surmising that other Maratha chiefs desired his overthrow, sought protection by an alliance with the Company in December 1802. But the very fact of British interference only succeeded in provoking further unrest within the Confederation, spearheaded by Scindiah of Gwalior. In the early afternoon of 23 September 1803, Major-General Wellesley encountered Scindiah and – unexpectedly – his entire army of 50,000 at the confluence of the rivers Kaitna and Juah near the village of Assaye. As a position it was 'confoundedly strong and difficult of access'.[42] Wellesley's own force numbered barely 7,000, of whom only 1,800 were British. Presuming that with two villages on opposite sides of the river it must therefore be fordable, he nevertheless pressed on. An impressive but hard-fought victory ensued. By the end of the year, Scindiah and his allies had sued for peace.[43]

Assaye was a significant victory, far eclipsing anything he had hitherto achieved. In later life Wellington was apt to regard it, even more than Waterloo, as his finest action. It prefigured his experience at Waterloo in two important ways. One was his personal bravery under fire. Colin Campbell of the 78th recalled that, 'The General was in the thick of the action the whole time […] I never saw a man so cool and collected as he was […] though I can assure you, till our troops got the orders to advance the fate of the day seemed doubtful.' The other was his reaction once the heat of the action had passed: he was much affected by the fact that 1,600 of his men became casualties in face of unexpectedly stout enemy resistance.[44] But some at home were less impressed. This was partly a case of the spectacular victory against superior odds being rendered necessary only because Wellington had not anticipated engaging Scindiah in such large numbers. 'It is obvious,' concluded the *Morning Chronicle*, 'that a bad General may by possibility gain a name merely through the intrepidity of his army in retrieving his blunders.' Even more though, as the newspaper continued with undisguised racial arrogance, it was a case of Wellington's army's bravery being bound to prevail as 'in no place is this more likely than in India, where European troops are brought in competition with the natives'. The latter feeling was widespread. Just weeks before Waterloo, an anonymous veteran complained bitterly that whilst Britain was celebrating its Peninsular War heroes, it was forgetting its Indian ones:

> The heroes (and they deserve that name) of the Peninsula must not laugh at the battles fought against the native Princes of Asia; for the Duke of Wellington will tell them, that neither in Portugal, Spain or France, did he fight harder or stand in greater peril than against the Mahrattas, at Assaye: and his loss on that occasion, in proportion to his numbers, was as severe as any of his battles in the Peninsula.[45]

Napoleon was not alone in thinking on the morning of Waterloo, that his adversary was merely a Sepoy general.

If Sir Arthur Wellesley, as he became in 1804, really wanted to make his reputation, it was clear that he would have to return home. He finally did so in 1805. India had provided him with invaluable training, both as a soldier and an administrator. Most of all, India made Wellesley rich. The £42,000 he took home was more than sufficient to provide for Catherine Pakenham. They married in April 1806. India did not, however, as reactions to Assaye exemplify, win him much by way of public recognition. News from India appeared intermittently in British newspapers, but without much comment. Between 1797 and 1801 moreover, the public could be forgiven for focusing on the possibility that the country might be invaded: the War of the Second Coalition began only weeks before the invasion of Mysore. The fear of invasion revived after Britain declared war on France in May 1803; it persisted for the duration of the Second Maratha War. India was a distant sideshow compared to events unfolding in Europe. Above all, Sir Arthur Wellesley continued to live in his brother's shadow. Before 1808, such references as there are in the British press to 'Wellesley' are overwhelmingly to Richard, ennobled as Marquis Wellesley in 1799. Sir Arthur was, understandably, perceived primarily as the military instrument of Richard's ambitions. When the former met Nelson at the Colonial Office on 12 September, the Admiral needed no introduction; Nelson, by contrast, had to ask an official for the identity of the soldier waiting to see Lord Castlereagh.[46]

The next three years would both reinforce the impression that the Wellesleys were a family cabal in which Richard was king, and confirm them as a political faction of consequence. Made increasingly uneasy by the style and substance of Richard's actions, the Board of Control recalled him; by 1806 he was facing charges of misgovernment and corruption. To help defend him, Sir Arthur was found a seat in Parliament. His interventions were few and mercifully brief: it must be considered doubtful whether many parted with the shilling needed to purchase his speech to a committee of the House on East India Company finances. Perhaps the aim was to bore his brother's critics to death. The case quickly collapsed, not least because the Wellesleys enjoyed informal support from the government.[47] And in March 1807 Sir Arthur joined the government (his brothers Henry and William also accepted appointments), when he agreed to serve as Portland's Chief Secretary for Ireland. As Thompson says, 'His military engagements in India may not have been fully understood or appreciated at home but his reputation was sufficient for him to be accepted into the high political circle in which his brother had moved before leaving.'[48] Improbable as it might now seem, it looked distinctly possible then that Sir Arthur would abandon his military career for one in politics. Not for the last time, however, Napoleon took steps that would shape Sir Arthur's destiny. France invaded Portugal in November 1807 and Spain in February 1808. When the popular Ferdinand VII of Spain was deposed by Napoleon in May, the Spaniards rose in revolt. English popular sentiment demanded action. It took the form of an expeditionary force of 9,000 men, which set sail from Cork, on 12 July, with Sir Arthur Wellesley at its head. Controversy thereupon replaced consensus. Why, ranted William Cobbett, with 291 generals available, had Wellesley been chosen? It seemed all too obvious to him that it owed everything to political jobbery.[49]

Of more immediate concern to Wellesley, as he disembarked at Mondego Bay, was the news that General Junot's force in Lisbon was larger than had been presumed. This was offset by tidings that an additional 15,000 men had been despatched from Britain, including Sir Hew Dalrymple, who would

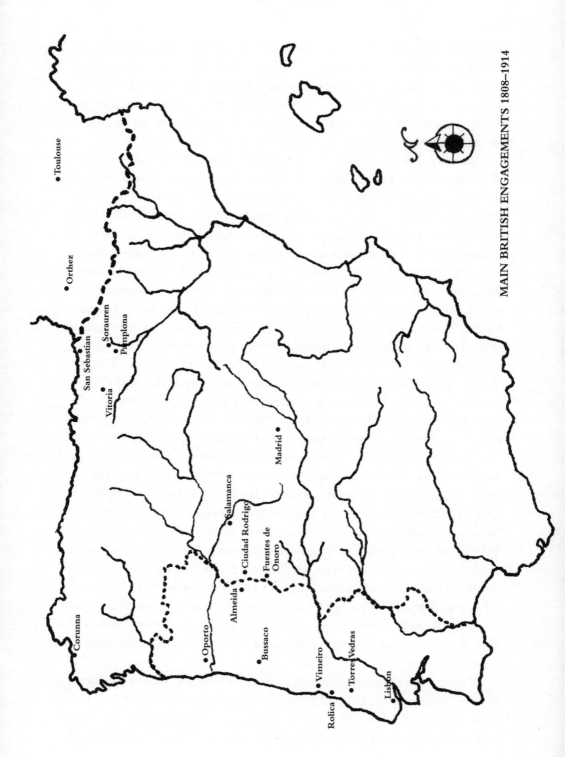

Toulouse

Orthez

Sorauren
Pamplona
San Sebastian
Vitoria

Madrid

Salamanca
Ciudad Rodrigo
Fuentes de Onoro
Almeida
Corunna
Oporto
Bussaco
Vimeiro
Torres Vedras
Rolica
Lisbon

take overall command from Wellesley with Sir Harry Burrard as his deputy. Before they arrived, however, Wellesley gained a limited victory over part of the French army at Roliça on 17 August. Four days later, he scored an altogether more satisfying one, as Burrard looked on, when Junot attacked him at Vimeiro.

Wellesley's success initially played well at home. The *Morning Post* carried an early, if idealised, account of him in action:

> since landing in Portugal Sir Arthur never went under cover at night, but always slept on the ground in the open air; he was the first up and the last down of the whole camp, sleeping constantly in his clothes […] he was cheerful, affable, and easy of access – enduring every privation himself, he was attentive to the wants of all, and ever active to obviate or remedy them […] In personal bravery he has been never excelled […] he was constantly in the hottest part of the action; wherever a corps was to be led on […] Sir Arthur was on the spot to head it […] Is it wondrous that such a man should be the idol of his soldiers, and the admiration of his brother Officers?[50]

Further recognition came with his first appearance in caricature.[51] But the caprice of press and public were never more evident than in the aftermath of Vimeiro. Sir Harry Burrard declined Wellesley's request to pursue Junot; Dalrymple, who arrived the day after Vimeiro, endorsed his deputy's caution. By the end of the month, they had brokered the Cintra Convention with Junot. The French agreed to leave Portugal, their transportation provided by the British. At home, this news transformed celebration into uproar. Ben Sydenham, an admirer of Wellesley, wrote that, 'It has excited universal indignation, such a ferment has never existed.'[52]

Whilst it was Dalrymple who had negotiated the armistice, it was Wellesley who bore the brunt of the indignation. This was partly because his superiors had ordered him to sign the Convention – the essentials of which he endorsed – but more because he remained a member of the government. Anti-government press organs, notably the *Morning Chronicle*, speculated openly about his generalship, insisting that his reputation rested on the too-narrow basis of Assaye. Speaking at a county meeting in Hampshire, William Cobbett, who detested both the government and 'that infernal family', smelt conspiracy. Why, he wanted to know, had part of the Convention only been published in French? 'My neighbours do not understand French; God forbid they ever should.'[53] Demands for an inquiry proved irresistible. They also allowed the Opposition to continue its attack: 'What a happy thing it is,' fulminated *The Times*, 'to possess rank and connection, and the means of patronizing friends and of serving dependants.'[54] Wellesley did not cut an impressive figure at the court of inquiry: when he appeared, on 22 November, he read a narrative of his involvement 'so rapidly [...] and in so low a tone, as to be scarcely audible without the bar'.[55] Much as Cobbett predicted, however, the inquiry exonerated Wellesley, Dalrymple and Burrard. Parliament then passed votes of thanks to Wellesley for his victories at Roliça and Vimeiro. These too, according to Wellesley's and the government's critics, were more politically expedient than merited. The Earl of Moira, for one, argued that as such votes 'were the highest honour that could be conferred on a subject, he thought they should be reserved for great occasions, and not lavished on every trivial advantage obtained over the enemy'.[56]

At the start of 1809, therefore, Wellesley's generalship, if not his personal valour, remained unproven with many. And whilst the events of 1808 had allowed him to emerge, at least briefly, from the Marquis Wellesley's shadow, he was encumbered by the new millstone that he had, through his political connections, been promoted beyond his competence. Events unfolding whilst the Cintra inquiry deliberated did not help. Sir John Moore, Britain's foremost soldier, popular with the Opposition, was killed on 16 January 1809 at Corunna, as the French successfully ejected his army from Spain. Less than three months previously Moore had predicted that if the French prevailed in Spain, it would be impossible to deny them Portugal too. One reason why there was remarkably little protest when, in April 1809, the government appointed Wellesley to head a new expedition to the Peninsula with the remit of defending Portugal from renewed French aggression, was the Opposition's consequent conviction that he would fail.

Matters did not transpire as they anticipated. In May, Wellesley crossed the Douro and took Oporto. In late June he struck into Spain where, on 27–28 July his Anglo-Portuguese Army fought a successful defensive action at Talavera. Walter Scott enthused that, 'His excellent conduct, joined to his high and undaunted courage, make him our Nelson on land.'[57] For his efforts Wellesley was elevated to the peerage as Viscount Wellington. But Talavera was not a decisive battle. Though Marshals Victor and Jourdan withdrew at its close, casualties were heavy – nearly 7,000 – on both sides. Mindful that another French Army was approaching from the north under Soult, Wellington saw no option but to retreat to Badajoz on the

Spanish-Portuguese border. Whilst there was some ringing of church bells in celebration when news of the battle reached home (for example in Bury St Edmunds), the ambiguous results of the battle ensured that it did not catch the popular imagination.[58]

Opponents latched onto the ambiguities. *The Times* accused Wellington 'of a degree of inconsiderateness' towards the wounded, even citing *Le Moniteur*, which predicted that, 'If he shall long command the English armies, we may flatter ourselves with obtaining great advantages from the brilliant combinations of a General so inexperienced in the trade of war.'[59] The Common Council of the City of London resolved that he 'had exhibited in the campaign of Talavera, with equal rashness and ostentation, nothing but a useless valour'. One of its number, Robert Waithman, who was to prove one of Wellington's most vehement and persistent critics, saw Talavera as part of an emerging picture of Wellington's desire for personal aggrandisement: 'his great anxiety appeared to be to gain laurels for himself'. Had the Cintra inquiry been conducted properly 'the country would, probably, not have now to lament the loss which we have sustained in Spain, from the hasty advance and precipitate retreat of Lord Viscount Wellington'.[60]

Wellington's ennoblement only added grist to the debate. What had he done to deserve it, asked the *Dublin Evening Post*? The answer, so far as it could see, was that he proceeded 'rashly, suffers himself to be deceived, is ignorant of the force and condition of his antagonist, is attacked, loses every fourth man in his army, retreats, and in one day he is raised to the dignity of a Viscount'.[61] The argument inevitably overspilled into Parliament when it passed a vote of thanks to Wellington for Talavera early in 1810. In the Lords, the Earl of Suffolk opposed the motion, arguing that Wellington's lack of caution, foresight and intelligence, had 'led to all the consequences of a defeat, instead of a victory'. There was more opposition a fortnight later when the Commons debated whether Wellington should be granted a £2,000 pension: that it was carried by 213–106 shows that Wellington was still some way from being recognised as a national hero. Not a few believed that a weak government had deliberately rewarded Wellington and talked up Talavera in an attempt to make some much-needed political capital. Though Wellington had resigned the Irish Chief Secretaryship when he left for Portugal, moreover, it was a government in which the Wellesley presence was as strong as ever: Richard, Marquis Wellesley, had become Foreign Secretary in December 1809, leaving a vacancy as ambassador to Spain, which Henry Wellesley would soon fill. Wellington himself later reflected on this stage of his career that there were even some at the Horse Guards who viewed him with suspicion owing to the fact that he had served his military apprenticeship in India, that he had political friends, and in consequence of his being 'a sprig of nobility'.[62]

An assessment of military realities too, though, informed the personal and partisan criticisms. Napoleon had scored a decisive victory over the Austrians at Wagram in July 1809. He announced that he intended going to the Peninsula in person with reinforcements during 1810. In face of such odds, *The Times* declared that 'our longer continuance there can be justified upon no principle of policy or even common sense'. In February 1810, Thomas Creevey confided gleefully to his journal that Wellington's 'career approaches very rapidly to a conclusion'.[63] Even as he wrote, however, Wellington was overseeing the construction of fortifications north of Lisbon. Taking advantage of natural topography, the three huge defensive lines of Torres Vedras caught the imagination of the British public like no other Wellingtonian position before Waterloo. As one much-reproduced eyewitness description put it:

> The lines may be said to defend a triangular portion of the kingdom of Portugal; possessing peculiar importance, by containing the capital, the port, and the grand depots [...] the French, even in the possession of the interior provinces, may be considered to have done nothing. Starvation is inevitable [...] The few directions in which a body of men could approach, are so commanded by artillery, that an effectual slaughter would be carried on during the time occupied in the most expeditious march. Ditches, palisades, and other works, tend greatly to the inaccessibility of the place.[64]

For much of 1810, however, the harbingers of doom looked liked being proved right; in the summer the French seized the fortresses of Ciudad Rodrigo and Almeida. It was not until 27 September that Wellington's Anglo-Portuguese force of 50,000 risked confronting André Masséna's army of 65,000 at Bussaco. Wellington's position, astride a long ridge with a reverse slope, would be brought to the mind of those who stood with him at Mont St Jean five years later. For the moment, what mattered was that they secured an emphatic victory before retiring to Torres Vedras. When Masséna reached it in mid-October, he could only rail at his adversary's lack of military sportsmanship: 'Lord Wellington, not daring to wait for us in the open country, endeavours to destroy everything which might subsist our army [...] no period of history furnishes an example of such barbarity.'[65] Finally accepting, in March 1811, that he could not go forward, Masséna withdrew into Spain. Portugal had been saved.

The news of Bussaco reached Britain in mid-October. It made an impact far greater and more favourable than anything Wellington had thus far accomplished. In the House of Commons, Spencer Perceval, Chancellor of the Exchequer, rejoiced at this vindication of the government's policy, adding that:

> Those, on the contrary, who have entertained the desponding idea that the sun of British glory was for ever set, must now congratulate themselves and the country on the proof that our military character never stood so high as at the present moment [...] We have a British army, composed of a general who has out-generalled theirs, and troops by whom their troops have been subdued.

The Lords followed suit in voting their unanimous thanks. Significantly, it was Lord Grey, reformer, and former Foreign Secretary, somebody hitherto unconvinced by Wellington's pedigree, who seconded the motion and described him as 'a great commander'. Though the *Morning Chronicle* cavilled, the press followed Parliament's cue. An article in the *British Review* dared to compare Wellington to Marlborough, even suggesting 'that his talents are, upon the whole, of greater promise; nor can we, by any exertion of philosophy, bring ourselves to despair of beholding him the instrument of as much good to prostrate Europe, as it received a century ago through the medium of his renowned predecessor'.[66]

Now for the first time too, anticipating genres that would follow Waterloo, widespread popular celebration of a Wellington victory is evident. Nobody caught the mood better than 'Hafiz' in his 'Sonnet to Lord Wellington':

> Though foul-mouth'd Faction thy fair fame abuse,
> And squinting Envy at thy merit sneer,
> Candour and Truth disdain their sordid views –
> To every friend of Freedom thou art dear.
>
> Then persevere in thy sublime career,
> By honour sanction'd, and by wisdom led;
> And teach the foe of Europe's peace to fear
> Britannia's bands – with Wellesley at their head:

While nations rescu'd from destruction's jaws,
Proclaim their gratitude, and thy applause.[67]

Not to be outdone, Philip Astley staged a military spectacle entitled 'Lisbon or Ruse de Guerre on the Banks of the Tagus' in the Strand's Pavilion Theatre. The performance included a song in which Mr Johnson declared that:

Our encampment was bristled with cannon,
To check Massena's ruse de guerre;
Lord Wellington will give him a drubbing,
If he approaches our right, left, or rear.[68]

Sadly, Mr Johnson's optimism was as misplaced as his lyrics were awful. The popular presumption that Masséna's retreat into Spain would presage further British and Wellingtonian triumphs in 1811 proved largely illusory. Bussaco was not destined to live in the national consciousness like Waterloo. Instead, for more than a year, the war became one of costly attrition. By his own admission, Wellington only narrowly escaped defeat by Masséna at Fuentes de Oñoro in early May. Though, a few days later, he took Almeida, the only Portuguese fortress still in French hands, his forces sustained heavy losses at Albuera in defeating a French army that was attempting to relieve its countrymen in the border fortress of Badajoz. Back in Britain, old doubts resurfaced. The *Liverpool Mercury* complained that, 'His Lordship seems rather to be feeling his way, than to be following any determined plan.' A month later it added that, 'His present position is neither threatening nor commanding.' Sir Francis Burdett, the Radical MP who remained steadfast in his criticism of the war, insisted that, 'There was no chance of our succeeding in driving the French out of Spain.'[69]

Burdett was wrong and forward momentum resumed in 1812. The Spanish border fortresses of Ciudad Rodrigo and Badajoz fell on 19 January and 6 April respectively; the latter, however, at a cost of 5,000 casualties. In another scene that would have echoes three years later, the sight of so many bodies in so compact a space moved Wellington to tears – though this quickly turned to fury as his men took revenge for their fallen comrades in an orgy of violence and dissipation. At home, a grateful Prince Regent raised him to an earldom and Parliament once more voted its unanimous thanks. Speaking in those debates, Lord Liverpool, the Secretary for War and the Colonies, noted the large number of casualties but 'hoped that the friends and relatives of those who so gloriously fell, would derive consolation from the fame of the illustrious dead'. The public at large certainly seems to have been more than happy to do so. By early May, Astley's Royal Amphitheatre on Westminster Bridge was advertising a sixteen-scene adaptation of the storming of Badajoz. For those who wanted to celebrate further, Henry Barker would soon offer a panorama of the bloody action in Leicester Square.[70]

'Lord Wellington has now a great game before him,' *The Times* enthused, as Wellington forged into Spain. It is perhaps partly for this reason that the press generally, from this point onwards, becomes more inclined to include details of military actions in its columns, usually in the form of eyewitness letters. The change of editorial tack was certainly propitious, for on 22 July, after a protracted game of military chess, Wellington seized on a gap in Marshal Marmont's forces to inflict a comprehensive defeat on him at Salamanca. A letter of 26 July, duly published, recalled that Wellington's words at the critical moment before the engagement were: 'Then, by God! We will attack them.' It was one of the first authentic Wellingtonian utterances to appear in print.[71]

Salamanca was Wellington's first major offensive victory of the war, paving the way for him to enter Madrid on 12 August. Britain was enraptured. The Duke of Clarence (the future William IV) said that only Roman history offered parallels: Salamanca should be compared with Caesar's triumph over Pompey at Pharsalus in 48 BC. Wellington was raised to a marquisate as the nation celebrated. Three hundred gathered for dinner and entertainment in Chichester, the same number as met in Liverpool. In Cornwall, Richard Hussey Vivian (who would be prominent at Waterloo and in the debates which followed it), was one of the cavalry officers who provided entertainment for eighty-six people at the Angel Inn in Helston.[72] But it was the illuminations in London (adorning both private and public buildings) that were most fully reported. When driving out to view them on 17 August the Marquis Wellesley, now unequivocally eclipsed by his sibling, was recognised by fellow spectators, who insisted on drawing his carriage back to Apsley House, his London residence. Between its gates he had placed a picture of Wellington with the words 'Portugal' and 'Spain' to the left and right, 'Salamanca' below, and just in case anybody had forgotten, 'India' above.[73]

But even Salamanca, as the virtually lone voice of Sir Francis Burdett pointed out, was no Blenheim. There were still 280,000 French troops in Spain at the beginning of 1812. If expelling them was the objective, Wellington had not been sufficiently resourced. By November, he was once more retreating to Portugal. It was, observed *The Times*, 'a melancholy view of the state of affairs'.[74] In fact, 1812 was decisive, but not in Spain. Napoleon had begun his fateful invasion of Russia in May; by October he was retreating from Moscow. Men were soon being siphoned off from the Peninsula as reinforcements. Wellington, meanwhile, used his appointment as Generalissimo of Spanish armies to augment his forces. By early 1813 he had more than 100,000 men at his disposal. Now at last he could think in terms of a war of liberation for Spain. Confirmation that the balance of forces had changed came on 21 June. Having invaded northern Spain in mid-May, Wellington crushed Joseph Bonaparte's army 100 miles from the French frontier at Vitoria. Incurring losses of 9,000 killed, wounded and captured, not to mention the mind-boggling riches contained in his baggage train, Joseph retreated into France.

Vitoria, like Salamanca, was well documented in letters that appeared in the British press. One claimed that:

> The moment that our brave fellows got possession of the enemy's baggage, all was riot – the army-chest was forced, and the men began to load themselves with bullion. To stop them was impossible. Some of the officers reported to the General that the men were plundering and carrying off the money. 'Let them,' was the answer of his Lordship, 'they have fought well, and deserve all they can find, were it ten times more.'[75]

Wellington was in fact furious – the pillage of the baggage train had interrupted the pursuit and prompted his comment that, 'We have in the service the scum of the earth as common soldiers' – but the public contented itself with the victory.[76] *The Examiner*, often critical in the past, thought 'the victory was won in a good cause'. As for Wellington, 'It is a general feeling throughout the army, that the great talents of their admired leader were never so conspicuous.' London was again swamped by illuminations with apparently only Sir Francis Burdett's home 'an invidious exception, displaying only a few dim candles'. In the provinces the eulogistic mood was epitomised by Mr Bromley, who spoke his own composition, 'Britannia's pride – Her Wellington!' in the theatre at Bury St Edmunds:

> A wond'rous era in the British Arms!
> Edward and Henry, Marlboro', Wolfe, in one
> We see concenter'd all – in WELLINGTON![77]

International musical recognition came in the form of Beethoven's minor, but popular, orchestral work, *Wellington's Victory*, which premiered in Vienna in December.

By 1813 fresh accolades (Wellington became a field-marshal in June), and formal parliamentary thanks were no longer deemed sufficient recognition of the national hero. The Earl of Roden chaired a meeting of Irish nobility on 20 July that, perhaps in a vain attempt to reclaim Wellington as one of themselves, agreed to subscribe for a monument to him in Dublin. By the end of the year on the British mainland, Lord Darnley was complaining, with their Lordships' concurrence, of the 'want of due attention to the erecting of monuments to commemorate the illustrious actions of such men as Lord Wellington and others'. Within months the women of Britain, at least, had responded to his call. The Duchess of York agreed to become patron of a subscription to raise a Wellington memorial. Charlotte, Duchess of Richmond, whose ball in Brussels on 15 June 1815 would soon immortalise her name, was one of the vice patrons.[78]

Though Vitoria was to be Wellington's last great victory before Waterloo, extracts from letters printed in the press thereafter allowed the public to follow his army's progress more closely than ever before.[79] By the end of October, the fortresses of San Sebastian and Pamplona had fallen, the last French toeholds in Spain. Wellington had already crossed into France on 7 October. With Napoleon having suffered a crushing defeat at Leipzig at the hands of Britain's allies in mid-October, the war was nearing its endgame. Over 600 attended a ball in Bury St Edmunds in December 1813 to celebrate the 'imminent liberation' of Europe. The ballroom was decorated with emblems of the allied nations but a transparency of Wellington took centre stage.[80]

As Wellington wintered at St Jean de Luz, published letters offered glimpses of the man. One reported that, 'He goes out hunting occasionally, and appears to enjoy the pleasures of the chase like a true sportsman, as if he had not any care on his mind. He enjoys excellent health and spirits.' A Slough butcher sent him a consignment of beef for New Year. His Lordship's acknowledgement ('it did not arrive in time for the New Year's Day'), was an early example of the terse replies for which he became famous in later life.[81] The beef having been consumed, the final push for victory began. Soult was defeated at Orthez on 27 February, a battle that concerned the British press principally because its hero had been wounded in the thigh by a spent musket ball.[82] But it was Napoleon who was spent. The March

1814 Treaty of Chaumont, in which Britain, Russia, Prussia and Austria pledged not to make a separate peace with France, signalled a final nail in his coffin. On 6 April Napoleon abdicated and was sent into exile on Elba as Louis XVIII returned to France. As one great warrior lost his most elevated title, so another gained his: on 3 May the former Arthur Wellesley became Duke of Wellington. Taking formal leave of his army at Bordeaux on 14 June, he set foot in England for the first time since 1809 nine days later.[83]

Britain could now take stock of Wellington and his army's achievements at first hand. Lord Grey, shedding all previous inhibitions, declared that the Duke had reached 'as high a pitch of renown as ever had been attained by any general or army of any age or country'. MPs followed suit in the weeks that followed, in what looks suspiciously like a competition for glory by association. Mr Whitshed Keene hoped that there would be a national memorial like that already projected for Ireland. From the Emerald Isle, Sir Frederick Flood insisted that there should also be a Wellington House and 'dwelt for a considerable time on the glory it was to Ireland to have produced such a man'.[84] Parliament voted the Duke £400,000, an erstwhile Wellington nemesis, Samuel Whitbread, having objected that the earlier financial rewards were too little. The Prince Regent ordained that 7 July should be a day of public thanksgiving for the end of the war. Wellington duly appeared, carrying the Sword of State, for the service at St Paul's.[85]

Sir Thomas Lawrence subsequently captured the powerful image of the Duke holding the Sword aloft in front of St Paul's. For the discerning, there was Nollekens' life-size and much-praised marble bust exhibited at the Royal Academy the previous year. The general public demanded more immediate and accessible images and mementoes of its hero. Wellington appeared in over twenty-five political caricatures in 1814, more than for the rest of his career to date combined. But his image was more likely to be found on such objects as snuff boxes, fans, bells, door stops, brooches, watches, razors, and barometers.[86] There was also an already established Wellington brand, including a Wellington coach with patent axle trees, and a Wellington costume for evening wear, worn over a white satin under-dress. For younger enthusiasts, G. Minshull and Sons astutely dedicated the second edition of their board game, 'The Rival Kings' to him. It was 'to be had at all the principal toy shops'.[87]

In fact, Wellington was in England only briefly during the summer of 1814. Away from the grand occasions, it is unsurprising that he was not generally recognised. When he first appeared in London on 23 June 'His

Grace was loudly cheered by the people to whom he was known'. For all that it was played, not many did see the conquering hero coming.[88] Even so, he was certainly more seen than heard. His fullest statement in public was made at a dinner in his honour on 9 July 1814 at the Guildhall when he was presented with the freedom of the City. He thanked Divine Providence, praised his brother officers, servicemen and allies; and professed himself ready to serve again should hopes of peace be disappointed.[89]

The public face of Wellington before Waterloo, therefore, was less the product of what people saw and heard than what they read about him. In no small measure, as has not been fully appreciated, the Duke was the creation of his despatches. Theoretically, these were formal and private communications to a political master, the Secretary of State for War and the Colonies, who forwarded them to the Crown. In practice, ministers alluded to them in Parliament, increasingly quoted from them verbatim, and released them to the press. As Wellington conceived them, his despatches were largely confined to facts. He usually covered such matters as events leading up to a battle, a description of where it took place, an account of the action itself, and then mention of units or individuals who had distinguished themselves. Though he was to be accused of too little in the last category, it was through his despatches that subsequent Waterloo legends such as Thomas Picton, Rowland Hill, William De Lancey, Alexander Gordon, FitzRoy Somerset and William Ponsonby first became familiar names with the British public. Foreign Secretary Lord Castlereagh, perhaps bankrupt of fresh superlatives after Vitoria, praised their modest narrative, 'a narrative which, by its noble plainness, exhibited the heart, the soul, the character and genius of the man – a narrative which delighted in the communication of deeds of glory, and confined itself to the description of achievements, unmixed with sentiments, and destitute of graces'.[90]

Castlereagh's inferences about Wellington are debatable. It was exactly because the Duke's despatches were such a blank canvas in what they revealed about the man, that both friends and opponents were able to portray him as they chose. In particular, it was on the various occasions when Parliament voted its thanks to Wellington that ministers sketched the character of the Duke 'known' by the British public before 1815. The artists in chief were Lords Liverpool, Bathurst, Castlereagh and the Marquis Wellesley.[91] They were assisted in their endeavours by newspapers such as *The Times* and *Morning Post*, which not only reported the debates in full but often adumbrated the main themes in their editorials.

Chief amongst those themes, beyond his self-evident skills as a general, was Wellington's standing with his men. As early as 1809 Castlereagh claimed that 'there was not a man, down to the lowest drummer in the army, who was not an enthusiast, that would cheerfully follow Sir A. Wellesley upon any service'. After Badajoz, Liverpool reported that the men viewed him 'with the most enthusiastic admiration'.[92] The Duke's reputation derived from his long-established personal bravery under fire and also, over time, from a perception that he was a talisman. One soldier in 1813 dismissed rumours that Napoleon himself might be about to appear against them with the remark, 'Let him come within sight, and the shadow of Lord Wellington's nose will frighten him back again.' The corollary of this was that Wellington was fast becoming indispensable – a view he shared – leading to the consternation of family, press and politicians when it was felt that his bravery led him to take unnecessary personal risks in the field. Privately, well before Waterloo, he was ascribing his own survival to a mixture of good fortune and Providence.[93]

That Wellington was also a disciplinarian, neither politicians nor press sought to deny. His circular of 28 December 1812 demanding order from his army was widely published. So was a soldier's letter of November 1813 that noted, 'Lord Wellington is very strict in keeping the army enjoined to the discipline in the General Orders: persons and property are respected as much as if we were in England.' But ministers and newspapers dwelt less upon Wellington the martinet than what they termed his humanity towards those serving under him. When the Lords gathered to vote their official thanks for Salamanca, Bathurst:

> was anxious to show, great as were Lord Wellington's military talents, how unwilling he was to risk the lives of his soldiers; how careful he was of the means of his country; and how willing to sacrifice even what must be most dear to a soldier – an opportunity of obtaining personal renown – if that opportunity must be purchased with too great a loss of men.[94]

That humanity, it was claimed, was extended to his adversaries too, in sharp contrast to the alleged brutalities perpetrated by French forces during the Peninsular War. Rather than extract retribution against Toulouse in April 1814, for example, 'Lord Wellington preferred, to the glory of heroes the destroyers of men and towns, the honour of preserving the lives and property of the peaceable inhabitants of a great city.' This was no more than was to be expected from the leader of the great cause that Wellington represented to the British public, what Grey had defined in March 1809 as a contest 'between justice, freedom, and public independence on the one side, and the highest degree of atrocity and oppression on the other'.[95] However idealistic this may have been in reality, at least to some extent, Wellington and his men had won their battle for recognition.

In retrospect, however, the celebrations of 1814 should be seen less as the feting of Wellington and his Peninsular army than, as the Prince Regent had ordered, an outpouring of thanks that a long and bloody conflict was over. This was a mature perspective to take. Since 1783, if one considers all theatres of operations and deaths from disease, not just in combat, it has been estimated that over 300,000 died. At the height of the struggle in 1809, one-sixth of Britain's adult population was under arms, approximately 768,000. By contrast, some 40,000 had died in the Peninsula. The Duke and his men were rightly amongst those being lauded, but the Crown, as Wellington would have insisted, was the natural focus for the nation. Events culminated in August with the serendipitous celebration of the centenary of the Hanoverian Succession. In London's Green Park there was a Temple of Concord together with a fortress 'exhibited as a mark of national esteem of our noble Allies, veteran chiefs, and brave heroes, who united in accomplishing the desirable event of a glorious peace, and the happy celebration of the House of Brunswick'.[96]

The other salient point discernible in Britain's 1814 celebratory events is the recognition that Napoleon's downfall had been the consequence of coalition pressure. Verses set to music and performed at Vauxhall entitled 'The Laurels of Wellington' were, as its subtitle made emphatically clear, 'An Ode to Peace obtained by the Allies'. Similarly, London's illuminations of 1814, unlike those following Salamanca and Vitoria, displayed a myriad of themes, 'our allies' and the restoration of the Bourbons being amongst the most prominent.[97] The emphasis on victorious monarchs in concert was also the unmistakeable message of a grand day in Oxford on 15 June. The Prince Regent's guests included both the Czar and the King of Prussia. A degree ceremony in the Sheldonian Theatre was interspersed with lines specially composed by Fellows. 'It is rather curious,' said *The Times*, 'that in these verses, the Duke of Wellington is scarcely noticed.'[98] But it was the newspaper that was missing the point. Most would now agree that the single most important event leading to Napoleon's downfall was his 1812 invasion of Russia. By comparison to this, the Peninsular

War was something of a sideshow. Moreover, qualification needs to be made even to the claim of the exclusivity of Britain's triumph there. Wellington himself conceded in 1820 that for all his success, 'those would form a very erroneous notion of the facts who should not attribute a fair proportion of it to the effect of the enmity of the people of Spain'. He might have added that in the wider scheme of things, Britain's greatest contribution to defeating Napoleon was not his but those in the naval and financial spheres.[99]

National celebrations after Waterloo would be different in their emphasis, for despite all that Wellington and those under him had achieved, the ultimate measure of their talents remained untested. A British soldier in France late in 1813 neatly summarised it, for he had heard rumours that Napoleon himself was about to take command against them:

> We wish most earnestly that this may be true; for I am sure there is not a man in this army, from Lord Wellington himself to the lowest soldier, that would not think it the happiest day of their lives to be placed fairly in front of the French, with Bonaparte at their head. If ever there was a day when British soldiers would be more than themselves, that day would certainly be the one.[100]

It certainly would.

2

Waterloo: The Battle of Giants

'Mein lieber Kamerad [...] quelle affaire!' These words, spoken to Wellington by Blücher when they met near the building known as La Belle Alliance on the evening of Sunday 18 June 1815, can reasonably be regarded as the first assessment of the Battle of Waterloo. That, at least, is how they appear to a British observer.[101] But Blücher had only just arrived at what had been one of Napoleon's battlefield vantage points; he can hardly have known much about what had unfolded in front of it over the previous twelve hours. It seems far more likely that his comment was a reference to the events of the previous four days. Blücher's greeting thus provides an example of one of the many ambiguities of Waterloo. For Britons, it is the name of the battle that, amid much else, consummated Wellington's reputation, but it is also the name given to the campaign that preceded it. A brief introduction to those events (not least with regard to what the Duke knew and thought at the time), is unavoidable: the hundred hours or so from 15–18 June would forge myths and create icons; it would also ignite controversies that continue to rage.

Wellington had not been idle since June 1814. He accepted appointment as ambassador to France and, having detoured en route to survey defences in the Low Countries, arrived in Paris on 22 August. Unfathomable as the British press professed to find it, the French did not share the view that Wellington's appointment was advantageous.[102] Fears that he might be assassinated persuaded the government to redeploy him as Britain's representative at the Congress of Vienna. He had been there only a month when, on 7 March 1815, news arrived that Napoleon had escaped from Elba. Britain immediately joined Russia, Prussia and Austria in forming the Seventh Coalition. Each pledged to put 150,000 men in the field: the man they denounced as an international outlaw would, they believed, be brought down by August.

The Duke arrived in Brussels on 4 April to assume command of Anglo-Allied forces in the Low Countries. His initial belief was that an invasion before 1 May would topple Napoleon before he could re-establish his hold over France.[103] But the Coalition was not yet ready. His mind thus turned to defensive preparations and liaison with the assembling Prussian forces based around Namur under the eccentric 72-year-old Marshal Blücher. On 3 May he had a satisfactory meeting with him at Tirlemont. Their two armies were, he believed, 'so well united, and so strong, that the enemy cannot do us much mischief'. He was therefore optimistic that 'we should give a good account even of Buonaparte'. A month later, at the start of June, he anticipated that operations against France would commence within the fortnight.[104]

In reality, the competing political and military constraints under which Wellington operated meant that he was less confident than the above summary suggests. Defending Brussels, for example, which was only 30 miles from the French border, meant that his initial dispositions were both further south and east from his main supply base at Ostend than strategic considerations alone would have deemed sensible. He was also hamstrung by his political masters not having given him the authority to invade. Given that Napoleon might not choose to rest on his laurels whilst the full weight of Coalition forces assembled against him, it was increasingly likely that he, not Wellington, would be the invader. Such an eventuality left Wellington militarily blindfolded since he neither knew for sure where Napoleon's forces were, nor where they would strike. It was therefore essential to keep his options open. For this reason his original deployment was in a wide defensive arc of 50 to 60 miles running roughly from Courtrai in the west to Enghien in the east. The Duke would be subject to much criticism for this, chiefly from those unappreciative that he was neither free agent nor clairvoyant.[105]

Wellington also lacked confidence in the polyglot force that was his army. 'It were to be wished,' admitted Horse Guards, 'that you had a more efficient army, composed of British materials.' Though Britons would laud the army that fought the Waterloo campaign, only 33,000 of the 95,000

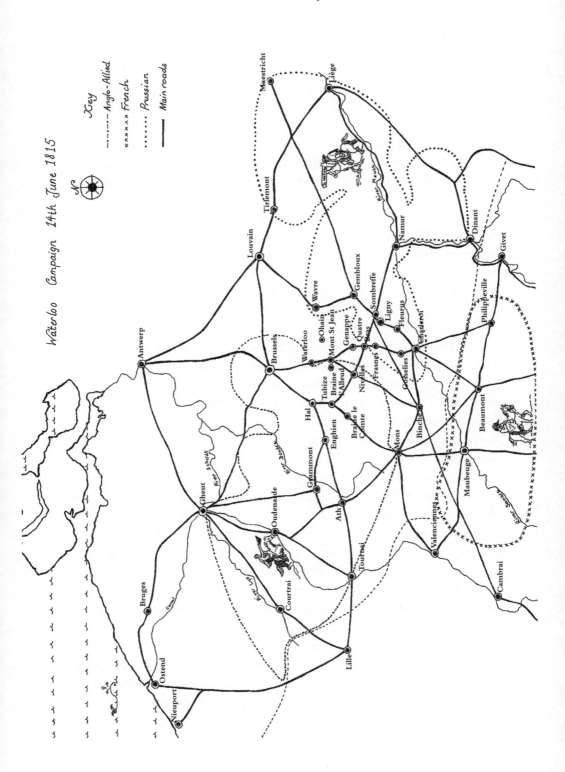

Waterloo Campaign 14th June 1815

Key

------- Anglo-Allied
×××××× French
.... Prussian
———— Main roads

men at Wellington's disposal were fellow countrymen, and most of them were not drawn from his battle-hardened regiments of the Peninsula. Of the rest, some 27,000 came from the German states of Brunswick, Hanover and Nassau. A further 8,000 Germans, based improbably in Bexhill, constituted the King's German Legion. The latter in particular might be relied upon, but the same could not be said of the 20,000 Dutch commanded by the young and inexperienced Prince of Orange. Even less faith could be placed in the 6,000 Belgians, some of whom had only recently been fighting for the French Empire, of which they had been part for the twenty years since 1794. The Duke might well be forgiven for describing as 'infamous' an army that spoke at least four different languages and lacked common equipment.[106] He was well aware that should Napoleon throw the full weight of his army against him, he would be both quantitatively and qualitatively outnumbered. Wellington's resulting caution was grounded on recognising this hard-nosed reality. The fact that he emerged victorious in the campaign has meant that posterity has tended to overlook his first priority of ensuring that he was not decisively defeated. To do this, the Duke needed a secure line of retreat towards his main supply base at Ostend or Antwerp beyond it. It was superfluous of the government to issue the euphemistic reminder that, 'Your Grace is well aware of the importance we have always attached to the possession of Antwerp and Ostend, not only as the means of providing for our communications with the army, but as securing a retreat in case of mischance.'[107]

Napoleon's deciding to strike west, in order to threaten Wellington's supply line at Ostend, was therefore a worrying possibility for the Duke. But the Emperor enjoyed the luxury of several options for an offensive.[108] He might have struck east beyond the River Meuse towards the Rhine Valley. This would have posed little immediate threat to Wellington; indeed it would have exposed the French left flank to both his and Blücher's armies. Both political and strategic logic, however, suggested to Wellington that Napoleon would opt for a more central thrust towards Brussels. The fall of a major city would rally support for Napoleon both in and outside France, perhaps even trigger the collapse of the Seventh Coalition. It would also open the way to Ghent, to which place Louis XVIII had decamped in ignominious haste. Wellington was very clear from the outset of the campaign that they should 'not let the enemy get possession of Brussels even for a moment'. He was less sure that he could guarantee it, especially if it risked the destruction of his army. Writing a few weeks after Waterloo, Lady Shelley, someone who enjoyed his confidence more than most, recorded that, 'my own impression is that [...] the Duke would have retreated in the direction of Hal, for he had declared at Brussels that he would not risk a defeat to preserve that city.'[109]

Wellington's presumption that Napoleon would seek Brussels as his first prize was correct, but it raised a further dilemma: along which of several roads would the blow fall? His conviction was that Napoleon would choose the main Paris to Brussels road running through Mons and Hal. Consequently, he believed that the initial attack would fall on Mons. The Duke was wrong, and he clung to his conviction until overwhelming evidence late on 15 June finally convinced him of his error. This was something else for which he would later be taken to task, for it meant that he was seemingly slow to react in support of the Prussians against whom Napoleon had decided to strike first. But to be guilty of over-caution was a lesser crime than to be fatally deceived – which is what would have happened had he allowed himself to be drawn east by a Napoleonic feint that left open both Brussels and his supply line. As he regularly insisted in later life, there 'never existed a man [...] in whose presence it was so little safe to make what is called a false movement'.[110]

Napoleon may not have induced the Duke to make the false step he dreaded but he did, for all Wellington's later denials, achieve an element of relative surprise at the start of the Waterloo campaign. Though Wellington was aware that French forces were concentrating around Maubeuge on 6 June – which still suggested Mons as their possible target – he wrongly discounted rumours a week later that Napoleon had joined them.[111] The Emperor was no apparition. His main attack was launched at 3.30 a.m. on Thursday 15 June along an 8-mile front towards Charleroi, which was in the Prussian zone for the defence of Belgium. This presented him with the option of a direct road to Brussels and also the opportunity, which he sought, of keeping the British and Prussian armies apart and defeating them separately.

Both the speed and clarity of communication do much to explain the movements of all the major actors during the Waterloo drama. During the crucial hours before the French attack, Wellington relied for information about what was going on in the area south of Mons from Major-General Sir William Dörnberg. At 9.30 a.m. on 15 June he wrote, without much apparent concern, that, 'I just hear the Prussians were attacked.' The Prussians themselves twice sent word to Wellington that this was so: first, from General Ziethen at Charleroi by 5 a.m.; later, direct from Blücher's headquarters. Establishing at what time those communications reached the

Duke has proved remarkably tendentious. Though the Prussians claimed that the first information was in Brussels by 9 a.m., Major-General Baron von Müffling, the Prussian liaison officer attached to Wellington, said the first news only arrived at 3 p.m.[112] The issue, for Wellington on 15 June anyway, was not so much 'when' as 'what': if this was the main French attack, what was its intention? By 7 p.m., and now sure of the former point, Wellington had issued orders for his army to concentrate with a view to marching at daybreak. But he was still uncertain on the latter point; hence his adding the strict rider that, 'This movement is not to take place until it is quite certain that the enemy's attack is upon the right of the Prussian army, and the left of the British army.'[113] For that, 'I must wait for my advices from Mons.' Only towards midnight did this arrive.

For this reason, it was his metaphorical dancing shoes, not his campaign boots, which Wellington put on that evening. His newly-wed Quartermaster-General, Colonel Sir William De Lancey, who went to his lodgings shortly before midnight, found him 'in his chemise and slippers, preparing to dress for the Duchess of Richmond's ball'. The ball assumed a mythical status after Waterloo, but it was hardly unusual: Wellington had given ones himself on 28 April and 7 June, and was planning another for the anniversary of Vitoria.[114] It made sense to go. His attendance would be reassuring to the anxious dignitaries of Brussels, and since many of his senior officers would be present it was a milieu in which pleasure could be mixed with any necessary business.

It was whilst Wellington was at the ball in Brussels, at around 1 a.m., that the Prince of Orange brought unexpected and unwelcome tidings. The main French advance was forging towards Sombreffe and the main Prussian force. Worse, the Prussian withdrawal from Charleroi had allowed a portion of that force under Marshal Ney to strike west into the Duke's sector towards Quatre Bras. Ney's orders were to occupy the strategically important crossroads where the Brussels to Charleroi road intersected with that from Nivelles to Namur only 20 miles south of the Belgian city. The situation would have been worse still had not generals Constant-Rebecque and Perponcher from the Prince of Orange's corps taken it upon themselves to occupy the position with a brigade.[115] The Duke withdrew to his host's dressing room. Chosen more for the fact that it contained a large map than the privacy it afforded, Wellington studied the map and declared that, 'Napoleon has humbugged me (by G-), he has gained twenty-four hours' march on me.'[116] He then left as unobtrusively as possible.

Wellington rose at 5 a.m. on 16 June and gave orders for Picton's Fifth British Infantry Division to advance to Quatre Bras. But still old doubts lingered. Ney was moving only slowly towards Quatre Bras. It was still conceivable that he might be headed towards Nivelles with the aim of turning Wellington's right flank. Picton's men were ordered to halt south of Brussels at Waterloo all morning. From there they could just as easily be directed towards Nivelles or Quatre Bras. Wellington passed them as he rode to the Quatre Bras position. He arrived at the crossroads by mid-morning. There were as yet only 6,500 men and guns to confront the approaching French force of 28,000. A less dilatory Ney could easily have seized the crossroads. That he did not may partly have been the consequence of Wellington's reputation: the circumspect General Reille, who was with Ney, could not believe that the Duke would not have hidden considerably more men than they could see before them.[117] The Duke meanwhile, wrote to Blücher at 10.30 a.m. from Frasnes, a hamlet just over 2 miles south of the crossroads, confirming that it was his intention to support him in his venture to give battle against Napoleon's main force in front of Sombreffe. Shortly after, with British forces approaching and Ney still yet to attack, he judged the position at Quatre Bras sufficiently quiet that he went to see Blücher in person. The two met at the Moulin de Brye at 1 p.m. On the condition that he was not attacked himself, Wellington confirmed his promise of support. Both the 'Frasnes letter' and his verbal commitment are problematic. It would be several hours before any of his men could reach the Prussian position, surely only a notional possibility anyway, given that a major engagement at Quatre Bras was almost certainly about to begin. Was Wellington, in being less than ingenuous, trying to steel the resolve of the Prussians, fearing that they might be tempted to fall back and leave him to face the French alone?[118]

By the time Wellington arrived back at Quatre Bras at 3 p.m., what had begun as a skirmish was quickly evolving into a full-scale battle. Crucially, from Wellington's point of view, though Ney was at last attacking in strength, the British were even more quickly reinforcing the position. With Picton's men arriving, Wellington's total force of 30,000 men outnumbered the French by the end of the day. Ney was thus unable to use the crossroads to turn east and attack the Prussian flank. To this extent, Wellington had provided considerable help to Blücher. The British saw this as sufficient reason to claim victory. More accurately, Quatre Bras had been bloodily indecisive. The Anglo-Allied force suffered the heavier of the heavy losses, some

4,800 as against 4,200 for the French. Wellington's fatalities included the Duke of Brunswick. The one who caught the popular imagination, though, was the exuberant and handsome 17-year-old Lord James Hay. Hours before, he had cut a dashing figure at the Duchess of Richmond's ball, but now, as the press whimsically put it, 'early closed an honourable career'. The same report noted that, 'The Duke of Wellington exposed himself as usual to imminent danger: the bullets, says our informant, were whizzing about him in every direction.'[119]

Quatre Bras was clearly no sideshow – Wellington's losses were amongst the highest he had ever sustained on a single day – but Ligny was the main battle on 16 June. Indeed, with 83,000 Prussians facing 65,000 French, the initial dispositions exceeded those at Waterloo. It was a battle in which Wellington was meant to have been the supporting actor to Blücher, a sort of Waterloo in reverse. But it was Napoleon who stole the show. Commencing at 2.30 p.m., the Emperor launched a series of frontal attacks around Ligny and the villages west of it. Five hours of bitter and costly fighting ensued before the French prevailed. The casualties, some 13,700 French and 19,000 Prussians, were enormous. It is staggering that twenty years later a Hanoverian veteran of 18 June could write, apparently without irony, that 'we had heard that the Prussians had taken part in a skirmish' at Ligny.[120] Gneisenau, Blücher's deputy, attributed the Prussian reverse to Wellington's non-arrival. The French General, Gourgaud, attributed Prussian losses to their having been on an elevated plain 'where they were absolutely unprotected, and exposed to all the firing of our artillery'. The Duke, for the same reason, had feared for Blücher's men. Napoleon therefore had it about right when, 'He attributed the battle of Ligny to the decided character of Blücher, and that of Quatre Bras to the necessity under which Wellington was placed of supporting the Prussian army.'[121]

By nightfall on 16 June Wellington had made up much of the twenty-four hours he had complained of losing. The French, by contrast, might have made more of the situation. Both Napoleon and Ney had summoned d'Erlon's I Corps of 20,000 men to their aid during 16 June: the bemused commander dithered and ended by assisting neither. Quatre Bras, perhaps even more so Ligny, would have turned out differently had he intervened. For despite having been beaten at Ligny, the Prussians were far from being destroyed. Logic suggested they would now retreat east away from Wellington and towards their supply line at Liège. With Blücher missing, initially presumed killed or captured after his horse had fallen on him, this

was Gneisenau's preference. But on 17 June, testimony to the old man's constitution and the restorative powers of gin and rhubarb, Blücher appeared
before Lieutenant-Colonel Sir Henry Hardinge, Wellington's liaison officer
with the Prussians, to inform him that other counsels had prevailed. They
would fall back northwards towards Wavre, 14 miles to the south-east of
Brussels.[122] Combined operations in defence of the city remained an option.

The story of 17 June is therefore one of which commander would respond
best. Though he later claimed that he literally saw that the Prussians had
been worsted at Ligny, the truth seems to be that Wellington at first inclined
to believe that they had had the best of the contest.[123] Since Hardinge had
suffered wounds necessitating the amputation of his left hand in the battle,
the Duke needed to be sure. Two squadrons of the 10th Hussars were sent
to establish the truth. Before 9 a.m. Wellington was in possession of the
facts, including the critical detail of the Prussians' falling back towards
Wavre. Captain Bowles of the Guards records Wellington as telling him that,
'Old Blücher has had a d–d good licking and gone back to Wavre, 18 miles.
As he has gone back, we must go too. I suppose in England they will say we
have been licked.' It is interesting that at such a moment Wellington could
still be concerned as to how news of his actions would play at home. But he
was typically decisive: 'I can't help it; as they are gone back, we must go too.'
By 10 a.m. the retreat was under way.[124]

The Anglo-Allied retreat from Quatre Bras was one of the smoothest chapters in the story of the campaign, thanks in no small part to the rearguard
provided by Uxbridge's cavalry together with the horse artillery. But it also
owed much to inaction on the part of the French. Ney did nothing by way of
harassing the allied retreat until 1 p.m. Like Wellington, he was unsure what
had happened at Ligny; now outnumbered at Quatre Bras, he was much slower
in finding out. Marshal Grouchy, who had been charged by Napoleon with
shadowing the Prussian withdrawal, displayed a similar torpor. But it was the
Emperor himself who set the tone of lassitude. Whilst Grouchy dealt with the
Prussians, he should have descended on Wellington's left flank. Had he done
so, with Ney re-engaging from the front, Wellington would surely have met
his Waterloo that day at Quatre Bras. The French might have been in Brussels,
as they planned, by Saturday night. By the time Napoleon's lancers appeared at
Quatre Bras at 2 p.m., his would-be victim had vanished. Wellington would be
forever mystified as to the reasons for his adversary's inertia.[125]

For Wellington's army, therefore, the dominant memory of the retreat
was less the pursuit from behind than the violent thunderstorm which

broke out overhead. Hope Pattison recalled that, 'The rain descended as if the windows of heaven had been opened, or the bars of the mighty deep unloosed [...] nothing that I have ever seen before or since can bear any comparison to this fearful visitation.' The Duke, less attuned to the Almighty, remembered it as 'the most terrible storm of rain that I have ever seen – our horses could not face it'.[126] Whilst it posed problems for all those that had to contend with it, life was inevitably harder for pursuer than pursued, especially the cumbrous French artillery. By nightfall on 17 June, Wellington's army had reached the relative safety of Mont St Jean.

The ridge of Mont St Jean lies roughly midway along the road from Quatre Bras to Brussels. Along it, thus bisecting the Charleroi-Brussels road lay another road running east to west from Ohain to Braine l'Alleud. A little to the north, on the edge of the forest of Soignes, lay the village of Waterloo where Wellington established his headquarters. Learning by messenger from Blücher at around 1 a.m. that the whole Prussian Army would cross from Wavre in the east to his assistance at daybreak, the Duke determined that he would stand and fight. He was still up at 3 a.m., for several letters were dated as being written at that hour. Though couched in a reassuring tone – 'all will yet turn out well', he informed Sir Charles Stuart in Brussels – they betray an unmistakeable subtext. The battle in the daylight hours might not turn out favourably. His female friend, Lady Frances Webster, was told that, 'The course of the operations may oblige me to uncover Bruxelles for a moment, and may expose that town to the enemy.' More explicitly still, the Duc de Berri was told to ensure that Louis XVIII was ready to make for Antwerp 'upon certain information that the enemy has got into Brussels'. The Governor of Antwerp was duly informed that there might be some unscheduled arrivals.[127]

Wellington's chief concern in the small hours of 18 June was what he considered the probability that Napoleon would attempt to turn his right flank. If successful, this would sever his supply line and route to Ostend. Though in his letter to the Duc de Berri he professed to think this unlikely, the same letter admitted the possibility that, 'It may happen that the enemy will turn us by Hal.' To minimise that possibility, Wellington made what many have come to see variously as his worst or most inexplicable decision of the campaign: to detach upwards of 18,000 men and 30 cannon under Prince Frederick of the Netherlands to Hal, 9 miles to the west of Mont St Jean. It was, in reality, a case of hoping for the best and planning for the worst. Such a strong force should be sufficient to prevent the success of the flanking manoeuvre he dreaded. But it could also serve a secondary purpose. Had he needed to fall back from Mont St Jean, Wellington might have been able to do so under cover of the forest of Soignes, but there would have been nowhere to mount another stand before Brussels. He would surely have opted to move in a north-westerly direction towards the relative safety of his supply base of Ostend where reinforcements were arriving daily. The force at Hal would help facilitate that movement. This is surely what he meant by his somewhat cryptic reference to Lady Frances Webster about being obliged to uncover Brussels. Ignominious perhaps it may have been, but tactical withdrawal was preferable to annihilation. As he said, the best test of a great general was, 'To know when to retreat; and to dare to do it.'[128]

Retreat, if it came, would be forced by the 71,497 men and 246 cannon opposite him.[129] The position of the French front line was marked roughly by the hostelry of La Belle Alliance, near where Napoleon was to establish his second observation post during the battle. To the left or west of it were General Reille's II Corps. On the other side of the main road to the east Napoleon positioned d'Erlon's I Corps. In front of them, he stationed his Grand Battery of 84 guns. Behind both d'Erlon and Reille there were cavalry divisions and behind them the reserves, which included Count Lobau's VI Corps. At the very rear of the position, either side of the farm of Rossomme – site of Napoleon's initial observation point – the legendary Imperial Guard awaited. Just over a mile south-east of La Belle Alliance, in a dip near the River Lasne, lay the village of Plancenoit.

Given his concerns as outlined above, Wellington readily admitted with respect to the disposition of his 67,771 men and 156 cannon that, 'I never took so much trouble about any Battle.'[130] Along the ridge, west of the crossroads on his right, he positioned many of his best forces, including the later fabled men of Maitland's brigade of the Guards Division. The trusted Lord Hill was placed in command of forces still further right, holding Braine l'Alleud, 2 miles distant. To the left, Wellington stationed the three brigades of Picton's Division with Vivian's and Vandeleur's cavalry brigades. Most of Uxbridge's cavalry, however, including the Household and Union Brigades, were initially massed in the rear centre of his line.

It was the salient features of the position itself, however, as much as the men holding it, that were destined for imminent immortality. Edward Cotton, participant and later guide, identified various strengths. The forward slope 'was a fairly steep glacis' presenting difficulty to attackers, the more so given that it was covered in tall rye and sodden from the previous

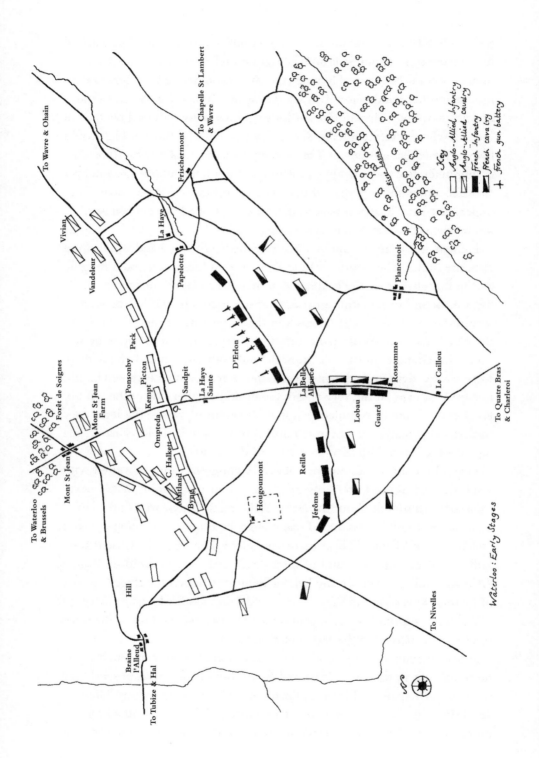

Waterloo: Early Stages

day's storm. Wellington's ridge also afforded its defenders the protection of thick hedges either side of the road. If not exactly the deep ravine later claimed by Victor Hugo, the road was certainly sunken several feet along a substantial length of the 2½ miles that made up the Duke's main battle-front. Behind the ridge there was also a reverse slope of the sort Wellington's experience had taught him to utilise so well. Captain Barlow noted that apart from the artillery, whose lack of manoeuvrability meant that it had to be placed on the forward slope from the outset, the army was 'perfectly concealed from the enemy who could by no means get a sight of its force or disposition'.[131] The flanks were also relatively secure. This was especially so to Wellington's left where trees, streams and the wet ground offered good protection, especially from cavalry. These natural defensive features were enhanced still further by the wooded hamlets of Papelotte, La Haye and Frischermont. On the right flank too, though, Cotton tells us that there were 'numerous patches of brushwood, trees and ravines [...] further protected by hamlets', principally Braine l'Alleud.[132]

What would soon be recognised as the most iconic landmarks of the main battlefield, however, were the farms of Hougoumont and La Haye Sainte. Their importance was later neatly summarised by Wellington when he characterised them as being 'like two bastions to the ridge between, and made the position a very strong one'. Hougoumont was an outpost on Wellington's right, almost midway between the rival armies. Sir John Sinclair described it only months after the battle: 'The buildings consisted of an old tower, and chapel, and a number of offices, partly surrounded by a farm-yard. There was also a garden, inclosed by a high and strong wall, and round the garden, a wood or orchard, and a hedge, by which the wall was concealed.' The whole was inspected by Wellington early on the eighteenth, who 'ordered Colonel Cooke to make loop holes in the wall: to throw down part of the garden wall: to raise a temporary rampart within it that the troops might be able to fire over it and to throw an abbatis [felled trees with their branches pointing out as an obstruction], across the Nivelles Road beyond Hougoumont.'[133] To hold it, the Duke initially sent four companies from the Guards Division together with some Nassauers, Lüneburgers and Hanoverians.

La Haye Sainte, by contrast, lay little more than 250 yards in front of the centre of Wellington's line. As Cotton said, it was 'far from being so commodious as Hougoumont, but considerably nearer our position, consequently easier of access, although more exposed to the enemy's attacks and cannonade'. It consisted of:

a farm-house, and court of offices […] being of a square form, with the house on the side nearest the position; a wall, with a gate and door, contiguous to the high road to Brussels on the left; the side opposite, and facing the enemy's position, one part of it a wall, and the rest a barn, with a very large gate leading direct into the fields.[134]

Defence of the complex was entrusted to a detachment of the King's German Legion with Major George Baring in command. More or less across the Brussels road from it was a sandpit containing men from the 95th Rifles.

Dressed in white breeches, blue frock coat and cloak, Wellington was cheered loudly as he rode along his line between 9 a.m. and 10 a.m. Having made some late adjustments for the defence of Hougoumont, he rode back towards the elm tree to the immediate south-west of the crossroads on the ridge, which was to serve as his most fixed point that day. All he could do then was wait. As events turned out, waiting was one of the main factors in what followed. Napoleon had planned on starting his attack at 9 a.m. It was nearly three hours later before he did: Lord Hill, who had two time-pieces with him, was adamant that his stopwatch showed the first shots to have been fired at 11.50 a.m.[135] The delay has usually been attributed to his waiting for the ground to dry out. This is not entirely convincing since the ground remained relatively soft all day. The weather too, remained unsettled: though paintings of Waterloo invariably suggest a dry day, Wellington was not alone in recalling that 'the day was dark – there was a great deal of rain in the air'.[136] There is probably more truth in the suggestion that the belated arrival of the French Army, still not fully deployed at noon, played its part. The Emperor too may well have been suffering from a bout of complacency: over breakfast in the farmhouse of Le Caillou he put his chances of success at 80 per cent and upbraided his marshals who advocated caution by famously rubbishing both Wellington's reputation ('Wellington is a bad general'), and that of his men. Certainly he anticipated no intervention from the Prussians.[137]

Compared to many engagements in which its two main protagonists had been involved, Waterloo was to prove a very simple battle. Napoleon's declared intent was to 'hammer them with my artillery, charge them with my cavalry to make them show themselves, and, when I am quite sure where the actual English are, I shall go straight at them with my Old Guard'. In agreeing that it was an unsophisticated affair, Wellington preferred a boxing metaphor: 'Never did I see such a pounding match. Both were what the boxers call gluttons [...] Napoleon did not manoeuvre at all.'[138] The Duke's objective was therefore simple enough: to withstand the blows. Modern accounts of Waterloo nevertheless tend to divide the battle into five distinct acts. Such divisions are useful in helping one to make sense of the many confused actions taking place, often overlapping or even simultaneous with each other. But it is equally important to remember that Wellington was afforded no such luxury. For him, it was more a case of being like a circus performer spinning plates than an actor who knew his lines for the clearly-delineated scenes of a scripted drama.

The first significant action of the battle was memorable because Wellington, like many in his army, could do little other than watch it. Presumably as a diversionary manoeuvre to induce Wellington to reinforce the position, thus weakening his main line, the French attacked Hougoumont. Shortly after midday, men from Jérôme Bonaparte's 6th Division succeeded in occupying the château's wood and orchard. But they could not take the château itself. Rather than desist, Jérôme insisted on committing more men to the assault. It is easy to forget, as the focus of Waterloo accounts turn elsewhere, and Hougoumont thus loses centre stage, that this battle-within-a-battle was to continue beyond 8 p.m. At its height, around 2 p.m., some 12,700 French had been drawn into the attack – clearly a disproportionate drain on their manpower given that the number of defenders at that time was only roughly a fifth of that quantity. From Wellington's point of view, the crisis period came early on, shortly before 1 p.m., when Lieutenant Legros and thirty men managed to force the north gate, only to pay with their lives when Sir James Macdonell and Sergeant Graham managed to force it closed again. In epitomising dogged British resistance against the odds in a fixed and identifiable part of the battlefield, it is easy to see why Hougoumont would figure so prominently in Waterloo mythology.

It was only at 1 p.m. that Napoleon finally fell on Wellington's main line. The prelude was half an hour's bombardment from his Grand Battery. This, because most of Wellington's men were still on the reverse slopes of Mont St Jean, 'produced but little effect'.[139] Its cessation signalled the advance of General d'Erlon's corps towards the centre-left of Wellington's position. They scythed through a Dutch-Belgian brigade and came dangerously close to breaking the Duke's line. That they did not owed much to the resolve of Lieutenant-General Sir Thomas Picton's 5th Division. Picton, an extrovert and eccentric Welshman – he insisted on appearing at Waterloo in civilian dress – was already well-known to the public from the Peninsular

War. Prominent at Quatre Bras, where he had sustained wounds which he concealed, he now consummated his fame by ordering the decisive charge that checked d'Erlon. Moments later, he died instantly from a bullet to the temple. He would be the British Army's most senior fatality that day.

Posterity would dwell not only on Picton's death but the charge by the Household and Union Brigades of cavalry, which transformed the repulse of d'Erlon's corps into something of a rout. Immortality was assured by their capture of two of the totemic French regimental Eagles. The capture of the Eagle of the 45th by Sergeant Charles Ewart of the Scots Greys was destined to be remembered as one of the most heroic deeds of the battle. Few accounts capture better the duality of heroism and horror that was Waterloo than Ewart's account of his feat in a letter to his father:

> it was in the first charge I took the eagle from the enemy; he and I had a hard contest for it; he thrust for my groin – I parried it off, and cut him through the head; after which I was attacked by one of their lancers, who threw his lance at me, but missed the mark, by my throwing it off with my sword by my right side; then I cut him from the chin upwards, which went through his teeth; next I was attacked by a foot soldier, who, after firing at me, charged me with his bayonet – but he very soon lost the combat, for I parried it, and cut him down through the head; so that finished the contest for the eagle.[140]

Someone else who took part in the charge, and who had received lessons in swordsmanship from Ewart, was 26-year-old Corporal Jack Shaw of the 2nd Life Guards. From Nottinghamshire farming stock, his physique and looks had commended him to the artist Haydon as a model, but he was best known across a broad social spectrum as a pugilist in London. Victories on Hounslow Heath on 8 April had made him Britain's unofficial boxing champion. Intoxicated on brandy, he was now wounded as a cavalryman, but succeeded in killing as many as nine of the enemy.[141]

Ewart's and Shaw's exploits notwithstanding, the action as a whole was of mixed military value, for the Union Brigade fatally over-reached itself in the charge. Even as they were swirling around the Grand Battery they were counter-charged by French cavalry. A third of their number became casualties, including their commanding officer, Major-General Sir William Ponsonby, who was killed. Wellington, who saw, but could do nothing to prevent this sequence of events, cannot have been happy: his priority was to conserve his forces in defending his position.

Shaw would eventually succumb to further wounds he sustained in the next main phase of the battle. Just before 4 p.m., Marshal Ney concluded that Wellington was in the process of ordering the very withdrawal which the Duke had feared might be necessary in his correspondence of the early hours. Though there was certainly discernible movement in his line, Wellington was in fact only bolstering his centre by moving forward three battalions of Brunswickers as those men who had been wounded moved back. Ney, looking up at the ridge and pumped on the adrenalin of battle, thought only of spreading chaos into what he imagined to be an attempted orderly retreat. His response is otherwise inexplicable: to attack, without the support of either artillery or infantry, an unbroken infantry position. The outcome was predictable. As ten regiments of cavalry, including the Chasseurs of the Imperial Guard, moved up the slope east of Hougoumont towards Wellington's centre-right, the Duke's infantry battalions formed into squares to receive them. His artillery supported them, the gunners running for relative safety within the squares as the French horsemen approached. Wellington himself, though he denied it, may have sought temporary sanctuary in one. Unable to break the squares, and suffering heavy losses, the cavalry had no option but to fall back. What remains inexplicable, since he now knew that no retreat was under way, is why Ney repeated the manoeuvre several times over the course of nearly two hours. Indeed, like Jérôme at Hougoumont earlier in the day, he substantially increased the numbers attacking, throwing not only Kellerman's division into the fray but also the Guard's heavy cavalry under Guyot. Observers on both sides would later describe Ney's actions diplomatically as 'premature'. Looking on at the time, a less reticent Marshal Soult declared that Ney 'is compromising us, as he did at Jena'.[142]

But this was Waterloo, not Jena, and Napoleon did nothing to extricate his wayward marshal. In any case, as with the British cavalry charge hours before, this sequence of events was more spectacular than decisive. Wellington's survival at Waterloo would depend upon his army's ability to withstand the effects of cumulative attrition. By late afternoon, there were signs that it might not. Specifically, La Haye Sainte, an excellent example of where the ebb and flow of battle makes the detail of events difficult to determine with confidence, was about to buckle in face of sustained French pressure. Men from the French 1st Division had surrounded the strategically important outlier by 2 p.m. at more or less the same time as d'Erlon's infantry were assaulting the main allied line. They forced the three companies of the 95th Rifles in the sandpit to withdraw and initially defied attempts to reinforce the château. They could not, however, secure the main farm building and some time after 3 p.m. its defenders were reinforced by three companies of the King's German Legion whilst the Rifles returned to the sandpit. A further 150 men, Nassauers, supplemented the garrison at around 5 p.m. It was not, therefore, men they ran out of but ammunition. Without it, those left had no option but to abandon the farm to the French.[143]

It was now 6.30 p.m. and the French determined to exploit their hard-won forward springboard into Wellington's centre. Artillery was hurried forward to inflict carnage on the Duke's now-precarious line. Wellington subsequently conceded that the château's loss had resulted in 'much of the injury done to the British Army on that day; and at all events their possession of this farm enabled them to make these repeated attacks on the centre of the Allied line'.[144] So did sharpshooters: it was from the vantage point of La Haye Sainte at about 7 p.m. that Lord FitzRoy Somerset, Wellington's military secretary, was hit by the musket ball that necessitated the amputation of his right arm.

The fall of La Haye Sainte was a major factor in persuading Napoleon that his opponent was on his last legs. To spearhead the delivery of the knockout blow, five battalions of the Middle Guard were assembled with three of the Old Guard in support. The Emperor himself moved forward with them at 7.30 p.m. as far as La Haye Sainte before handing over to Ney to lead the attack on Wellington's centre-right. Not for the first time that day, they underestimated the resolve of Wellington and his men. Even as the Guard was forming up, the Duke had reorganised and reinforced his centre by moving Netherlanders across from his left together with the light cavalry forces commanded by Sir John Vandeleur and Sir Hussey Vivian. Since he could see that they would bear the brunt of the approaching storm, the Duke also instructed Sir Colin Halkett and Sir Peregrine Maitland to deploy their brigades into lines of four. What followed was remarkably described in a letter written by Captain Digby Mackworth of the 7th Fusiliers, less than four hours later:

> The cannonade continued without intermission, and about 6 o'clock we saw heavy columns of Infantry supported by Dragoons forming for a fresh attack, it was evident it would be a desperate and, we thought, probably a decisive one; everyone felt how much depended on this terrible moment. A black mass of the Grenadiers of the Imperial Guard with music playing and the great Napoleon at their head came rolling onward from the farm of 'La Belle Alliance'; with rapid pace they descended the opposite heights, all scattered

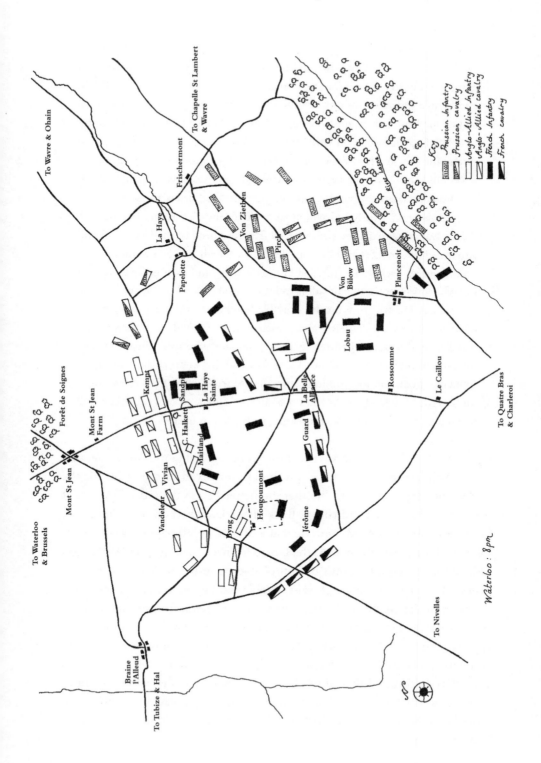

To Chapelle St Lambert & Wavre

To Wavre & Ohain

Frischermont

La Haye

Von Ziethen

Pirch

Papelotte

Von Bülow

Plancenoit

To Wavre & Ohain

To Waterloo & Brussels

Forêt de Soignes

Mont St Jean Farm

Kempt

Sandp.

La Haye Sainte

La Belle Alliance

Lobau

Rossomme

Le Caillou

To Quatre Bras & Charleroi

Mont St Jean

C. Halkett

Maitland

Vandeleur

Vivian

Byng

Hougoumont

Guard

Jérôme

To Nivelles

Braine l'Alleud

To Tubize & Hal

Waterloo : 8 pm

Key

Prussian Infantry

Prussian cavalry

Anglo-Allied Infantry

Anglo-Allied cavalry

French Infantry

French cavalry

firing ceased on both sides, our little army seemed to collect within itself, the Infantry deployed into line, and the Artillery charged to the muzzle with grape and canister, waited for the moment when the enemy's columns should commence the ascent of our heights; those spaces in our lines which death had opened and left vacant were covered in appearance by bodies of Cavalry [...] The French moved on with arms sloped au pas de charge: they began to ascend the hill, in a few seconds they were within a hundred paces of us, and as yet not a shot had been fired. The awful moment was now at hand, a peal of ten thousand thunders burst at once on their devoted heads, the storm swept them down as a whirlwind which rushes over the ripe corn, they paused, their advance ceased, they commenced from the head of their columns and attempted to extend their front, but death had already caused too much confusion among them, they crowded instinctively behind each other to avoid a fire which was intolerably dreadful; still they stood firm – la garde meurt et ne se rend pas. For half an hour this horrible butchery continued, at last seeing all their efforts vain, all their courage useless, deserted by their Emperor, who had already flown, unsupported by their comrades, who were already beaten, the hitherto invincible Old Guard gave way and fled in every direction. One spontaneous and almost painfully animated 'Hurrah,' burst from the victorious ranks of England, the line at once advanced; general officers, soldiers all partaking of one common enthusiasm. The battle was over.[145]

Mackworth did not, of course, witness every detail. He did not know that it was Wellington himself who was directly involved in the order for the British infantry to open fire. Neither did he see that as the Guard recoiled it was further battered by a brilliant flank attack launched on the initiative of Sir John Colborne's 52nd Foot. Be that as it may, he was right that the decisive punch had been thrown. As the Guard fell back in confusion, Wellington judged that he could assume an improbable offensive. At 8.30 p.m. he signalled the general advance. The last notable resistance came from members of the Imperial Guard under the direction of General Cambronne near La Belle Alliance. His scream of 'merde' or, for more tender sensibilities, an approximation of Mackworth's 'la garde meurt et ne se rend pas', would come to symbolise French defiance at Waterloo no less than Hougoumont's defenders epitomised that of the British. Militarily, it was inconsequential. Wellington later remarked that the French implosion was 'one of the most remarkable phenomena of sudden and total rout of a disciplined army he had ever seen'.[146]

So why had it been so sudden and total? The explanation lies in accepting that Wellington's perspective from the crest of Mont St Jean on 18 June entirely neglects the events which unfolded that day to the east. Determined to honour his promise to support Wellington, Blücher's Prussians in the shape of Bülow's IV Corps had intended setting out from Wavre at daybreak. Unimpeded, they might have covered the 10 miles to Mont St Jean by 2 p.m. An unlikely cocktail of congestion, a fire in the town and the rain-sodden roads in fact meant that 'the troops got on very slowly'.[147] By mid-morning, however, they were well under way, followed by Pirch's II Corps, Ziethen's I Corps and Blücher himself. By 1 p.m. the leading units were at Chapelle St Lambert, less than 5 miles away. With a telescope Napoleon could see them for himself; he responded by despatching part of Lobau's VI Corps to block their advance. What the Emperor had wanted to see was evidence that Grouchy and his force of 33,765 would interpose itself between the Prussians and Mont St Jean. He did not. Grouchy had spent most of 17 June assuming that the Prussians were retreating south-east of Ligny to Namur rather than north to Wavre. He realised the gravity of his mistake at Gembloux at 10 p.m. that night. Even then he dithered until 8am on the morning of 18 June before setting off for Wavre. By the time he approached the town, he was several hours behind Bülow. It was then a case of the interceptor being intercepted: Lieutenant-General Thielemann and 15,200 men of the Prussian III Corps had been left behind for that purpose. It was 4 p.m. before Grouchy's men seriously assaulted Wavre; they would never reach Mont St Jean.

Even without being harassed from the rear, however, the Prussian forces continued to make only slow progress. Moving along what were no better than trackways, much of the terrain in front of them comprised the Bois de Paris, punctuated by ravines, streams and the occasional small settlement. Whilst the battle for Hougoumont raged, French cuirassiers swirled around La Haye Sainte and d'Erlon's cavalry contested the main ridge in early–mid-afternoon, the leading units of Bülow's corps were struggling through the defile of the River Lasne. Not until Ney was launching the first of his suicidal cavalry attacks were the first significant Franco-Prussian cavalry encounters taking place on the edge of the Bois de Paris. It took an hour for the Prussians to clear the wood and for Bülow to be ready to strike towards the village of Plancenoit at the rear of the main French deployment in front of Mont St Jean. By 5.30 p.m., outnumbered before the weight of Bülow's corps, Lobau had fallen back to the village, surrendering

it altogether after another hour's bitter close-quarter fighting. To retrieve
the situation, Napoleon needed to send eight battalions of the Young Guard
under General Duhesme, to retake it.[148]

But the Prussians could now only be delayed at best. The leading men
of Ziethen's I Corps had reached Ohain by 6 p.m. Blücher's instinct was to
divert them south to assist the attack on Plancenoit; the timely intervention
of Müffling persuaded him that they would be better used by proceeding
on to Wellington's east flank: Papelotte became a metaphorical hinge for the
coming together of men from Wellington's and Blücher's armies. Crucially,
it was Ziethen's arrival that allowed Wellington to move men across from his
left to his hard-pressed centre and right.[149] Even without Ziethen, Bülow's
corps, ultimately 32,000 strong, was soon reinforced sufficiently to enable it
to take Plancenoit for a second time. They in their turn were to be driven
back at 7.30 p.m. when two battalions of Napoleon's Old Guard were com-
mitted to the fray. By then, Napoleon was in the process of overseeing the
deployment of the main body of the Imperial Guard for what would be his
final assault on Wellington. He was powerless to do anything about the third
and final Prussian capture of Plancenoit by the 5th Infantry Brigade of the
Prussian II Corps at 8 p.m.

Establishing precisely the Prussian contribution to the outcome of
Waterloo remains controversial. Some 72,000 Prussians marched to
Wellington's assistance; by the end of 18 June his own army numbered perhaps half that. From Napoleon's perspective, from mid-afternoon there were
two armies to think about; by early evening it could even be said that he
was fighting two battles. Lobau's corps sent towards Plancenoit numbered
approximately 7,000; the various battalions of the elite Imperial Guard sent
to assist them, nearly 5,000. Thus a sixth of Napoleon's battlefield strength
was diverted to protect his right flank and rear, not to mention his being
deprived of Grouchy's 33,000 men tied down by Thielemann's Prussians at
Wavre. If one includes them in the calculations, the Prussians by themselves
confronted over 40 per cent of the French forces in action on 18 June.

The fact of the Prussians' imminent arrival may also have contributed to
the shape of events on the slopes of Mont St Jean; just possibly to the frenzied nature of Ney's cavalry attacks; certainly to Napoleon's brusque rebuttal
of his Marshal's request for more reserves. The final attack of the Old Guard
too, can be seen as a last desperate throw of the dice to smash Wellington's
line before the French Army was crushed vice-like between the jaws of
its enemies. The Prussian casualty figures alone – 7,000 at Waterloo and

another 2,500 at Wavre – tell us that however late their arrival at Waterloo, their contribution was something more than peripheral. Above all, and a fact Wellington never denied, the Prussians turned what would have been an indecisive victory for him into a comprehensive one. Without them, the Duke's depleted and exhausted forces would have been unable to exploit fully the fruits of their sustained and heroic defence. With them, more than willing to conduct a brutal pursuit, not least by Brunswickers intent on avenging their Duke who had fallen at Quatre Bras, the dividend for victory was enormous. Reports of the Prussian Army's savagery lingered long and made Britons uneasy, but as Captain Barlow put it, 'Their co-operation was really most important as it so totally annihilated and dispersed this once formidable army that it never afterwards appeared in a regular and organised body.'[150] The campaign, in other words, would have had to continue. It did. But the Prussians took the lion's share in it and there was no need for a further great battle. The campaign, if not the Battle of Waterloo, was emphatically an allied victory in which British soldiers accounted for only roughly a sixth of the fighting strength.[151]

How Wellington would formally gauge the contribution of his ally remained to be seen, but his initial reaction to the day's events just ended is well-documented. First was his recognising the good fortune that had allowed him to survive the battle unscathed. Uxbridge, who sustained the most famous wound of the battle even as the French Army was disintegrating, was remonstrating with him not to expose himself to unnecessary danger when his own right knee was shattered by grapeshot. In the Duke's version of the incident in July 1815, he replied, 'Oh, damn it! In for a penny, in for a pound is my maxim, and if the troops advance they shall go as far as they can. A few moments after this Lord U. was wounded.' This is less colourful than the popular version originating with Horace Seymour, Uxbridge's aide-de-camp. He told Croker that, 'He was next Lord Anglesey when he was shot; he cried out: "I have got it at last." And the Duke of Wellington only replied: "No? Have you, by God?"' Either way, however, it confirms the truth of Wellington's admission to Lady Frances Webster that, 'The Finger of Providence was upon me and I escaped unhurt.'[152]

At least Uxbridge survived. The Duke felt keenly the loss of those close to him who did not. One was his aide-de-camp, Lieutenant-Colonel Sir Alexander Gordon. Gordon's thigh had been shattered at 6.30 p.m. near La Haye Sainte; his dying in Wellington's bed at Waterloo nine hours later reduced the Duke to tears. Another was his Quartermaster-General,

Sir William De Lancey. De Lancey had been riding beside Wellington at 3 p.m. when struck by a spent cannonball. Eight ribs having been detached from his spine, De Lancey finally passed away on 26 June. The memory of what happened to him lingered long in Wellington's mind. Small wonder that he told Dr Hume in the early hours of 19 June that, 'I don't know what it is to lose a battle, but certainly nothing can be more painful than to gain one with the loss of so many of one's friends.'[153]

But there were competing emotions too. One, given the clear evidence only hours before the fighting started that he was less than sure about the likely outcome, was relief. It was encapsulated in his admission to Creevey that Waterloo was 'the nearest run thing you ever saw in your life'. There was also professional pride in his own performance: he was far from being alone in thinking that, 'I don't think it would have been done if I had not been there.' Creevey was at pains to note that Wellington's tone in saying this was not one of triumphalism, but there can be no gainsaying that the Duke was also experiencing a measure of exhilaration. The great Napoleon, he informed his mother only hours after the event, had 'fought the battle with infinite skill, perseverance, and bravery'.[154] And yet, after confronting him for more than eight hours, certainly for longer than he had reckoned on before a substantial Prussian intervention was in evidence, he had prevailed. Many of the above elements are apparent, as well as his remarkable attention to detail, in a now unfamiliar letter Wellington wrote to Sir Charles Flint in the early hours of 19 June. Amongst the Waterloo fatalities was Lieutenant-Colonel Charles Fox Canning who had been carrying Wellington's despatch box:

> Poor Canning had my small dispatch box in our battle yesterday, and when he was killed it was lost. I shall be very much obliged to you if you will send me another of the same size as the last, with the same lock and key and leather cover &c., as soon as possible. Let it have in it a small silver or thick glass inkstand with one of Bramah's patent penholders and one of his pens. What do you think of the total defeat of Buonaparte by the British Army? Never was there in the annals of the world so desperate or so hard-fought an action or such a defeat. It was really the battle of the giants. My heart is broken by the terrible loss I have sustained of my old friends and companions and my poor soldiers. I shall not be satisfied with the battle, however glorious, if it does not of itself put an end to Buonaparte.[155]

It is clear from this letter too, that Wellington was of the opinion that Waterloo had been a victory for the British Army: not an allied victory, and still less a Prussian one. Such an opinion, that British forces could claim the laurels of Waterloo because they had done most to endure it, is not incompatible with a version of events which holds that the Prussians had contributed more to the Waterloo campaign. Given the physical and mental strain he had had to bear over the previous twenty-four hours, as also such relatively trivial practicalities as his need for a replacement despatch box, it was understandable that the Duke's thoughts focused primarily on the battle just ended. Whilst it is not inconceivable that the letter is an example of Wellington's deciding how much of the truth to relate, the context in which it was written surely makes it more probable that he was express-ing his real visceral emotions in its closing lines. Moreover, the sentiments they reveal were not without substance. The Anglo-Allied losses, just over 17,000, represented about 25 per cent of his starting strength. Of these, approximately 3,500 were killed and 10,200 wounded. British regiments had suffered particularly badly, incurring perhaps two-thirds or more of the losses.[156] He repeated his belief that it was the dogged British soldier who had prevailed in the letter written to his mother. It ended 'your affect and dutiful son'.[157]

Lady Mornington's awkward son had come a long way. In the wake of Waterloo the Marquis Wellesley referred to 'my brother's transcendent increase of glory'. A few days later the Countess of Pembroke's view was that Wellington had 'now proved himself to be beyond all doubt a very great man'.[158] And so it was, with his and their reputation secure, that men from Wellington's army encountered men from Blücher's at La Belle Alliance on the night of 18 June. Prussian bands played 'God Save the King'; the British replied with three cheers for Prussia. It was an unforgettable scene. When the two victorious commanders met there in person at about ten o'clock, at what had so recently been Napoleon's headquarters, the ines-capable symbolism of their rendezvous point commended itself to them too. The *Morning Post*, at least, reported as fact that 'they agreed to call this famous battle by so auspicious a title, "The battle of La Belle Alliance"'.[159] Wellington made no such commitment. The battle of posterity was about to begin.

3

The Battle of Posterity: Opening Shots 1815–1818

O n the morning of 18 June 1815 Mr Sutton, who made his living by running passage vessels from Essex to Belgium, was in Ostend. Confident that he was sufficiently apprised of recent military developments, he returned to his native Colchester by means of one of his own ships and thence to London. *The Times*, hitherto confused by competing rumours and conflicting stories emanating from French and Dutch press sources, was persuaded by his account. It was published on 21 June. Napoleon, it reported, had driven in the Prussian position at Charleroi and was intending to separate the two armies and take Brussels, which 'would give great éclat to the opening of the campaign'. But he had been thwarted. The British had had the better of a battle between Nivelles and Fleurus. This enabled the two allied armies to join at Genappe 'so that on the 18th Buonaparte was constrained altogether to abandon his attempt; and before Mr Sutton came away, the cannonading in the line of retreat sufficiently proved that the French troops had sought refuge within their own frontier'. The Duke's genius had thus prevailed over Napoleon. 'We have strong reason to believe,' claimed the editorial, 'that he was completely deceived by the Duke of Wellington, who affected total inattention to the movements of the enemy, insomuch that his Grace was actually engaged at a ball in Brussels when news arrived of the attack on Charleroi.'[160] This was an interesting spin on who had been surprising who. As an account of what had happened more generally, it was also seriously deficient.

The official news of the Waterloo campaign, together with the two captured French Eagles, was entrusted to Major Henry Percy. He reached Downing Street shortly before 10 p.m. on 21 June.[161] This was early enough for the *London Gazette* to publish it the next day. Compared to news of Wellington's Peninsular War victories, which typically took two to three weeks to arrive, this was remarkably quick. It was one reason why Waterloo made such an impact. Within days, the broad outline of the battle had become familiar to the general public. Within weeks, they were equally well versed in the details of the exploits of some of its noteworthy participants. This was partly the consequence of the familiar official despatches and parliamentary thanks. But exponentially more so than over the previous seven years, it was also the product of soldiers' letters, detailed histories, exhibitions of art and memorabilia, poetry and prose, memorials, even personal visits. Waterloo became a self-generating industry in a way that the Peninsular War, or certainly its constituent battles, did not. Reasons for this are obvious enough: the campaign had been brief, bloody, conclusive and dramatic. The Spanish General, Miguel Alava, put it well on 20 June when he described Waterloo as 'the most important battle that has been fought for centuries, in its consequences, its duration, and the talents of the chiefs on both sides; and because the peace of the world, and the future security of all Europe, may be said to have depended on its result'.[162]

Another key reason why Waterloo came to assume a rapid and important place in the national consciousness was the part presumed to have been played in it by the British Army. One of the by-products of Wellington's achievements in the Peninsula had been to drag the army's reputation up with his own. As Lord Liverpool couched it diplomatically, in moving thanks to him for the defence of Portugal, though the army had been great under Marlborough, 'In more recent periods, circumstances had induced us to attend more to maritime affairs.' Wellington's exploits 'had clearly shewn us the value of our military character'. By 1814, the song 'Wellington for Ever' proclaimed in its chorus:

Britain's chief, WELLINGTON,
Lion's hearts have his men
They always are ready,
Steady, boys, steady,
They'll fight and they'll conquer again and again.

But Britain's celebrations in 1814 had also acknowledged the reality that Napoleon's first abdication had been the consequence of a long-term collaborative effort. Waterloo could more plausibly be presented as a triumph for British arms. The British public were now to believe that Wellington's 'scum of the earth' were authentic heroes.[163]

Wellington himself remained integral to the story. But he would not dominate it in the way in which he had dominated popular media coverage of the Peninsular years. The range and variety of sources feeding the unending public fascination with the battle made it impossible for it to be otherwise. In any case he was, as Commander-in-Chief of the army of occupation in France, largely absent from Britain for over three years after Waterloo. That the story of the battle was told in his absence did not mean that he was uninvolved in its creation. He gave leads and was consulted, even trying on some occasions to control the process. He recognised – perhaps slowly and certainly not without irritation – that, ultimately, he could not do so; this would not stop him from trying. By the time he returned to England, effectively for good at the end of 1818, a popularly accepted version of the Waterloo saga was well established, if not entirely settled or uncontested.

Wellington's most important contributions to the fashioning of the Waterloo story came in the twenty-four hours after the battle. He had returned to his headquarters, an inn in the village of Waterloo known locally as Jean de Nivelles, not much before midnight. His sleep was interrupted at 3.30 a.m. by his surgeon, Dr Hume, who roused him with the news that his aide-de-camp, Colonel Alexander Gordon had just died. Within half an hour the Duke had set to work on his campaign Despatch. The resulting document would be the first published British account of the action; it was this that Major Percy bore to London on 21 June. In due course its writing would itself become one of the iconic scenes of the story: Lady Burghersh painted it on the basis of information supplied to her by Wellington in 1839. A version of her work, which appeared in the hugely popular *Illustrated London News* shortly after Wellington's death, further embedded the image in the national psyche.[164]

The Waterloo Despatch assumed the format Wellington had refined in the Peninsula. He shed tears as he embarked upon it, and desisted part way through when the news of General Ponsonby's death caused emotion to get the better of him. He completed it when he was in Brussels later that day. It was compiled partly on the basis of what he had seen for himself but also from what his personal staff, trained in such experiences, gleaned from their movements around the scene of action. He also drew on reports gathered by senior officers, both written and oral, which he summarised. The finished document, addressed to Earl Bathurst as Secretary of State for War and the Colonies, succeeded in being as detached in tone as it was brief in length. It stands in marked contrast to the personal letters he was writing during the same hours.[165]

As was his wont, Wellington began by setting the scene. Napoleon had concentrated his forces and attacked the Prussians. Claiming that 'I did not hear of these events till in the evening of the 15th', he responded to the news only when he 'had intelligence from other quarters to prove that the enemy's movement upon Charleroi was the real attack'. He acknowledged that the next day the bulk of the French forces were engaging Blücher, but that he was 'not able to assist them as I wished, as I was attacked myself'. Both allied armies were then obliged to fall back. But the Despatch is not the place to turn for an account of the battle of 18 June. Wellington succinctly describes the Waterloo position but devotes only two brief paragraphs totalling fewer than 150 words to the various assaults on his main line. They provide neither a sense of the battle progressing ('repeated attacks of cavalry and infantry occasionally mixed, but some times separate'), nor a clear sequence of events. The cavalry charge ordered by Uxbridge before mid-afternoon, for example, one of only three specific actions mentioned, appears at the end of this section. The other two referred to are Colonel Macdonell's sustained defence of Hougoumont with the 'utmost gallantry' and the Duke's belief that, owing to a want of ammunition, La Haye Sainte had fallen early on. Of Napoleon's final attack he writes only that 'after a severe contest, [it] was defeated'.

Where Wellington does offer something by way of analysis is in how the battle climaxed. In words that would inspire many a poet and artist, he wrote that:

> having observed that the troops retired from this attack in great confusion, and that the march by general Bülow's corps [...] upon Planchenois [*sic*] [...] had begun to take effect, and as I could perceive the fire of his cannon, and as Marshal Blücher had joined in person, with a corps of his army to the left of our line by Ohain, I determined to attack the enemy [...] The attack succeeded in every point.

The battle was gained. But rather than exult in his success, Wellington was relatively restrained, concluding that 'the army never, upon any occasion, conducted itself better'. Some thirty-five or so senior officers are then listed by name as having distinguished themselves, including a number who had been killed or wounded. This led to his penultimate point that 'such a desperate action could not be fought, and such advantages could not be gained without great loss; and I am sorry to add that ours has been immense'.

Wellington's final observations, before news of fresh fatalities prompted him to detail them in a postscript, are at once the most telling and controversial part of what he wrote:

> I should not do justice to my feelings, or to Marshal Blücher and the Prussian army, if I did not attribute the successful result of this arduous day to the cordial and timely assistance I received from them.
>
> The operation of General Bülow upon the enemy's flank was a most decisive one, and even if I had not found myself in a situation to make the attack which produced the final result, it would have forced the enemy to retire, if his attacks should have failed; and would have prevented him from taking advantage of them if they should unfortunately have succeeded.

As he had throughout his time in the Low Countries, Wellington was acknowledging that he might have been worsted by the French. In explaining that he had not been, his formulation of words can be taken to imply the belief that he might have won the battle alone, for the Imperial Guard was defeated and he was able to take the offensive even as the Prussians were still attacking Plancenoit. And yet he is categorical that it was the arrival of the Prussians that had contributed decisively to the shape of events. The more one reads his words, the more ambiguous and contradictory they become.

Unsurprisingly, the Waterloo Despatch has regularly been subjected to microscopic analysis. Wellington gets some details wrong. Blücher, for example, was not outnumbered at Ligny; the first big attack on Hougoumont did not start at 10am; Uxbridge's cavalry charge secured two Eagles, not one. So too, he errs over the fate of some individuals. He lists Colonel Ompteda for praise, unaware that he was dead; Sir William De Lancey is recorded as dead – Wellington believed he had witnessed the death – when he still lived. Many matters go unrecorded: why had he not personally secured Quatre Bras; why did he not mention Colborne's flanking manoeuvre against the Imperial Guard; why, generally, was there not more praise? Did he deliberately falsify some details he did include, such as the time he heard of the initial French advance?

Wellington's Despatch has recently been described by Adam Zamoyski as 'a fascinating document in relation to the known events, as it clearly sets out to falsify the record by marginalising the Prussian role in the victory'.[166] The seeking of both personal and national advantage is given as the reason for this. It is a tendentious set of claims. One must be very sure before ascribing such base motives to the Duke. That the Despatch did bring personal and national glory does not prove that these were his intentions when writing it. If they were, he need not have mentioned the Prussians at all, nor alluded to the possibility of his defeat. Instead, he could have used the sort of language employed by Alava, cited above, or in the first Dutch bulletin issued at 3am on 19 June, which said that, 'The army of Field-Marshal the Duke of Wellington covered itself with glory. The victory was complete. The enemy was totally defeated and put to the rout.' In this account the Prussians are mentioned only as an afterthought: 'Prince Blücher having joined the Duke of Wellington, their armies are pursuing the enemy beyond Genappe.'[167]

The Despatch should be seen as what it was, the report Wellington was obliged to make to his political masters on the operations of the British Army. It was by definition biased. Couched in his characteristically sparse style, what is most surprising about it is that he says so much about his Prussian allies and in such a laudatory way, far more than he confided in his private correspondence during the same hours. He would rarely, if ever, go so far again in acknowledging their contribution. Viewed overall, as an historical account of the events it describes, the Despatch was an understandably imperfect first draft. This was because it was written on the basis of conflicting and incomplete information, and when he was in a state of extreme stress and fatigue. It is, however, consistent with what he believed to be true at the time as revealed by what he wrote in his first letters home after the battle. Where the Duke would prove unreasonable in future years was in maintaining that nobody could – or should – write a more accurate account of events.[168] Though there was some logic to his point that no other participant was better placed to do so, it does not follow that he got things right. Specifically, even if he really believed during the afternoon of 18 June that the Prussians were not having a significant impact upon the French Army until late in the day, he would not modify his position when due reflection and further evidence might suggest the truth to be otherwise. He wanted his first draft, albeit duly clarified, to be the final word.

One point on which Wellington would have the final word, in Britain at least, was on the choice of name for the battle of 18 June. There is a long-standing myth that Wellington opted for Waterloo because it had a British ring to it.[169] The French, by contrast, were initially inclined to call it the Deroute de Fleurus. More serious competition was provided, as Walter Scott noted, by La Belle Alliance, the name pressed especially by the Prussians.[170] Müffling's account of the campaign refers to Waterloo as La Belle Alliance; the official Prussian despatch was headed Battle of La Belle Alliance (Waterloo). Gneisenau devoted the final two paragraphs of the latter to arguing the case, 'that this battle should bear the name of La Belle Alliance' above all because, 'There […] it was, by a happy chance, Field Marshal Blücher and the Duke of Wellington met in the dark, and mutually saluted each other as victors.' The name would also symbolise the alliance of armies and nations. Czar Alexander I endorsed the point when he visited the battlefield in September, accepting a glass of wine proffered from the inn and observing, 'Yes! It is really the fair Alliance both in respect to the States, and the families.'[171]

In Britain too, for perhaps up to two weeks after the event, the name of the battle hung in the balance. The *Morning Post* of 26 June reported on 'the tremendous battle of La Belle Alliance', whilst the *Royal Cornish Gazette*, referring to Waterloo, added in parentheses 'or, as it has, perhaps more properly, and certainly more happily, been called, of La Belle Alliance'.[172] The Poet Laureate, Robert Southey, was just one of many Britons who preferred La Belle Alliance. Three weeks after the event in Paris, Captain George Barlow was still calling Waterloo by the name of La Belle Alliance. Contrary to myth, Britons experienced no problem with the name. It was at once romantic, symbolic and more accurate than Waterloo. Some early British visitors to the battlefield were surprised to find La Belle Alliance bearing many scars of battle when buildings in Waterloo were unmarked.[173]

One person, Wellington, decided what the battle would be called. The Prussians admitted as much in asking that the British contemplate calling it La Belle Alliance. Had Wellington acceded to their request, the British would undoubtedly have embraced it. But the Duke seems never for a moment to have considered it. There was, on one level, nothing surprising in his opting for Waterloo. His usual habit was to name his battles after his headquarters. He headed and wrote most of his victory Despatch from there. His instructions for 17 June were that his forces should fall back to Waterloo. One veteran, who knew his chief well, noted in a letter home of

20 June that the battle, having been fought at Mont St John, should be designated as such, but that 'it will probably be called, Waterloo'.[174]

There is no denying, however, that Wellington quickly displayed sensitivity in face of the suggestion that La Belle Alliance would be more apposite. Waterloo commended itself to him in part by drawing attention only to the battle of 18 June; not to the more general allied campaign of which it had been the culmination. Waterloo also focused attention on the British position at the start of the battle when Prussians were in short supply. La Belle Alliance inclined one to think about the end of 18 June, the French position and the Prussians; both literally and figuratively, it would have suggested the British and Prussians to have been something like equals. Waterloo left Blücher and the Prussians only as an adjunct to victory. This is not simply speculation. Southey found that part of his article on Wellington for the July 1815 *Quarterly Review* had been added to, specifically a clause 'saying that the good sense of Europe had rejected the name of Belle Alliance for the battle as being some degree false'. He rightly suspected Wellington's friend, John Wilson Croker, to be the author of the interpolation; he was aghast to discover that Croker had made it after consultation with the Duke himself. More suggestive still of Wellington's desire to downplay the rival pretensions of La Belle Alliance is that within a year he rubbished the fact that his encounter with Blücher took place there at all, insisting bizarrely, that, 'It happens that the meeting took place after ten at night, at the village of Genappe.'[175] He never would erase the imagery of La Belle Alliance, but could at least content himself that he had won the battle of names. Even Southey recognised that 'once it had been named for Waterloo a word so English in its appearance would prevail'.

It was thus Waterloo to which the British press devoted enormous attention from 23 June onwards. The earliest reports followed Wellington's Despatch closely, buttressed usually by some commentary and reference to parts of his private letters, which had been immediately made public by their recipients. Specifically, these included those to Lord Aberdeen and the Duke of Beaufort, condoling with them respectively on the death of Colonel Gordon and the wound to FitzRoy Somerset. Both were taken by the newspapers as confirmation of Wellington's humanity; both letters too, included variants on the theme that winning a battle was only slightly less tragic than losing one. Wellington's letter to Sir Charles Flint lamenting the losses sustained by his 'poor soldiers' was also alluded to – but not the portion where he might be construed as exulting in victory. Instead it was Wellington's

humility and fastidious preparation that was emphasised with direct reference from his letter to his brother William that, 'Never before was I obliged
to take such pains for victory, and never before was I so near being beaten.'[176]

The Duke's Despatch, and specifically its encomium of the Prussians, also
provided a cue for parliamentarians. In the Lords, Bathurst said that though
Wellington would not have been defeated had the Prussians not arrived, he
could not have taken the offensive without them. *The Times*, too, judged
that without the arrival of Bülow's corps, Wellington would probably not
have ordered the advance, 'which decided the fate of the day', adding a few
days later that 'we must not be backward in expressing our admiration of the
persevering bravery of our gallant Allies, the Prussians whose acts converted
an orderly retreat into a total and irretrievable rout'.[177] Its comments were
occasioned by the publication in full of the Prussian despatch. The newspaper particularly approved of the fact that it gave 'full and liberal praise
to the English', in particular approving of the comment that, 'The English
army fought with a valour which it is impossible to surpass.' In fact, for
those readers who chose to read and reflect on the despatch for themselves,
the most interesting part of it was not, as *The Times* insisted, whether the
battle should be called Waterloo or La Belle Alliance, but rather the Prussian
perspective on their contribution to the victory. Believing the Anglo–Allied
army to be outnumbered (Gneisenau's figures of an 80,000 Anglo–Allied
army ranged against 130,000 French were considerably awry), 'it was not
possible but that such heroic exertions must have a limit'. Bülow's engaging
the French right flank from 4.30 p.m. was therefore essential. Even so, at
7.30 p.m. 'the issue of the battle was still uncertain'. At that point, however,
Ziethen's corps appeared in strength: 'This moment decided the defeat of
the enemy.' It triggered the collapse of the French right, 'while, at the same
time, the whole English line advanced'.[178] It had not appeared quite like
that from where Wellington was positioned on Mont St Jean, but in the
heady days of late June 1815 most Britons were too euphoric to notice.
They would generally always be more ready to acknowledge the contribution of their Prussian ally than the Duke and his inner circle.

The British appetite for details of Waterloo appeared to be insatiable
during the summer of 1815. That is the inescapable inference one must draw
from the columns of both national and provincial newspapers, which regularly included letters from soldiers who had fought in the campaign. The
letters, usually anonymous and to parents, made much reference to Picton,
Ponsonby and Uxbridge; many dwelt also on the steadfastness of the infantry,

and the charge of the British cavalry, which had led to the capture of two Eagles. Most salient, though, were the number of letters whose writers professed to have witnessed Wellington cool under fire, or even close enough to have heard him issuing orders. The *Morning Chronicle*, for example, published an account that insisted Wellington had exclaimed, an hour before the end of the battle, 'Would to God that night or Blücher would come!' At the end of October, the *Lancaster Gazette* was one of the last provincial newspapers to print a version of Wellington's supposedly having said, 'Up, Guards, and at them again!' as the Imperial Guard met its nemesis.[179]

Apart from the official British and Prussian accounts, the other important 1815 overview of events that appeared in the press was that written by General Manuel Alava. Alava was Spain's Minister Plenipotentiary to the King of the Netherlands in 1815. A friend of Wellington's from the Peninsula, he took it upon himself to join the Duke on 18 June. Old habits dying hard, he was actively engaged at Waterloo. His Despatch was written on 20 June but only appeared in the British press from early August. Though it 'contains some statements not exactly correct', Wellington rated it second only to his own as a description of the action.[180] This was presumably because it accorded with his own sentiments, especially perhaps Alava's conclusion that 'it may be asserted, without offence to any one, that to them [Wellington and the British Army] both belongs the chief part or all the glory of this memorable day'. The two may well have discussed the day's events, for only Alava had eaten with Wellington on the night of Waterloo. If so, they agreed to differ over some details for Alava has the battle starting at 11.30am as against Wellington's 10am. Alava also ventured the suggestion that it was Napoleon's sighting the Prussians that precipitated his increasingly frenzied attacks from late afternoon. Where he is most original though, is in dividing the battle into four distinct phases. These comprised the initial assault on Hougoumont; second, d'Erlon's infantry attack repulsed by Picton's infantry and the heavy cavalry; third, the massed attacks by French cavalry from mid-afternoon; lastly, the final offensive by the Imperial Guard. Alava had provided the British public with the best early coherent narrative of Waterloo.

They were soon provided with many more. Even before the end of 1815, one could obtain a third edition of Lieutenant-General Scott's *Battle of Waterloo* at 5 shillings or a fifth edition of a British staff officer's account for 6 shillings. By the time the first anniversary of the battle came around, there was a sixth edition of James Simpson's *Visit to Waterloo*. In the same month,

Robert Hill's *Sketches in Flanders and Holland*, containing thirty-six plates and fifty views, was being advertised for a hefty five guineas.[181] By then, Waterloo had entered the national lexicon. One of the earliest examples comes from May 1816. A body of agricultural labourers was reported as having descended upon Great Bardfield in Essex with a view to destroying its threshing machines. Undeterred, Mr Spicer and his neighbours 'determined to resist the attack of the rioters, and by a Waterloo movement got between the mob and the barn where the machine was deposited, and dared them to advance'.[182]

For those who wanted something other than the printed word to satisfy their appetite for what had taken place on 18 June there was much more. Prints of the heroic Corporal Shaw in action were particularly popular. One artist who responded to the demand was George Jones, whose resemblance to Wellington meant that he was occasionally mistaken for him. Serving with the army of occupation, he would earn the epithet 'Waterloo Jones' for his various sketches of the battle. A number of them were used as illustrations for one of the best known early accounts, *The Battle of Waterloo by a Near Observer* (1817). In February 1816 twenty artists competed for a 1,000-guinea prize when their works went on view at a public exhibition in London's British Gallery. *The Times* thought it premature: 'how is an historical picture, worthy of the admiration of an enlightened people, to be designed and executed in six months?'[183]

More commercially successful was Henry Barker's panoramic painting of the battle housed in Leicester Square. Entry cost a shilling. So popular did it prove that an elevated stage was added for ease of viewing. It closed on 1 May 1818 prior to embarking on an equally lucrative provincial tour. Competition was provided by a Waterloo museum opened at 97, Pall Mall in November 1815. For 1*s* 6*d*, the public could view more than 1,000 exhibits, including one of Marshal Ney's batons. It was wound up in a two-day sale in March 1817.[184] Theatregoers to Sadler's Wells, meanwhile, had been able to watch Mr Sloman perform *Waterloo, or Wellington Forever* within days of the battle. Not to be outdone, Astley's Royal Amphitheatre advertised a new song by Mr Herring entitled 'Waterloo, or Buonaparte Defeated'. At the close of its 1817 season, Mr Barrymore promised his patrons that 1818's 'campaign' would 'obtain for him a Waterloo victory over every other general in the theatrical field of battle'.[185] The greatest coup, however, was effected by William Bullock. He bought the coach used by Napoleon at Waterloo, which Blücher had sent to London as a present for the Prince Regent in January 1816. Exhibited at the Egyptian Hall in Piccadilly, it created a sensation, not least because part of the exhibit was Jean Hoorn, one of Napoleon's coachmen, who had lost an arm in the battle. Well over 200,000 had paid to see it by August. A provincial tour quadrupled that figure. Two years later, an 'unusual assemblage of persons' was attracted to Tattersall's near Hyde Park corner for an auction whose lots included the four horses that had pulled the coach. With more humour than imagination, Richard Tattersall himself conducted the bidding for 'Bony the first etc.' They made 73 guineas for the Prince Regent. A different sort of humour is revealed in letters to the press complaining about the nuisance that was Waterloo cracker fireworks and that 'vagabond boys [...] pay off old grudges against the old and infirm, by means of this weapon'.[186]

If these various and vicarious entertainments proved insufficient, people could view the site of battle for themselves. A month after Waterloo it may well have been Mr Sutton (the failed military analyst), who was advertising crossings from Colchester to Ostend as the 'most cheap, expeditious, and pleasant route to Brussels, [and] the field of Waterloo'. Europe had been closed to Britons for much of the long Revolutionary Wars; their cessation made foreign travel all the more attractive. A visit to Waterloo, if only as part of a more general European tour, quickly became more or less compulsory. A widely-published letter of mid-August 1815 thought it odd that more people were not taking advantage of the opportunity.[187]

In fact, as Wellington complained at the end of 1817, many did. Early illustrious tourists included Czar Alexander, King William of the Netherlands and several Prussian princes who were guided around the field in September by the Prince of Orange. The Duke too would pay several visits to the scene of his victory – surely the ultimate guide – before his return to England. More typically, John Scott, the literary editor, who was at Waterloo in July 1815, found himself in the company of 'a host of my countryfolk, of each sex, and every age, profession, residence, and condition'. They were not the earliest visitors. That dubious honour belonged to Belgian peasants. A sergeant in the Royal Artillery, writing to his father in Edinburgh from Paris in September, recalled that, 'I saw several men and women from the adjacent villages stripping the dead; and I am told that these wretches plundered many of the wounded.' The plunder included teeth. One visitor to the battlefield from Brussels on 19 June recalled that 'some Russian Jews were assisting in the spoliation of the dead, by chiselling out their teeth! – an operation they performed with the most brutal indifference. The clinking hammers of these wretches jarred horribly upon my ears.' Not so, presumably, for the chisellers. Those in search of dentures might pay them up to £2 for a single tooth. Healthy teeth from young men both looked better and lasted longer than prosthetic alternatives.[188] So plentiful were they that 'Waterloo teeth' became well known in both Europe and the United States.

But the scavengers left plenty behind for the early visitors. A Reverend Rudge vividly described the detritus of war:

> Every part of the field of battle was strewed with different articles belonging to those who had fought and bled. Every thing around attested the horrors of war, and the march of devastation. On every side were scattered the arms and clothing of the slain; shoes, caps and belts, and every other military appendage, either stained with blood, or covered with dirt. In the corn fields, which had been completely ploughed up by the trampling of the horses, and the movement of the soldiers, a number of books, cards, and letters were seen.

The roof of La Haye Sainte was 'pierced with a thousand holes'.[189] A group from Leeds who visited the battlefield on 30 August found that La Belle Alliance 'is now used as a sort of inn for the sale of bad small beer, and dignified with the pompous designation of The Wellington Hotel'.[190]

The collection of Waterloo memorabilia was an inevitable by-product of this embryonic tourist trade. For all that Britons declaimed against scavenging by Belgian peasants, some were perfectly prepared to indulge in some petty scavenging of their own. T. S. Lea, a Kidderminster carpet manufacturer who visited the field on 28 September, borrowed a hatchet in order to extract bullets from the trees. Their lower reaches denuded of the lucrative lead balls, local peasants subsequently used ladders to retrieve those in the upper reaches. Unlike Lea, most British visitors were content simply to buy from them. As they walked the field in October, a group from the north of England was pestered by Belgian peasant boys proffering buttons, eagles and musket balls. In August Walter Scott had bought two cuirasses and a French soldier's memorandum book.[191] He reported that French muskets were so plentiful that they could be bought for 7s 6d each in Brussels. Though appalled by what he had seen on his visit, the Reverend Rudge picked up a small piece of skull. It was at least easier to carry around than the 12-pound cannonball found by John Scott.[192]

One spot, perhaps above all others, proved a magnet for these early visitors. This was the elm tree that Wellington had designated as his nominal command post close to the crossroads of Mont St Jean on 18 June. Unsurprisingly, the many musket balls the earliest visitors remarked on seeing embedded in it, had all disappeared by September. The artist David Wilkie complained that this, of all trees, had been desecrated in such a way but saw nothing untoward in removing 'a good sized branch'. An account published in 1818 described what remained of:

> an old picturesque tree, with a few straggling branches, projecting in grotesque shapes from its ragged trunk […] it still retained, however, the vitality of its growth, and will probably for many future years be the first saluting sign to our children and our children's children, who, with feelings of a sacred cast, come to gaze on this theatre of their ancestors' deeds.[193]

Sadly, they would not.

Though the battlefield quickly resumed its former guise as unremarkable farmland, the flow of visitors to Waterloo continued unabated, attracted by a burgeoning of memorials. A rapid popularity attached to the building known as 'the Maison Paris' next to the inn that had been Wellington's headquarters. Owned by a retired forester, it was here that the wounded Marquis of Anglesey (as Uxbridge had become), had had his leg amputated. The limb had then been placed in a coffin and buried in the yard of the property, surmounted at first by Michaelmas daisies and then a willow tree. The Bishop of Norwich's wife visited there on the first anniversary of Waterloo and was shown 'as a relic almost as precious as a Catholic bit of bone or blood, the blood upon a chair in the room where the leg was cut off'.[194] Across the road, opposite Wellington's former headquarters, an unofficial memorial centre was provided by the church of St Joseph. There were at least two marble tablets there by the end of 1815. In 1817, a man from Liverpool found it 'nearly covered with monuments to the memory of British officers […] every English reader, whilst his heart is touched with the deepest sympathy, must feel himself elated in belonging to a country which has produced instances of such unparalleled heroism.' On the battlefield itself, he could not but notice the newly-completed monument to Colonel Alexander Gordon paid for by his six siblings and the 'plain mural monument' at La Haye Sainte. Hougoumont, 'a heap of ruins', was sufficient monument in itself.[195]

Visitors to the battlefield clearly needed direction. Captain Mercer had not even finished breakfast on 19 June when a carriage from Brussels disgorged its passengers to examine the field. In speaking to one of them about the previous day's events, Mercer had acted as the first, albeit involuntary, battlefield guide.[196] The man who became the intending visitor's must-have guide, however, was Jean Decoster. Tall, in his early 50s 'and of a robust appearance' in 1815, he had been selected on the morning of 18 June by three French generals as a local who could be of use to Napoleon in describing the terrain before him. He was with or near him throughout the day, even on occasion being given snuff by the Emperor. Only in the early hours of 19 June was he relieved of his duties near Charleroi, recompensed with a single Napoleon and deprived of his horse. But the canny peasant did not need Walter Scott to advise him that he had been indirectly presented with a potential fortune. When his January 1816 testimony of his day at Waterloo was published, his financial future was secured.[197] There cannot have been many days thereafter when his recollections and services were not in demand.

But what did this mania for visiting Waterloo mean? Stuart Semmel has recently suggested that early travellers to Waterloo wanted to venerate a tangible past at first-hand in its wholeness – an objective that sits rather awkwardly alongside their competing desire to bring back parts of it! In any case, the Waterloo they visited was already an imagined or interpreted past, whether it be through the plethora of written accounts and images or through the medium of guides such as Decoster. The true explanation is perhaps much simpler. Those who went to Waterloo shortly after 1815 were mostly described in neutral terms as visitors. Some were pilgrims; the majority we would characterise as tourists. They were all drawn by the enormity of the events that had taken place there on 18 June. Some paid homage, more were simply curious. There was nothing new about visiting and desecrating battle sites. Whilst in Paris with the army of occupation, the enterprising Colonel Woodford excavated the field of Agincourt for a period of two to three weeks unearthing, amongst other things, stirrups and spurs. He did so unmolested: Agincourt had not excited general public interest for several centuries. What brought most people to Waterloo, therefore, was a mixture of fascination and fashion. The poet E. S. Barrett observed that most visitors returned from early-post-1815 Europe either 'Beparised or Bewaterlooed'. It quickly became unfashionable not to know at least 'one honest gentleman, who has brought home a real Waterloo thumb, nail and all, which he preserves in a bottle of gin'. It may safely be concluded that Wellington was not much impressed by any of this. He observed with wry irony to Lord Limerick that, 'I hope the next battle I fight will be further from home. Waterloo was too near: too many visitors, tourists, amateurs, all of whom wrote accounts of the battle.'[198]

Lord Byron, Robert Southey and Walter Scott were amongst those 'amateurs' who visited Waterloo partly in search of literary inspiration. Poetry, not least theirs, was to play an important part in memorialising the battle. There was a feeling that it was a more appropriate art form than prose for an event so recent and gigantic in scale. Not everybody agreed. Wordsworth, for example, was initially so overpowered by what he had heard about it, that he was persuaded 'rather to decline the subject than to grapple with it', except perhaps in some distant future. But he was unusual. As early as 27 June, the *Morning Chronicle* had Wellington improbably addressing his army after Waterloo in verse, exhorting it onwards to Paris.[199]

Best known of the less ephemeral offerings, of course, is Byron's *Childe Harold's Pilgrimage*. The first two cantos, describing a pilgrim's travels and reflections, appeared in 1812 and had made their author famous. Only weeks after Waterloo, one correspondent from Paris was reporting overhearing an argument that, 'Lord Byron qua Poet was a greater man than the Duke of Wellington qua general and that *Childe Harold* would be read when nobody would think of Waterloo.' Byron visited Waterloo early in 1816 and rode over the field twice, principally to find the spot where Major Frederick Howard of the 10th Hussars had been killed. Howard was a son of the Earl of Carlisle who had briefly acted as Byron's guardian. Equally dutifully, Byron sent a piece of round shot, French badges and cockades to his publisher, John Murray.[200]

By June 1816 the third canto of *Childe Harold* was complete. In journeying through Belgium (thence onwards to the Rhine and the Alps), his hero inevitably stops at Mont St Jean:

> And Harold stands upon this place of skulls,
> The grave of France, the deadly Waterloo!

It was not part of Byron's purpose, however, to analyse the battle. Whilst he acknowledged the bravery of the ordinary British soldiers and featured Howard prominently, Wellington, whose politics he disliked, is not even mentioned. Instead, the most memorable lines were inspired, as Byron

explained, by the fact that, 'On the night before the action, it is said that a
ball was given at Brussels.'[201]

> There was a sound of Revelry by night;
> And Belgium's Capital had gather'd then
> Her Beauty and Her Chivalry.

Thus Byron's imagination immortalised the Duchess of Richmond's ball
for posterity. It also probably explains why so many came to believe that it
was held on the eve of Waterloo, not Quatre Bras. Such a detail was inconsequential juxtaposed against the powerful image of youthful manhood
enjoying itself when only hours later:

> Who could guess
> If ever more should meet those mutual eyes;
> Since upon Nights so sweet such awful Morn could
> rise?

The more typical approach to Waterloo was taken by the Poet Laureate,
Robert Southey. Somebody who had celebrated news of the battle by
going with Wordsworth and other Lakeland acquaintances to the summit
of Skiddaw, where they ate roast beef and plum pudding whilst singing the
national anthem, might reasonably be expected to write about it.[202] The
'Poet's Pilgrimage to Waterloo', a narrative poem of his walk from Brussels
to Mont St Jean, duly fulfilled that expectation. Like many, Southey regarded
June 1815 as having eclipsed the nation's exploits of a century before:

> And even our glorious Blenheim to the field
> Of Waterloo and Wellington must yield.

Roughly a quarter of the poem is given over to an account of the battle
with very considerable attention paid to the devastation in and around
Hougoumont. But it is Wellington to whom the day belongs:

> The leader, on whose equal mind
> Such interests hung in that momentous day;
> So well had he his motley troops assigned,
> That where the vital points of action lay,

> There had he placed those soldiers whom he knew
> No fears could quail, no dangers could subdue.

In 'Poet's Pilgrimage', it is Napoleon who is not mentioned at all. The Prussians too, appear only in one line to rout the French ('Consummated their great and total overthrow'). It is the Duke's,

> Our great Commander's eagle eye
> Which comprehended all, secured the victory.

Published in 1816, the poem was a commercial and critical success. It generated £215 within two months of its first publication. The June 1816 *Monthly Review* declared that, 'The Pilgrimage to Waterloo appears to us to be [...] the best of the numerous effusions on that victory.' By the end of 1817, the second edition could be bought for 10*s* 6*d*.[203]

The Duke did not meet Southey until 1824. Generally, he did not like poets. 'I hate the whole race. I have the worst opinion of them. There is no believing a word they say – your professional poets, I mean – there never existed a more worthless set than Byron and his friends for example.' A relative exception to his rule was Walter Scott, who had idolised Wellington since at least the Battle of Talavera. Scott spent a fortnight in Brussels in August 1815 and then three weeks in Paris, seeing Wellington 'repeatedly', even sitting next to him at supper, 'by special invitation', where he heard all 'about his campaigns & particularly about the Battle of Waterloo'.[204] With the benefit of such privileged access he duly completed the manuscript of 'The Field of Waterloo'. It was published on 23 October with an initial print run of 6,000. Like Southey he judged the battle to be greater than that of Agincourt or Blenheim. So too, he left the reader in no doubt whose contribution was decisive:

> But HE, his country's sword and shield,
> Still in the battle-front revealed,
> Where danger fiercest swept the field,
> Came like a beam of light,
> In action prompt, in sentence brief –
> 'Soldiers, stand firm!' exclaimed the Chief,
> 'England shall tell the fight!'

Scott was savaged by the critics. As the anonymous author of 'On the lamented fall of a late poet in "The Field of Waterloo"' put it:

> On Waterloo's ensanguined plain
> Full many a gallant man was slain,
> But none, by sabre or by shot,
> Fell half so flat as Walter Scott.[205]

The public, however, disagreed. 'The Field of Waterloo' was in its third edition by the end of 1815 with people encouraged to buy it if only because profits were being donated to the Waterloo Fund.[206]

More durable in literary terms was Scott's January 1816 *Paul's Letters to His Kinsfolk*. Comprising sixteen chapters – or letters – to his relations, they are a good example of a popular contemporary literary genre. In Scott's case, however, they were far more than fiction, corresponding closely with what he had written in his private correspondence. This was in turn based on research and his first-hand dinner experiences, for example Wellington's claims that he was confident of holding out all day on 18 June without Prussian help; similarly that he could have conducted a retreat through, and defence of, the forest of Soignes long enough for the Prussians to have come to his assistance the next day. Though not purporting to be history as such, letter eight provides a detailed account of Waterloo, including what Sir Colin Campbell thought to be 'the best and most correct [account] that had yet been published' of Wellington's ubiquitous directing genius during the battle.[207]

Whilst it is reasonable to suppose that Wellington did indeed utter the sentiments Scott ascribes to him, one should bear in mind that he was meeting him nearly three months after the battle and that he knew Scott would almost certainly publish. Some retrospective embroidering was inevitable. Gone, therefore, are Wellington's concerns that he might not be able to save Brussels; banished too, the idea that there was any doubt that his army alone could have prevailed or that the battle was a close run thing. More reliable, perhaps, in terms of what the Duke really thought, is the record of a conversation he had with Thomas Sydenham on 14 July, when memories were still raw. Compared to a month before, it offers us a more nuanced assessment of how well British troops had performed at Waterloo but is chiefly important for providing us with a more definite and coherent view of how the battle climaxed than that contained in his Despatch:

I observed that in talking of the Battle of Waterloo, he invariably mentioned it with some expression of horror, such as, 'It was a tremendous affair', 'It was a terrible battle', 'it was a dreadful day', holding both his arms above his head and shaking his hands. He repeatedly said he had never taken so much pains with a battle; that no battle had ever cost him so much trouble or anxiety; that he owed the victory entirely to the admirable conduct of old Spanish infantry (meaning the regiments which had served under him in Spain), which he says he is certain is the best infantry in the world; that the other English regiments, though they behaved tolerably well, yet often in the course of the day shuffled, got unsteady, and alarmed, and that it required great exertion to keep them together. As for all the rest of the troops, they repeatedly gave way, and would probably have left the field altogether if they had not had the infantry to rally under […] I asked the Padrone what had led to the sudden and general extinction of the French army. He said that a general attack on the left of his line having entirely failed, the enemy retired with great precipitation and in much disorder. Soon after this he observed the fire of Bülow's columns advancing rapidly on the flank and rear of the enemy. He then saw he could attack the enemy with certain success and immediately ordered the whole line to advance.[208]

In other words, Wellington was now unambiguous that he had defeated the Imperial Guard before the Prussian intervention became consequential. Neither, in this fresh telling of the story, was his German ally deemed to have been decisive. This may well be what the Duke saw and what he remembered – or what he thought he saw and remembered. More probably, it was the version of events he had settled on after a month's reflection. Either way, it had become, at least for him, the unalterable truth.

The Duke was clearly happy, as his conversation with Sydenham illustrates, to talk informally about Waterloo. Croker, who dined with him in Paris in July, reported him 'in exceeding good spirits; he was ready enough to give details of his battle'. Peel confirmed much the same thing. Wellington was even prepared to take the time and trouble to think about, and nominate, Corporal James Graham to the Reverend J. R. Norcross as a man deserving of an annuity for bravery during the defence of Hougoumont.[209] Perhaps, now beginning to enjoy his victory and surrounded by friends, he genuinely believed that his account of events would come to be accepted. In Britain, at least in broad terms during his lifetime, it would be.

But, as he quickly discovered, acceptance would not extend to every salient point. Wellington particularly objected to elements of Southey's article

on himself for the July 1815 number of the leading Tory intellectual journal, the *Quarterly Review*. Southey, though relatively less laudatory about
Wellington and Waterloo in his prose than in his poetry, was hardly overly-
critical: his article accepted the Duke's contention that the battle was won
before the weight of Prussian numbers became significant and credited him
with being 'everywhere; always where the struggle was most arduous'. But
his proofs did dare to suggest that the Duke had been caught somewhat
off guard on 15 June and that the Prussians had contributed materially to
the day. As he put it, 'Even if the British Army had not repulsed the enemy,
assailed him, and already driven him to flight, this movement of the Prussians
[on Napoleon's right] would have been decisive.' Via Croker in Dublin,
forewarning of the piece reached Wellington in Paris. Even though, on
the latter point at least, Southey was only really paraphrasing the Waterloo
Despatch, the Duke bridled. As Southey, in turn incensed, recorded, two
interpolations were added to what he had written: 'the first was to deny
in the most audacious and insolent terms that the Duke of Wellington had
been surprised, and that of the second to deny in the same manner that any
merit whatever was due to the Prussians in the victory!' Having got wind
that something was amiss (publication of the July number was delayed until
late November), Southey used his own reputation to insist that Croker's
supposed emendations be omitted. Wellington and his proxy were defeated.
John Taylor Coleridge judged it 'a compleat trial of principle [...] he has
[...] exposed himself to the full weight of the Duke of Wellington's personal
indignation for the sake of historic truth [...] Lord Wellington has behaved
as smally as Southey has greatly.'[210] It was a sign of things to come.

Even as this tussle was unfolding, Croker proposed, at the start of
August 1815, that he might himself write an account of Waterloo. Though
Wellington hardly enthused at the suggestion, he responded to his friend
with the promise that, 'I am most ready to give you every assistance and
information in my power.' Ten days later, he duly obliged, providing him
with answers to a list of queries, including when the battle had started and
the loss of La Haye Sainte. But his earlier caveats had hardened by then into
the conviction that, 'You may depend upon it you will never make it a satisfactory work.' Croker thereupon deferred to the Duke's recommendation
'to leave the battle of Waterloo as it is'.[211] Other would-be authors received
shorter shrift. William Mudford, for example, was refused permission to
dedicate his account of Waterloo to him the following spring. At the same
time, Sir John Sinclair, the former Scottish MP and agriculturalist, recalled

that his soliciting Wellington's help for a history of the battle had elicited the less-than-helpful response that:

> I can give you no information that would be of any use to you. My mind was so completely occupied with the great events of the battle, that I could not pay any attention to its minor details. All that I can tell you is, that we met the enemy; that we fought a battle; and that we gained a victory.[212]

This was partly literary license on Sinclair's part but it was true that he, like Croker, had been favoured with the considered opinion that 'the Duke entertains no hopes of ever seeing an account of all its details which shall be true'.[213]

Wellington's responses raised the not unreasonable questions, asked by Mudford and Sinclair, as to whether he was opposed to all histories of the battle, and, if not, what sources might with propriety be used? The Duke, it turned out, was not opposed to Britons having an accurate history:

> but I do object to their being misinformed and misled by those novels called 'Relations', 'Impartial Accounts,' & C. & C., of that transaction, containing the stories which curious travellers have picked up from peasants, private soldiers, individual officers, & C. & C., and have published to the world as the truth.

An accurate history could be written only on the basis of reliable, official reports. But Alava's had got some details wrong, whilst Müffling's was flawed by his having been off the field towards the end of the battle. Thus he could refer them 'only to my own despatches published in the "London Gazette"' – in other words the Waterloo Despatch was definitive![214] It was a circular and, in Wellington's mind, neat argument.

If he honestly believed it, Wellington's logic was also naive. Though he was genuinely disgusted with all that he had read about Waterloo, he could not stop fresh outpourings on the subject. It also raises the question of why the official Prussian record of the campaign should be viewed as being of inferior authority to his. Arguably the best way of arbitrating between the two is to consider the French perspective. Napoleon, after all, was better placed than anyone to pass judgement on the relative importance of the Anglo-Allied and Prussian forces ranged against him. Decoster's testimony appears to lend weight to Wellington's version of events, that the British had won the battle. Bonaparte, he maintained, watched as the Imperial Guard was 'annihilated in an instant [...] when he saw the old guard destroyed, he lost all hope; and, turning to Bertrand, said, "All is now over – let us save ourselves.'"[215] It is to Wellington's credit that he never cited this, consistent as he was in deriding peasants as the lowest of all possible sources. Decoster is nevertheless supported by other accounts from the French side. An anonymous Frenchman's account of the battle relating 'that the French army was disordered, and even beaten, before the arrival of the Prussian troops' was widely republished in the British press. The newspapers also reproduced a letter of 18 July from an anonymous sailor – Napoleon had surrendered himself to British custody three days earlier – claiming to have heard him say that:

> never was a battle so severely contested as that of Waterloo […] they were only overcome by the superiority of British discipline and British intrepidity. He was astonished at the firmness with which his charges were received and repulsed by our troops […] and he feels no hesitation in saying that the Duke of Wellington was a better general than himself.[216]

The latter account, if true, may well have been an attempt by Napoleon to ingratiate himself with his captors. If so, it failed. His incarceration on St Helena did not thereafter predispose him favourably towards his jailers. Whilst there, he was served as secretary for a time by General Baron Gaspard Gourgaud. In 1818, Gourgaud's account of the Waterloo campaign – by proxy, Napoleon's – was published in English. It caused a furore, given added grist by the fact that Gourgaud was then living in England, albeit in the process of being deported, controversially, under the terms of the Aliens Act. *The Times* dismissed him as 'this silly man' and refused to give credence to this 'very foolish account of the battle of Waterloo'.[217]

Gourgaud's book is very obviously an exercise in self-exculpation tempered by sour grapes: Napoleon insisted that he was badly let down by Grouchy and Ney; by all the laws of probability he ought to have triumphed on 18 June. There is little on Wellington as such, though the Duke is censured for not knowing where the French were before 15 June, and for fighting in front of a forest at Mont St Jean. He should also have retreated further north and joined with the Prussians before risking battle. What raised British hackles most, however, was that the explanation for Waterloo's outcome accorded more with Gneisenau's despatch than Wellington's. Napoleon, through Gourgaud, claimed that without the necessary diversion of Lobau and sections of the Imperial Guard, the full weight of the French

Army would have won the day by 3 p.m. Instead, Ziethen's arrival impacted decisively upon the morale of both the Anglo–Allied and French armies.[218]

Napoleon was clearly inconsistent in explaining his defeat. In his mind, the main point was that he should not have been defeated. What to him was the incidental detail of whether a British or Prussian Army had prevailed largely depended upon his mood. Sir Thomas Reade, who spoke with him on St Helena, had it right when he said that Bonaparte had told him:

> that the Duke of Wellington, ought, if he had been a good general, to have retreated, and not made his stand where he did. Yet, at other times, feeling peculiarly indignant at the Prussians, he, of course, will not allow them to have had any share in the result of that action, but describes his defeat to the firmness of the English infantry alone, by which all his plans were disconcerted.[219]

The publication of Gourgaud's account was nevertheless taken sufficiently seriously that it prompted a substantial letter to the British press saying that it offered a different interpretation from the one the British had become used to. It restated at length the Wellingtonian line: that the Duke had acted cautiously but prudently on 15 June. Whilst not denying that the Prussians made a contribution to the success of the day, Wellington had ordered his army to advance with the French already in confused retreat. The letter is simply signed as being from 'a British officer present'. Given that he was evidently well-informed, he was presumably somebody senior, possibly FitzRoy Somerset.

The Duke may possibly have sanctioned the anonymous letter himself. If he did, it was unnecessary. By 1818, both press and public had a firmly established view on both Wellington and Waterloo. Lord Anglesey put it neatly, at a grand public reception at Lichfield in Staffordshire to welcome him home, when he said that 'our troops under any other commander must have failed, and with any other troops under that great chieftain, the struggle must have been unsuccessful'.[220] The public too, shared Wellington's view that the battle had been both horrible and glorious. Little attempt was made to disguise the former. As early as 23 June, French losses were put at 35,000, the allies at 10,000. This was not so very far wrong. Such colossal casualty figures on a battlefield only roughly 4 square miles in size make it comparable to the slaughter of the Somme a century later.[221] In terms of casualties sustained per yard, it was arguably worse. Neither did reports confine themselves to impersonal statistics. One soldier's letter published in September, describing the battlefield on 19 June, confessed that:

I never think upon it but with horror. Death had reaped a plentiful harvest
and displayed his ravages in their ugliest forms. Poor mutilated wretches still
lay in the agonies of death, calling or making signs for a drop of water. There
was none to be had [...] here a dead man served for a pillar to his dying companion – others lay, as it were, holding each other in a last embrace.[222]

Nor, it was made clear, was there much dignity in death. Rare exceptions
were Sir Thomas Picton, whose body was brought home, in due course
to rest in St Paul's Cathedral; and Major Frederick Howard's, whose
remains would ultimately find their way to the family mausoleum at
Castle Howard.[223] The norm, though, as Hope Pattison recalled, was that,
'Preparations were soon set on foot to bury the dead by digging large
trenches, into which they were thrown promiscuously – friend and foe
together.' T. S. Lea, who detoured to Waterloo whilst travelling abroad pro-
moting his carpet making business, reported the further detail that 'after
some difficulty' the Prussians had forced 4,000 peasants to undertake the
gruesome task over a three day period. Two mass graves, each 60 feet long
and 9 feet wide, had accounted for the bulk of the corpses, whilst seven or
eight smaller graves had been necessary for assorted limbs. On his visit to
Waterloo a few weeks later, the Reverend Rudge was shocked by the reality
of death at the site of one of the mass graves beside Hougoumont:

The smell was here particularly offensive, and in some places, parts of the
human body were distinctly to be recognised. The earth with which they had
been covered, had sunk in, and exhibited here and there an arm and a human
face, the flesh nearly wasted away, and the features of the countenance hardly
distinguishable from the change they had undergone.[224]

Such was the fate of the fallen. The publication of such details could not but
make an impact. Dorothy Wordsworth recorded that, 'The particulars of the
battle of the 18th are dreadful. The joy of victory is indeed an awful thing, and I
had no patience with the tinkling of our Ambleside bells upon the occasion.'[225]

Like her brother, however, Dorothy Wordsworth's sentiments about
Waterloo did not reflect mainstream public opinion. So far as the latter was
concerned, any shock and revulsion very rapidly gave way to celebration
of what Wellington's army had achieved. This was true even amongst those
who had taken part in the battle (including Wellington himself), and had
lost friends. Captain Barlow, for example, lost his 'two most intimate friends'

but called Waterloo the 'field of honour'.[226] Britons rationalised the slaughter by seeing it in traditional terms. The language and images used were ones of necessary Christian sacrifice for the advancement of national glory. Individuals were not forgotten entirely – Picton and Ponsonby, as the most senior fatalities in a deferential society, were much alluded to – but like all the fallen they were idealised as heroes who had given their lives in a righteous cause. Such were the themes of the outpouring of prose and poetry in the weeks and months after the battle. The 15-year-old RGT's 'Thoughts on the Battle of Waterloo at Night', for instance, took solace in the fact that the fallen heroes who had died to 'save their country from despotic sway' would meet in heaven:

> Yet, what's more noble think? Or what's more brave?
> What greater fame or honour doth afford?
> Britannia ever mourns a soldier's grave,
> Who falls thus wielding the triumphant sword.[227]

If such sentiments were unoriginal, the public response to them following Waterloo was unprecedented. The most practical manifestation of this was the Waterloo Fund. This had its origins in two meetings held in London. On 28 June, bankers and merchants gathered at the City of London Tavern to consider a public subscription 'for the relief of the sufferers in the late glorious battles'. The other, for the same purpose, took place on 11 July at the Thatched House Tavern in Westminster with the Duke of York in the chair.[228] Amounts great and small flooded in. The Common Council of London voted £2,000. At Thornton in Yorkshire, the Reverend Patrick Brontë dedicated the collection from his thanksgiving service on 23 July. The fund reached £100,000 by early August. Within a year it approached £300,000. In spring 1817 it was announced that applicants now had until Waterloo Day to apply for its £457,576 1s 9d. Wellington was consulted about how this might most fairly be done.[229]

There was also Waterloo prize money. This ranged from Wellington's £61,000 to £2 11s 4d for corporals, drummers and privates. Beyond monetary reward, the War Office announced that all who had served in the campaign would be credited with two years service and be known as 'Waterloo men'.[230] The Duke himself was instrumental in moving for a Waterloo medal, further proof of how special he deemed the achievement. Indeed, his recommendation 'that we all should have the same medal' is one

of the most egalitarian statements he ever made.[231] Some 39,000 were issued
in 1816–1817. It was the first time that the British government had issued a
medal to all soldiers present at an action.

Other commemorative initiatives followed. The Prince Regent led the
way by creating a Waterloo Chamber at Windsor Castle. An estimated crowd
of 20,000 gathered at Portsmouth to witness the launch of the 84-gun
Waterloo adorned with a full-length figure of the Duke. Eight miles north,
on the old A3 road to London, supposedly because several returning veterans chose to settle at what had been known as Waitland End, Waterlooville
was born. Additions to existing settlements to mark the battle were especially common. In Truro, the corporation marked the second anniversary
of the battle by laying the foundation stone for a Waterloo Crescent, the
principal building in which was Wellington House. Nearly all the properties
in London's newly-completed Waterloo Place had been let by the start of
1818.[232] The phenomenon did not escape Jane Austen's notice. In *Sanditon*,
her unfinished novel of 1817, Mr Parker proudly shows a visitor the fruits of
his attempts to turn a Kentish coastal village into a fashionable resort:

> You will not think that I have made a bad exchange when we reach Trafalgar
> House – which by the bye, I almost wish I had not named Trafalgar – for
> Waterloo is more the thing now. However, Waterloo is in reserve – and if we
> have encouragement enough this year for a little Crescent to be ventured
> upon – (as I trust we shall) then, we shall be able to call it Waterloo Crescent.[233]

Dedicated memorials appeared too. One on the Marquis of Lothian's estate,
standing 100 feet high, was dedicated as early as mid-October. The four
sides read respectively 'Victory', 'Waterloo', 'Wellington' and 'To Wellington
and the British Army'.[234] The House of Commons petitioned the Prince
Regent for a national memorial on 29 June. Members responded warmly
to Castlereagh's proposal that, unusually, it should be dedicated to all those
who participated in the campaign since 'every soldier in the ranks throughout our whole army had behaved during the whole of the action, with the
most undaunted courage, and with unexampled coolness, patience and perseverance'. Charles Williams-Wynn went so far as to propose that the names
of all the fallen be inscribed on any monument. But Wellington was in no
danger of being eclipsed. The Duke of York had already privately informed
him that 'though the firmness of the troops is beyond all praise yet the
success must ever in justice be acknowledged to proceed from your own

personal conduct and presence of mind'.[235] Wilberforce proposed that only a palace could now fairly reflect the nation's gratitude to the Duke.

The parliamentary debate of June helped fuel a more general one in the months that followed as to the precise form of a national memorial. Most favoured traditional pillars or arches. With a perspicacity that would not be realised for a generation, *The Times* thought that a triumphal arch surmounted by an equestrian statue of Wellington at Hyde Park Corner 'would be a strong and permanent record of national greatness'. One correspondent believed that a sculpture of Wellington delivering the already immortal, 'Up, guards, and at them!' would gain public approval. Doubtless with an eye to employment for himself, the architect, James Elmes, suggested creating a 40-acre village in north London with houses named after individual heroes of the campaign.[236]

Another with a possible eye to self-advancement was Wordsworth. A day before Parliament returned to the question on 5 February 1816, he had overcome his initial reluctance to write about Waterloo by publishing lines intended for inscription on a public memorial:

Heroes! – for instant sacrifice prepared;
Yet filled with ardour and on triumph bent
'Mid direst shocks of mortal accident –
To you who fell, and you whom slaughter spared
To guard the fallen, and consummate the event,
Your Country rears this sacred Monument!

MPs in fact met to discover that their broad unanimity on the question of six months previously had partially evaporated. The euphoria engendered by Waterloo had given way to inter-service rivalry. Castlereagh attempted to defuse this by proposing that the Waterloo memorial proceed alongside one to Nelson, Trafalgar and the navy, since 'the house would be anxious to hand those exertions down to posterity in a manner that should avoid the indication of any preference, and place both services on a footing of equality'. He was not entirely successful. Was Trafalgar, it was asked, really as significant as Waterloo? Might not a single monument to all who had served in the war – Tierney argued strongly for a church – be more appropriate?[237]

Castlereagh's motion for two monuments was eventually carried. The deadline for designs to be lodged with the British Gallery was set for 1 July. In spring 1817 William Wilkins' design for the Waterloo memorial was chosen from amongst 200 others. Costing £200,000, his proposed 280-foot ornamental tower was to have stood in Portland Place facing Regent's Park. Like the one to Trafalgar at Greenwich, it was, for reasons not entirely clear, never built.[238] The national memorial to Waterloo was instead a bridge. Shortly before the battle's first anniversary, it was announced that a clause would be added to the Bill for the projected Strand Bridge to rename it. Designed by the Scottish engineer, John Rennie, the Waterloo Bridge Company was empowered to raise half a million pounds for its construction. Its completion provided the focus for the celebrations of the battle's second anniversary. The Prince Regent, flanked by Wellington and the Duke of York, officially opened it on 18 June 1817. The project was hailed enthusiastically by the press:

> No mode of perpetuating great deeds by works of art is more consistent with good taste than where such works combine, in a high degree, what is ornamental with what is useful. Monuments of this kind have stronger claims on public respect than the costly construction of pillars, obelisks, and towers.[239]

At 2,890 feet in length it was indeed monumental. But it hardly represented the thanks of a grateful nation. The taxpayer had not had to bear the cost. Four toll houses were an integral part of the bridge's construction, with a penny toll levied on those wanting to use it.

Catalysed by economic hard times, the inevitable waning of public euphoria over Waterloo led to other memorials being less grand than had originally been projected. The same day that Waterloo Bridge was opened, the foundation stone of Robert Smirke's Irish memorial was laid in Dublin's Phoenix Park. It was scheduled for completion by 18 June 1819. However, despite the fact that £20,000 had been quickly subscribed, the funds ran out before a statue of Wellington could be added to the 210-foot column. Plans to erect a monument to the Duke and Waterloo on the Blackdown Hills in Somerset had also begun well. Some £1,700 was raised and 10,000 attended the ceremony to lay the foundation stone in October 1817. Six acres of land around the memorial were to be tenanted by three former servicemen, respectively from England, Scotland and Ireland. Their duties included maintaining the 4-acre memorial site and helping to oversee an annual athletics festival on 18 June. But the four Waterloo cannon to decorate the base of the Egyptian-style triangular column never arrived. It was completed, minus a statue of Wellington, only in 1854.[240]

The Somerset site owed its selection to the fact that it overlooked the town of Wellington, the supposed ancestral home of the Duke's family. After Waterloo, the question of where his home would be could not be deferred indefinitely. His initial preference was for a Somerset estate, though the media was far more exercised by the question than he was. The architect, Benjamin Dean Wyatt, spent three years investigating possible properties in at least six different counties. His search finally bore fruit in 1817 when Lord Rivers' Stratfield Saye estate on the Hampshire-Berkshire border came onto the market. The sale was completed for £263,000.[241] Most people, Wellington included, assumed that the relatively unimpressive house would be demolished to make way for a grand Waterloo Palace to rival Blenheim. That it did not owed much to the Duke's being content simply to improve what he had. As was the case with the national memorial, however, the nation had not matched its actions to its words.

Wellington's indifference to the failure of a palace to materialise in Hampshire is also to be explained in terms of how his life unfolded. Stratfield Saye would prove to be less a palatial home than a comfortable winter hunting retreat. His principal residence would be 149 Piccadilly, better known to contemporaries as No. 1, London or Apsley House. The Duke bought this on generous terms in 1817 from his financially-embarrassed elder brother, the Marquis Wellesley. It provided him with a London base for what he must have already decided would be a busy public life, not a sedate and glorious retirement, on his return to Britain.[242]

Wellington was not permanently absent from Britain in the two to three years after 1815. His visits were nevertheless brief and sporadic: in summer 1816 when his return included a visit to Cheltenham; most extensively, when he was present for the 1817 Waterloo anniversary celebrations.[243] Most of his time, however, was passed either at his base in Cambrai or in Paris, interlaced with regular visits to the Low Countries. As Commander-in-Chief of the 150,000-strong allied army of occupation in France, the British press occasionally mentioned his whereabouts, but generally regarded his activities as unexceptional. The chief instances before 1818 when this was not true were the execution of Marshal Ney by firing squad in December 1815, and a libel trial brought against the *St James Chronicle* in February 1816 following articles alleging that Wellington had conducted an adulterous relationship with Lady Frances Webster. Neither episode notice-ably damaged the Duke's reputation with most Britons. The consensus was, as the Duke insisted, that Ney's fate was an internal French matter.

Meanwhile, the libel case ended with the newspaper having £2,000 damages awarded against it. Some might even have agreed with Wellington's barrister's line that his client 'might be looked up to by Christendom as the tutelar saint of the moral world'.[244]

These exceptions apart, Wellington was arguably less of a fixture in the national consciousness after 1815 than at any time since 1809. His virtual disappearance from political caricature between Waterloo and 1819 is one measure of this. The year 1818, however, did mark something of a return to prominence for him. This was triggered, literally, when a pistol was discharged at the Duke as he returned to his apartment on the Avenue des Champs-Élysées during the night of 11 February by a fanatical Napoleonic veteran, André Cantillon. The allied press was outraged. As the *Austrian Observer* put it, 'The man whom he attempted to assassinate does not appear here in his own individual character: he belongs to Europe – nay, to the human race.' A fortnight after the event, normality of sorts appeared to have returned for 'the Duke of Wellington is remembered only as a personage who now and then gives a dinner, has an audience at Court, and hires Grassini to sing for him'. In fact, Cantillon's arrest and trial filled inches of column space for most of the year.[245] By then, Wellington had long since been focused on other matters. He had come to the conclusion that the intended five-year term for the army of occupation was not only unnecessary but counter-productive in that it helped fuel French revanchist sentiment. His argument that the force both be reduced in size and withdrawn early proved persuasive. By November 1818 the last troops had left. For someone who had spent almost all of the previous decade away from his native land, it was news indeed when the Paris papers reported that Wellington was leaving too, adding that, 'It is said that he will not revisit the Continent for a considerable time.' Before the year was out, the British press was able to confirm rumours that he would join the government. On New Year's Eve it was reported that the Duke had started work as Master-General of the Ordnance.[246] The Hero of Waterloo, hitherto a quasi-mythical figure, so far as the British public was concerned, would now become real.

4

Heroes and Villains: Wellington, Waterloo and other Battles 1819–1832

S
ir William Fraser was one of many who believed that Wellington's reputation rose after Waterloo. Large crowds regularly gathered to see him. On 28 September 1819, when he received the freedom of Plymouth, untold numbers pressed for 'a transient view of the deliverer of Europe'. Four days later, in Exeter, he was reported to have shaken hundreds of hands in fifteen minutes. When he stayed with the Duke of Buckingham in 1827, a 450-pound Wellington pudding was prepared for children on the Stowe estate. A Mr Makepeace, who claimed to have lost his nose and part of his face to the last cannon shot fired by the retreating French at Waterloo, was especially keen to see him. In the same year a Wellington autograph from 1814 was sold for £1 6s. The Duke was even reported to be popular in China, an approximation of his name in Chinese suggesting that he was 'perhaps descended in a direct line from the five-clawed dragon, who, it seems, is the guardian saint of the Celestial Empire'.[247]

In fact, Wellington's popular standing would fluctuate wildly in the first decade or so following his return to England. Even his devoted admirer, Mrs Arbuthnot, records how as early as September 1820, 'the Duke told us the people had shouted to him as he went down to the House in the morning, "No hero, We want no hero!!"' She decided that 'his unmerited unpopularity did not extend beyond the Radicals of London'. But this was untrue. Though most newspapers ignored or downplayed it, there were, for example, reports of popular dissension when he attended a public dinner in his honour at Winchester in March 1821.[248]

The increasing public ambivalence towards the Duke was at root the consequence of his decision to become Master-General of the Ordnance in Lord Liverpool's government. If his objective had been simply the preservation of his heroic status, there would be much truth in Alava's judgement 'that the Duke of Wellington ought never to have had anything to do with politicks – that he ought to have remained, not only as the soldier of England, but of Europe, to be ready to appear again at its command whenever his talents and services might be wanted'.[249] Wellington believed that he could act as an independent servant of the State, insulated from the excesses of party politics. He made it a condition of accepting office that he would not necessarily be bound by the anyway imperfectly developed doctrine of collective cabinet responsibility: if the government resigned he would not necessarily feel obliged to resign with it. Events quickly exposed the limitations of his premises. His eminence, ability and instinct to fight for causes in which he believed ineluctably dragged him to the forefront of political controversy. He rapidly became identified in the popular mind with the forces of reaction. Whilst the battlefield site, and those who fought at it retained their special allure with most of the nation each Waterloo Day during the 1820s, its victor would increasingly become associated, across the political spectrum, with the French variant of his name, 'Vilainton'. More accurately perhaps, to risk an unavoidable pun, it might be suggested that a pair of Wellingtons emerged. By 1832, the gulf between the two, one the hero of Waterloo, the other the villain who had destroyed the Protestant constitution whilst, paradoxically, having opposed Parliamentary Reform, would appear to be unbridgeable.

Wellington had hardly been conceived of as a Liberal before 1819. Having attended the Congresses of Vienna and Aix-la-Chapelle he was associated in the popular mind with the Russian, Prussian and Austrian autocracies, which constituted the Holy Alliance. He was also a close friend of the Foreign Secretary, Byron's bête noire, Lord Castlereagh. But it was the Duke whom Byron likened to the first murderer in Macbeth as 'the best of cut-throats', a backhanded compliment if ever there was one, for:

You have repaired Legitimacy's crutch,
A prop not quite so certain as before.[250]

Wellington's true political colours would be confirmed for many by his behaviour during the series of domestic popular agitations of 1819–1821. During the summer of 1819 there were mass meetings across the industrial north, Midlands and western Scotland, demanding a melange of reforms that included universal suffrage, annual parliaments and the repeal of the 1815 Corn Laws. At Blackburn in July, one of the speakers was a Waterloo veteran 'who begged pardon for having fought in so bad a cause'. The most famous gathering took place on 16 August at St Peter's Field, Manchester. Sixty thousand assembled to hear Henry 'Orator' Hunt address them. Concerned that Hunt would incite disorder, the local authorities ordered the local yeomanry cavalry to assist with his arrest; in the confusion, men from the 15th Hussars joined them. In the ensuing crush hundreds were injured and about a dozen left dead and dying. The latter included 18-year-old John Lees from Oldham. He had survived the French cavalry in 1815 to return to his trade as a cotton spinner. At his inquest, William Harrison testified that his friend had indeed been at Waterloo 'but never in such danger as there; at Waterloo there was man to man, but there it was down-right murder'.[251]

The Duke joined the rest of the government, however, in defending the actions of the Manchester authorities. Nationwide, the Opposition tried to canalise popular anger over the Peterloo Massacre by trying to organise a series of county meetings to censure its decision. A requisition calling for such a meeting in Wellington's Hampshire was amongst them. It failed to materialise, owing to a strong counter-requisition, to which the Duke was a signatory. This earned him the opprobrium of the Opposition's Lord Brougham, who argued, with some logic, that as a member of the government under scrutiny, Wellington should have maintained the political neutrality of which he boasted. It is no surprise to learn that the Duke was one of the principal targets for the Cato Street conspirators, who intended to assassinate the cabinet in February 1820.[252]

The following year brought Wellington no respite from either Brougham or controversy. Brougham was chief attorney to the popular Caroline of Brunswick (sister to the Duke who had been killed at Quatre Bras), the estranged wife of the profligate George IV. When the latter became king in January 1820, the Duke was prominent in his government's negotiations to reach a settlement with her. When these failed, George insisted that ministers introduce a Bill divorcing her. As Wellington rode from the Lords during the hearings that summer and autumn, he was 'assailed by every species of noise that by possibility could denote popular disapprobation'. Such was the fear of popular unrest in London by the end of 1820 that it was estimated that there were enough men and guns in the capital to win another Waterloo.[253]

It was Wellington's role in the Hampshire public's response to the Queen Caroline affair that really damaged his political reputation, at least with progressive commentators. On becoming Lord Lieutenant of the county in December 1820, he agreed to present a loyal address to the King signed by the county's predominantly Tory gentry. Hampshire's leading Opposition figures, meanwhile, had held a county meeting, attended by some 5,000 freeholders, deprecating the government's actions against Caroline. Sensing blood, Opposition peers accused the Duke of denying the Hampshire freeholders their voice. Wellington protested his innocence, insisting that as the address, in his view, represented the county's voice, 'it was not necessary to go through the farce of a county meeting'. This belittling of a long-accepted constitutional right of assembly was far and away his biggest political gaffe before 1830. Creevey recorded that he 'was pummelled black and blue' by the Opposition leadership. As late as 1832, an ironic poem against him included the lines:

I never saw a reason
For heeding those mob-farces miscalled 'meetings'.[254]

By early 1821, therefore, any political honeymoon period for the Duke had long since passed. In caricatures, memorably Hone and Cruikshank's 1819 parody 'The Political House that Jack Built', he was 'Waterloo Man', Lord Liverpool's hired assassin. Even *The Times* thought that he 'has become less admired and less popular, with every year that he has formed part of the Civil Government, and almost with every vote that he has given on questions of national politics'. 'Military men,' the paper concluded, 'are seldom very sound or generous politicians. Their instinct is so strong on the side of power, that they would [...] extend to whole nations the discipline inseparable from an army.'[255]

Wellington's waning popularity, accompanied, as the Peterloo sobriquet exemplified, by the resurfacing of popular ambivalences about the army, did not, however, have any discernible impact upon the numbers of people wanting to visit the sites where both had prospered together. The Duke himself was there at least three times during the summer of 1821, in September by royal command, when he acted as guide to George IV. Anglesey too visited at around this time, supposedly dining with his son at the table on which his leg had been amputated. In 1828 he told Creevey that 'the people of that house have made the Lord knows what by people coming to see the grave of my leg which was buried in the garden!'[256] For ordinary mortals, the guide of choice, until his death in the mid-1820s, remained Jean Decoster. In the summer of 1824, he was reported to be living in a roadside cottage about a mile from Waterloo church and that 'so many and constant are his visitors, English and Prussian (but few French), that at this season of the year, long days, his only employment is acting as a guide to the visitors'. The following year a Mr J. Deville and his party were hugely impressed by him, not least because he apparently knew every general officer's name from the battle, and 'our feelings were kept alive [...] in a manner I never before experienced'. Doubtless, like everybody else, Decoster embellished his account with each retelling – by October 1822 he was insisting that pigeons had not returned to Hougoumont until three weeks after the battle. Suspicions also lingered that his sympathies, like that of many Belgians, had lain with Napoleon. For this reason, Lieutenant-Colonel Peter Hawker labelled him 'disgraceful' when he made the obligatory Waterloo visit as part of a European tour in spring 1821. Hawker had nevertheless actively sought him out to act as his guide.[257]

Hougoumont, with or without pigeons, seems to have remained relatively unaltered for most of the 1820s.[258] An 1822 visitor described it as 'a complete ruin' except for the chapel containing its fifteenth-century crucifix, the Christ figure charred, some said miraculously, only at its feet. The only 'addition' was visitors' autographs on the walls. Some of these, in particular Sir Walter Scott's and Lord Byron's, quickly became attractions in themselves. Only by the end of the decade had new gates been erected to replace those 'so much disfigured by the shots that they resembled a sieve'. In the orchard, one visitor recounted dining on as many strawberries and cherries as 'any person could reasonably desire'.

La Haye Sainte, by contrast, had been repaired and re-inhabited. The same visitor who had dined al fresco at Hougoumont reported arriving there on a feast day and found himself eating amongst young peasants who sang and laughed over a good meal, the garden 'full of flowers, and redolent of sweets'. Recalling what had passed there a little over a decade before, he reported that 'Recollections of this kind at dinner do not serve to improve the digestion.'

However young, the feasters can hardly have been ignorant of La Haye Sainte's role in the battle, for there was a pyramidal memorial to the men that had defended it. Other memorials included the black gothic arrow-head one to the Prussians at Plancenoit, completed in 1818, and another to the Hanoverians, begun in autumn 1826, consisting of a pillar topped with a statue of victory.[259] A more implausible 'memorial' was a table at La Belle Alliance, said to be the one used by Wellington and Blücher when they met there on the evening of 18 June. Perhaps it provided a resting place for the visitors' book that was in evidence by 1822. Away from the three famous buildings, however, the general view was, as one 1822 visitor wrote, that farming had 'entirely obliterated the traces of the dreadful conflict'. In particular, the two mass graves around La Haye Sainte containing an estimated 6,000 bodies had been entirely levelled by ploughing. It looked so ordinary that Samuel Taylor Coleridge, who visited the field in 1828, professed to be totally unaffected owing to 'the total deficiency of memorable places to excite any interest in him unless they possessed some natural beauty'. He was surely being obtuse. William Wordsworth, his travelling companion, 'keenly inspected the field of battle, insatiably curious after tombstones, and spots where officers had fallen (the Duke of Brunswick, Picton, Ponsonby, etc)'. For him, as on his first visit in 1820, the predominant feeling remained the 'horror breaking from the silent ground'.[260]

Wordsworth was largely, one presumes, imagining the horror, but it was still tangible. The anonymous visitor of 1822 recorded that, 'In traversing the field [...] we found several skulls, bones, and musket-bullets, which the plough had recently turned up.' In 1824 a former colonel in the Portuguese Army noted that the trade in battlefield memorabilia was so profitable that 'there are a host of young Paysannes accost the visitor [...] with shot, grape and musket, which they sell for half a franc a piece'. By the end of the decade, a Monsieur Saintine reported that though 'great quantities' of swords and muskets were still being found, their price had been depressed by the rumour 'that the inhabitants had a regular manufactory for these articles'. By contrast, the verisimilitude of skulls, 'which are excellently done up', his guide assured him, was impeccable since 'whenever we want any bones or skulls we mark the place, [where the ears of rye were darker] go at night, and dig them up'.[261]

It was not just local peasants who were alleged to have violated the graves of the fallen. The *London Observer* of 18 November 1822:

estimated that more than a million of bushels of human and inhuman bones were imported last year from the continent of Europe into the port of Hull. The neighbourhood of [...] Waterloo, and of all of the places where, during the late bloody war, the principal battles were fought, have been swept alike of the bones of the hero and of the horse which he rode. Thus collected from every quarter, they have been shipped to the port of Hull, and thence forwarded to the Yorkshire bone-grinders, who have erected steam-engines and powerful machinery, for the purpose of reducing them to a granulary state. In this condition they are sent chiefly to Doncaster, one of the largest agricultural markets in that part of the country, and are there sold to the farmers to manure their lands. The oily substance gradually evolving as the base calcines, makes a more substantial manure than any other substance, particularly human bones. It is now ascertained beyond a doubt, by actual experiment on an extensive scale, that a dead soldier is a most valuable article of commerce; and, for ought known to the contrary, the good farmers of Yorkshire are, in a great measure, indebted to the bones of their children for their daily bread. It is certainly a singular fact, that Great Britain should have sent out such multitudes of soldiers to fight the battles of this country upon the continent of Europe, and should then import their bones as an article of commerce to fatten her soil![262]

This is a remarkable account. Byron, amongst others, commented on how crops grew best over mass gravesites but those were in situ. If true, this commercialisation of Waterloo heroes is a telling comment on what society thought of, and did for, the ordinary soldier. It was a far cry indeed from the idea, briefly floated by some in 1815, that all the fallen should be memorialised by name. Britons, and their Waterloo allies, still had a long road to travel before the sanctity of battlefields was properly recognised. The idea of Waterloo in the public imagination as a place of heroism, rather than a site of mass slaughter, was ever-increasingly in the ascendant during the 1820s. Wordsworth's reaction was a minority one. Visitors happily took home human bones, presumably because they viewed them more as trophies of the great national triumph than as human remains deserving of individual respect. Such a mindset would explain the absence of any significant outcry to the *London Observer*'s report.

One memento Waterloo visitors of the 1820s could no longer take home with them was pieces of the elm near the crossroads, which had been Wellington's command post. The farmer on whose land it stood complained that he was losing half an acre's crops annually to the feet of tourists anxious to set their eyes on what contemporaries agreed was the most celebrated tree in British history since Shakespeare's mulberry. Since, by the autumn of 1818, it was anyway as good as dead – it was reported that the trunk was completely stripped of its bark to at least 3 feet above ground level – he determined to fell it. Serendipitously, on 27 September, the day before the axe was due to fall, one man who visited the scene was John George Children, a Fellow (later President) of the Royal Society and trustee of the British Museum. He persuaded the farmer to sell it to him.[263] This did not spare the elm its fate but it did ensure portions of it a more verifiable posterity. Two chairs, fashioned from it by Thomas Chippendale the younger in 1820, were duly presented to the Duke and George IV. The latter kept his at Windsor Castle, perhaps near the snuff box made partly from the same tree, which Sir Walter Scott gave him in 1822. A third chair was created from wood presented to the Duke of Rutland, Children's friend from university, whose son had served in the 10th Hussars at Waterloo. Portions of the remainder were incorporated into a work-table made by William Lovett 'with a silver plate let into the top stating this'. Lovett, subsequently a founding father of the Chartist movement, detested Wellington's politics; Lovett the patriot and apprentice craftsman was clearly proud of his vicarious association with Waterloo.[264] His is a nice example of someone who could conceptualise two Wellingtons.

The loss of Wellington's elm was more than compensated for by the creation of the Lion's Mound, an initiative that would change the topography of the battlefield forever. In 1819, King William I of the Netherlands instructed his chief engineer to produce plans for a memorial on the site where his son, the Prince of Orange (in Wellington's 1824 description 'a brave young man but that's all'), had been wounded at Waterloo shortly before 7 p.m.[265] Work was properly under way by spring 1824; 2,000 men with 600 horses and carts were being employed on the project by the summer. In the process of constructing an artificial hill over 130 feet high and 1,700 feet in circumference, they were to move well over 300,000 cubic yards of earth. This came mostly from the ridge at the centre of the Anglo-Allied line, effectively removing the southern bank of Wellington's sunken road towards La Haye Sainte. Surmounting a pedestal at the top of the mound was a 31-ton cast-iron lion, some 21-feet long and 12-feet high, with a paw resting on a globe. It was formally put in place on 30 October 1826. J. Deville described it as 'a most stupendous work' that brought to mind the similarly proportioned Neolithic chalk mound of Silbury Hill near Avebury in Wiltshire.[266]

Contemporaries were divided as to the merits or otherwise of *La Butte du Lion*. The Reverend William Falconer, who observed the mound as a work in progress in 1825, thought that it disturbed the dead. This did not prevent him from picking up a rib disturbed by the work, though he did put it down again only to discover the next day that a less respectful visitor 'had probably secured it as a relic'. Wellington was also unimpressed. Like Falconer, he first saw the mound in 1825 when guiding a Mrs Parnther over the battlefield. This seems the most likely occasion for his supposed remark that, 'They have spoiled my Battle-field.'[267] Belgians were also less than enamoured. In 1830, on gaining independence, there were rumours that some would attempt to destroy the lion, which they regarded as a symbol of their having had to live under a Dutch yoke as part of the United Kingdom of the Netherlands since 1815. Above all, inevitably, it was the French who objected to the 'modern pyramid'. Monsieur Saintine related to his compatriots in 1829 that the lion was 'looking towards, and apparently threatening' France. But most tourists loved it, for the panoramic vantage point it afforded of the battlefield. By 1830, map sellers and two women selling cakes, wine and gin were on the lion's pedestal to greet them.[268] Such was the genesis of what would become known as *Le Hameau du Lion*.

The erection of official allied memorials on the battlefield prompted the *Morning Post* to ask why, 'England, that supplied the transcendent Genius who planned, and the main bulk of the heroic army who achieved that most glorious victory – England is the only nation whose triumphs rest unrecorded by a single national monument.' By the same date, regret had also been expressed that there was no official act of remembrance each 18 June, pointing out that in Belgium, public officials attended *Te Deums* in the principal churches:

> We love these patriotic rites to the shades of departed heroes […] Why do we suffer the great day in question, to pass by unheeded in the march of time? Why is not some national solemnity appointed to mark its return? Some public scenes at which children may learn to lisp the name of Wellington, and prattle, even in their sports, of Waterloo![269]

An editorial suggested one possible answer: 'In times of peace, we are certainly not fond of recurring to the triumph of war in a public way, as we would not wish to excite any angry feeling in the bosom of those once respected as gallant enemies but now esteemed as honourable friends.'

For a few others at least, the reluctance to celebrate 18 June stemmed from the belief that Waterloo had marked the triumph of *ancien régime* ideals and the government (of which Wellington had become a member), to which they were opposed. There had always been some who thought that the Duke had been the instrument of those intent on upholding despotism. Byron, for one, asked:

> And I shall be delighted to learn who,
> Save you and yours, have gained by Waterloo?[270]

Those who agreed with him included Robert Waithman, who became MP for the City of London in June 1818. He proclaimed at a celebratory dinner in his honour that, 'The Battle of Waterloo was the Ministers' battle, in which neither this country nor the Continent gained any benefit [great applause].' Similarly, John Cam Hobhouse, who only narrowly lost the 1819 Westminster by-election, refuted allegations that he had referred to 'the carnage of Mont St Jean' but 'would content himself with remarking, that British soldiers had never been employed on a more unfortunate occasion than the battle of Waterloo'. And at a dinner in Edinburgh to remember Charles James Fox's birthday, Lord Erskine told assembled guests that Britain found itself 'even after a kind of miracle in our favour, at the battle of Waterloo, in a state of Europe far less favourable to our prosperity, than probably would have been its condition if we had left France, in the beginning of her Revolution'. Certainly it was easier to forge a national consensus about the meaning of Trafalgar: in 1805 a charismatic hero had died in a battle that was won by a Britain fighting against an enemy that planned to invade her.[271]

Such sentiments, however, did not reflect the popular mainstream. More representative of what was going on was the ironic advice contained in *Freeman's Journal* under the headline 'on the privilege of being disagreeable'. It included the injunction for, 'All Englishmen travelling on the continent: to shew a due sense of their own superiority, and a becoming recollection of the battle of Waterloo.'[272] The truth is that many Britons did continue to commemorate Waterloo, so much so that a disgusted French press was complaining at the end of the 1820s that were they to mark their martial triumphs on the same scale 'there would be no end to them'. Though church services were relatively rare, church bells were commonly rung on 18 June in British towns and cities from Scotland to Cornwall. By 1821 too, there were public memorials inside St Paul's Cathedral to Lord James Hay (General Maitland's youthful aide-de-camp who had died at Quatre Bras), and Sir William Ponsonby and Sir Thomas Picton, the senior generals who had fallen. The latter was also remembered by an obelisk to him near Carmarthen. Opened to the public on Waterloo Day 1828, 10,000 had attended the ceremony to mark the laying of the foundation stone on 16 August 1825. Picton's Waterloo medal was placed beneath it. And though the long-talked about Waterloo column failed to materialise, the memorial initiated before Waterloo by the ladies of England was completed. Dedicated to Wellington 'and his brave companions in arms', an 18-foot statue of Achilles, its head said to have been based on the Duke's, was unveiled in Hyde Park on Waterloo Day 1822. Cast from cannon taken at Vitoria, Salamanca, Toulouse and Waterloo, it was the first public statue in London of a nude male. Offended sensibilities were mollified by the addition of a strategically-placed fig leaf.[273]

It was, however, celebration rather than commemoration that was the salient feature of each 18 June. In London the best known event was the fete held in Vauxhall Gardens. That which took place in 1827 was 'one of the most grand and extraordinary perhaps ever witnessed in this country'. The centrepiece was a re-enactment of the battle on a site of several acres – which became known as the Waterloo Grounds – with underground gas pipes used to provide fire. Many veterans took part. The following year local residents complained that the noise was a 'moral nuisance' that 'could only be compared to the cannonading of a town'.[274] The only regular event to rival it was J. M. Amherst's *The Battle of Waterloo*, staged at Astley's Amphitheatre from 1824. It provided the perfect vehicle for the famous equestrian performer, Andrew Ducrow, who had taken over the business from its eponymous founders. Running initially for 144 nights, it was destined to be revived for over half a century. Both Vauxhall and Astley's, however, were eclipsed in scale by the one-off regatta on the Thames organised by the Duke of Clarence as Lord High Admiral on Waterloo Day 1828, purportedly the first event of its kind since the reign of Charles II. Wellington, who at various times attended both Vauxhall and Astley's, arrived at 4.30 p.m. He was 'hailed by loud cheers' from vast crowds on either bank as he was rowed to the state cabin of Clarence's barge.[275]

In the provinces, travelling panoramas of the battle remained popular. One, consisting of ten scenes painted on 10,000 square feet of canvas, complete with a piper from Waterloo, could be viewed in Glasgow until it closed early in 1821. A decade later, Mr Laidlaw's panorama in Brighton proved 'a resistless magnet with the military, and their many friends cannot but be influenced by their example'.[276] Waterloo Day itself became an obvious midsummer date to choose for other celebratory events. In 1819, for example, 18 June was chosen to open a new stretch of the Lancaster Canal; in 1825 the day was picked to launch steam packets at Liverpool and Chester. Somewhat incongruously, the annual Maying at St Cross near Winchester was also moved to 18 June to mark Waterloo.[277] Meanwhile, near Chelmsford in 1825, a Waterloo veteran named Mr Graham chose 18 June to ascend in a balloon: 'It is to be hoped that his courage will in future be guided with more prudence,' noted a concerned editorial. Such admonitions did not deter a Mr Green from undertaking a similar stunt near Exeter on 18 June 1828 during which, for reasons best known to himself, he despatched a cat safely to ground via a parachute.[278]

Above all, ordinary Britons took advantage of 18 June as an opportunity to eat, drink and make merry. There were public dinners in Aberdeen, a ball and supper at Ipswich; the people of Pontefract held a dinner dance to celebrate the completion of their Waterloo monument.[279] Military personnel regularly played host: in 1826, Colonel Horner and the officers of the North Somerset Yeomanry Cavalry patronised a grand gala event at the Sydney Gardens in Bath; in 1832 an estimated 400 attended the fancy dress ball and dinner given by the Plymouth garrison. Soldiers might in their turn be feted by locals: detachments of the Scots Greys were entertained at Ipswich in 1825.[280] A typical statement of what they all believed themselves to be celebrating – the quasi-myth of Waterloo as a purely British victory – was given eloquent expression by an editorial in the *Morning Post* to mark the battle's tenth anniversary. It was, the paper said, one 'which seemed to absorb and eclipse all the former triumphs of our arms, by its splendour and the importance of its results, and which shed a lustre on Old England and unparalleled perhaps in the annals of the world'.[281]

As well as being sponsors and guests at public gatherings, the military also marked Waterloo Day with its own series of events. Those on duty on 18 June wore laurel leaves in their caps. Those who had actually fought in the campaign were excused duty and received an extra day's pay. With over 70 per cent of officers who had served in the campaign (1,646 of 2,281), still in the army in 1827 it comes as no surprise to learn that many dined together, for example those from three regiments of the Guards who met in London's Thatched House Tavern that year.[282] One supposes that such occasions were more given over to reflection than most. A few were explicitly so. Arguably the most notable occurred in 1829. Sixteen veterans of the 92nd processed behind a piper from their barracks in Limerick to Sir Denis Pack's grave in County Kilkenny. Here they placed laurel on the grave of the man (Pack died in 1823), in whose brigade they had served at Waterloo.[283]

Their unusual act of remembrance concluded, however, the sixteen veterans conformed to the far more typical programme of dinner where, 'animated by an ample supply of mountain dew, the brave fellows passed a delightful evening, and "fought their battles o'er again, and told how fields were won"'. Mountain dew, in its various alcoholic forms, seems to have been the absolute prerequisite for any gathering of Waterloo veterans. Most passed off unremarkably. Even some excesses were reported with an indulgent pen. In 1826, after a suitably liquid commemoration of 18 June, a private who had served with the 42nd in 1815 appeared before magistrates in Marlborough Street. He was charged with being drunk in the streets, and had refused the watchman's entreaties to go home 'saying that he had been at Waterloo, and as he had not been compelled to retreat there, he would not fly before a watchman'. The magistrates offered to let him go if he would promise not to get drunk again before the following 18 June. The veteran thought this impossible 'for there is the Anniversary of the battle of Vitoria to come, then that of Salamanca, and – but I cannot recollect them all, but I must get drunk upon those days, and then, you see, we shall have the battle of Waterloo round by then. This is the effect of being always victorious.'[284]

Similar episodes were not always so amusing. On Waterloo Day 1816, Benjamin Twigg and John Moody were amongst twenty celebrating at The White Lion near the Tower of London. Drawn into an argument by a Spanish sailor, they were both fatally stabbed. Sadly, this example of alcohol-induced violence was not unique. Exactly five years later, five soldiers were charged with the murder of William Cogle, who died from his injuries following a heated altercation in Westminster. The coroner's jury expressed regret that 'during the last two Anniversaries of the Battle of Waterloo, the drunken and disorderly conduct of the soldiery in this neighbourhood has excited considerable alarm'. The Duke of York ordered that troops should be confined to barracks for future celebrations.[285] It made little difference. In 1823, dragoons stationed in Canterbury met, appropriately enough, at The Duke of Wellington 'to regale themselves, and talk over the merits of the battle: after some little time, they were joined by others, principally broom-dashers, and both parties got into warm altercation; at length, each man arming himself with whatever came first to hand, a desperate fight ensued, and many of them were most severely bruised'.[286] For all that he was criticised for it, there was some substance in Wellington's contention that British soldiers were 'the scum of the earth […] fellows who have all enlisted for drink'.[287]

Such stories only received the amount of column inches they did because the participants had been at Waterloo. To have survived the battle and then still be cut down prematurely was deemed a newsworthy bitter irony. Shortly before Christmas 1825, Major Whitefoord, a captain in the 15th Hussars at Waterloo, who carried a bullet inside him from the day, was killed in a shooting accident near Ipswich when his friend slipped and discharged his gun. A Lieutenant Grant, who had led the charge of the 42nd Highlanders, was run over and killed by a stagecoach on or about Waterloo Day 1827.[288] And the battle itself was still numbering its victims, for several veterans who died during the 1820s were said to have succumbed to injuries sustained in 1815. Lieutenant W. P. Fortescue of the 47th died in June 1821 after a 'decline brought on by a severe wound through the body, received at the battle of Waterloo'. In 1828, R. Bamford Hesketh of the 3rd Guards died in Denbighshire 'after a long and painful illness from a wound sustained at Waterloo'. But none was as stoical as William Addiss, a former grenadier from Herefordshire, who died in Dublin on Waterloo Day 1822. As he slipped away, he bade his mother decorate his room with laurel and wore his medal – which he asked to be placed on his coffin. His last reported words were 'that it was a day on which a soldier ought to be proud to die'.[289]

Even for those who survived Waterloo and had left the army, the fact of their having served in the campaign meant that they remained of public interest. Few can have led such an esoteric existence, however, as Mr Thompson, billed in 1821 as a 7-foot Scottish giant who had fought at Waterloo, and who was one of five 'natural curiosities' who could be viewed during market week in Derby. More predictably, a good number found temporary or permanent employment in the various fields of law enforcement. Several Waterloo veterans were amongst those sworn in as special constables at the end of 1823, including one who had survived forty-three sabre wounds in the battle. John Briggs of the 1st Life Guards found a new life as lodge turnkey at Worcester Jail until his death in November 1826. At Waterloo he had been one of those who had helped carry Lord Uxbridge from the field. Professional policing offered another obvious opening. Best known is Charles Rowan. He had attended the Duchess of Richmond's ball and served with the 52nd Light Infantry at Waterloo. In 1829 he was appointed Senior Commissioner of the newly created Metropolitan Police.[290] A decade later he was one of a three-man royal commission whose report led to the creation of county constabularies.

Other veterans found themselves on the wrong side of the law, proof of the truth of Wellington's warning to Croker a month after Waterloo that 'every man you see in a military uniform is not a hero'. One was found guilty of bigamy at the Sussex assizes in 1818. In August 1819 Ralph Wright was found guilty of rioting in Macclesfield. Two more were sent from Huddersfield to York Prison charged with treason in April 1820. In September 1823 Robert Gill was hanged at York Castle for robbery; George Pitchford was executed at Warwick in 1824 for coining base money. Two years later, John Sutton and William Butt were found guilty of poaching on Lord Stamford's estate and shooting at his gamekeeper, whilst in 1829 John Wilson was convicted of burgling a Cambridge widow.[291] Some of these instances, at least, were the consequence of economic hardship or political Radicalism. Others accepted their misfortune stoically. One such was George Thorp. Twice wounded at Waterloo, he found work for a time as a white-metal manufacturer. When he became unemployed, however, his wife and three children ended up in the workhouse, where one child perished. Thorp was eventually put to work breaking stones on the road of Shales Moor near Sheffield, but died of weakness in 1827. The press invited donations for his surviving family for, 'A grateful country cannot now recompense him.' Even before he died, a desperate Thorp had attempted suicide. At least two other veterans succeeded in doing so in 1830. One of them, Sam Wright, the keeper of the Marylebone watchhouse, had been unable to support his young family.[292]

A few of the Waterloo 'heroes' who remained in the news were drawn from the army's many female camp followers. One of the most colourful characters known to the London authorities during the 1820s was Ann Jones, better known by her alias 'Waterloo Tom'. Her husband, who had served with the 7th Light Dragoons, was killed in the battle. She, however, had mounted his horse and rescued a Captain Lance, only to be wounded herself. Subsequently she was granted the not ungenerous pension of 1s 9d daily. In the summer of 1822, however, she was arrested for a ninth time charged with vagrancy in Camberwell and sentenced to a month in Brixton Mill. In 1824 she was sentenced to another month for vagrancy in Chancery Lane. She was arrested for a sixteenth time shortly before Waterloo Day

1825 and by the end of the year was being charged with breaking a pane of glass in a confectioner's window in Oxford Street. Thereafter she disappears from the record.[293]

The most remarkable story of the period, however, was that of David Sutherland. He was found destitute in Covent Garden in spring 1831. It transpired that he had been born the night before the battle (according to some accounts, actually during it), near Hougoumont, a fact which must qualify him as the youngest person present on 18 June. His father in the 42nd was killed that day by a musket ball to the head. The regiment had thereupon effectively adopted both him and his mother as mascots. They had followed it to Gibraltar where the mother died. But the boy returned with it to Scotland, until in 1830 he was turned out of the barracks at Stirling Castle for having brought in alcohol. A few months later he took a boat to Woolwich. Pending proof of the tale, a Mr Campbell of Knightsbridge offered him a position in his household.[294]

The Waterloo Fund was presumably meant to have prevented at least some of the stories of human misery mentioned above from arising. By Waterloo Day 1819, its governing committee had investigated 7,531 applications and voted one-off donations totalling £192,844 to wounded servicemen and their dependants. Annuities totalling £22,142 had been granted to 727 widows, 977 children and 277 disabled NCOs and privates.[295] This constituted an impressive record but the Fund was, inevitably, far from being a failsafe.

Wellington is sometimes criticised for not having done more to assist his comrades-in-arms. The charge is understandable but unfair. It would be long after his death before the State accepted that it had an ongoing responsibility to former servicemen and their families. His main contribution to Waterloo commemoration was the less burdensome dinner he hosted at Apsley House every 18 June, primarily for surviving officers of the campaign. In 1821, which seems to have been the first time the press noted the event, forty-two were present, including George IV. The following year, when the gathering was more widely reported, about sixty attended. Bathurst, still Secretary for War and the Colonies, received what was effectively an invitation from the Duke for that occasion, the earliest extant such document. By 1823 the event was becoming so well established that newspapers were recording that the invitations in general had gone out. For the tenth anniversary gathering, two military bands were engaged to provide music in the grounds.[296] The only year during the period when the dinner did not take place at Apsley House was in 1829. Instead, guests converged on 10 Downing Street, probably because the 90-foot Waterloo Gallery at Apsley House was then under construction. Following its completion in 1830, it became the fixed venue for what was increasingly referred to as a banquet.[297]

Wellington himself was not short of dinner invitations. He could rely upon his hosts to remind guests of his indispensable contribution to Britain's victory in the war in general and at Waterloo in particular. The Duke was brief and platitudinous in returning thanks on such occasions. This could be interpreted as meaning that he was cold, but most took it as proof of a self-effacing nature in a man who was proud of his officers and men and what they had achieved together. It was an arrangement in which both hosts and their honoured guest tacitly agreed to marginalise or even overlook altogether the contribution of Britain's erstwhile allies. On 27 December 1820, for example, when attending a grand dinner in Chester, Wellington reflected that it was the British Army, now increasingly maligned, which had 'rescued Europe from the grasp of tyranny, and its services never can be forgotten, however its noble deeds may be treated by the folly of some men, and the wickedness of others'.[298] His most expansive remarks made in public about the Waterloo campaign during this period came at a dinner in London in May 1825. Of all his triumphs, he declared, the 1815 campaign was unparalleled and had:

> produced consequences which were unheard of as the result of any event of that description in modern times, or, indeed, in any times. It completed the military glory of this country. It relieved mankind from the apprehension of a return to that horrible, revolting, and degrading tyranny which had been imposed upon nearly all the world except the people of this country. It enabled his Majesty's government to effect the peace of Europe upon terms most honourable to ourselves and as such have led us to the greatness and prosperity we now enjoy.[299]

Radicals baulked at the details, but it was a good summation of the Establishment view of what Waterloo meant: Britons should be proud of their nation, their soldiers and, though Wellington did not say it, their hero.

On the details of the battle itself, however, Wellington made no substantial public comment: the record, as he had stated it in the Waterloo Despatch, should continue to speak for itself. A rare, albeit inconsequential, exception occurred at Cheltenham in 1828 when a veteran accosted him, claiming to have given him water to drink at Waterloo. He received a peremptory, 'Be off, you scoundrel [...] I never took a glass of water during an engagement in my life.'[300] In private, by contrast, Wellington would still quite happily talk about the campaign. Such conversations show him remaining true to his line that the battle was a victory for himself and his British soldiers. In face of suggestions to the contrary, it was, if anything, a position in which he became increasingly entrenched. Just how far he really believed all he said, was deceiving himself, oversimplifying, or genuinely confused, is impossible to say: almost certainly all four. His comments do at least suggest which aspects of the campaign lingered longest in his memory, in some instances perhaps, because they weighed most heavily on his mind.

Foremost amongst his pronouncements was his estimation of Napoleon as an opponent whose presence on a battlefield equated to 40,000 men.[301] Though Wellington was adamant that Bonaparte would have been better served by a defensive strategy in 1815 ('we should then have had great difficulty in dealing with him'), he told Greville in 1820 that the offensive manoeuvres of 15 June were the 'finest thing that ever was done – so rapid and so well combined [...] The Duke says that they certainly were not prepared for this attack.' This was one of only two occasions after Waterloo when Wellington admitted to having been surprised – albeit in the campaign, not the battle – a charge that he otherwise disingenuously denied, and in public his admirers rubbished. The other, surely a revealing contradiction, came in 1823 when he at first asserted to Mrs Arbuthnot 'that was all nonsense, that it was quite ridiculous to talk of his having been surprised', but then added that 'if I was surprised, if I did place myself in so foolish a position, they were the greater fools for not knowing how to take advantage of my faults'.

That both his friends and foes had been guilty of faults in 1815, Wellington was more than willing to explain. Chad recorded that he had explicitly told Gneisenau that the Prussians would be worsted if they insisted on fighting in their chosen position at Ligny. Gneisenau had replied only that 'our men like to see their Enemy'. Thus unheeded, the Duke returned to save the situation at Quatre Bras ('By God If I had come up 5 minutes later the Battle was lost'), in the process tying down Frenchmen who would have been better employed securing a more decisive victory against Blücher. The French compounded their error, he believed, by not moving against him earlier and in greater numbers on 17 June. This contrasted sharply with 'the extraordinary celerity with which the allied armies were got together'.

As for Waterloo itself, like everybody else, the Duke tended to exaggerate when it came to numbers: he told Greville that he had only 50,000 men at Mont St Jean. One should also treat his 1821 claim to Chad that it was he who repulsed what was presumably d'Erlon's massed infantry attack ('I brought the 95th to play upon the flank of the French who were at it, with the Highlanders, & this broke them'), as the comment of an excited battlefield guide. Similarly, his 1824 admission to Mrs Arbuthnot that having painstakingly placed every regiment himself 'he was quite tranquil as to the issue' may reflect more an outward than inward calm. The latter contention was confirmed by Alava, however, at the same dinner party: he recalled finding Wellington under the elm tree on 18 June concerned primarily for the well-being of Lady Charlotte Greville!

On the point that Wellington was immensely proud of his dispositions for 18 June, we can be more certain. It was why he was so irked when critics suggested that his chosen battlefield position was a poor one: he would countenance the possibility that he might have had to retreat but not the accusation that to do so would have been impossible. Mrs Arbuthnot was told forcibly in 1823 that, 'I could have got into the wood, & I wd have defied the Devil to drive me out!' This had not proved necessary, not least because of his eye for the ground. Standing near the Gordon memorial in 1821, he asked Chad to 'observe with this hollow Road & la Haie Sainte and Hougoumont, how strong the position was'. He told Greville that it 'was uncommonly strong' with the two farms 'admirably situated and adapted for defence'. This was why he was repeatedly so vexed that the latter should have fallen, something he ascribed to the commanding officer's failing to create an opening through the back wall which would have allowed his men to import ammunition.[302] But the temporary loss of La Haye Sainte did not obviate his insistence that Napoleon had therefore been wrong to launch a frontal assault; he should have tried to outflank him via Hal. The Duke told Greville in 1820, prematurely as it turned out, that he was surprised not to have been more censured for sending a substantial portion of his own force to Hal in anticipation of such a manoeuvre.

Such a move would, at the very least, have drawn him away from the Prussians. Towards his ally, the Wellington of the 1820s was clearly not the generous Wellington of the Waterloo Despatch. He told Lady Shelley that Blücher's main achievement had been to avoid Grouchy and arrive at Waterloo 'in order that the Prussians may profit by their victory'. Equally small-minded was his contention that though he had seen them from 10am 'that they had only one Corps of 30,000 […] & that they did not chuse to deboucher & come into action "till their whole force had joined"'. Mrs Arbuthnot, who surely derived her view of the battle exclusively from her hero, recorded the obvious untruth of 'the arrival of the Prussians, who did not get upon the ground till eight at night & not till the Duke had charged the French line & they were flying in every direction'. 'I beat them', was Wellington's 1823 summation to her of what had happened to the French Army.[303]

Quite often, Wellington's comments on Waterloo were made in response to what he or his interlocutor had just read on the subject, for example Gourgaud's 1818 account of the campaign or Maximilien Foy's more general history of the war, which appeared posthumously in English in 1827. The book criticising Wellington's conduct at Waterloo that excited greatest public interest in 1820s Britain, however, was *Napoleon in Exile*. It was published in 1822, a year after Bonaparte's death. The author revealed nothing substantively new. But unlike others who would write at first hand of the former Emperor's time at St Helena, he was a Briton, Dr Barry O'Meara. In various conversations Napoleon had told him that if either Grouchy had arrived at Waterloo, or at least prevented the Prussians from intervening, Wellington would have lost. Moreover, nobody would have escaped since retreat was impossible from the Duke's poorly chosen position. Instead, 'destiny, decided that Lord Wellington should gain it', albeit assisted by 'the firmness and bravery of his troops' but above all by Blücher's arrival. The latter thus deserved greater credit. Wellington, by contrast, was 'a man of little spirit, no generosity, and without grandeur of the soul'. He was also guilty of 'folly' in not having fallen back on Antwerp, where the combined strength of the allies must have prevailed; he had allowed himself to be surprised and needlessly given battle alone.[304]

Mrs Arbuthnot was furious that 'such stories shd go down to posterity uncontradicted, that the next generation wd really believe that he was surprised, & give all the credit of the victory to the Prussians'. Wellington professed not to be concerned. After all, the French '[might] talk & write themselves sick, that they never could alter the fact that their army was annihilated'. But he cared more than he liked to admit. He obtained a copy of O'Meara's work and annotated the several charges levelled against him by Napoleon concerning his performance during the Waterloo campaign. There is a cross at the point where Napoleon claimed that it was 'the arrival of Blücher, to whom the victory is more to be attributed than to Wellington, and more credit due as a general'.[305] In literary terms, Napoleon was far more successful in keeping his two antagonists apart after the battle, than he had been in military terms during it.

O'Meara's book, portions of which were widely reproduced in both national and provincial newspapers, was just one example of the continuing avaricious public appetite for anything related to 1815. *Stories of Waterloo*, a very popular three-volume anecdotal work, appeared in 1829. Still one of the best known memoirs, Captain John Kincaid's *Adventures in the Rifle Brigade*, first appeared in 1830. The 1832 annual report of the Liverpool Mechanics and Apprentices Library noted that accounts of Waterloo were amongst the most requested items. Launched three years before, the *United Service Journal* was yet another organ through which material could reach an insatiable audience. The very first number contained a striking eyewitness account of the battlefield on 19 June by an English denizen of Brussels and, like O'Meara's book, was widely syndicated to the press.[306]

But it was the roles of the two principal antagonists at Waterloo that continued to dominate literary outpourings on the subject. A comment on this came in the form of an 1824 essay, 'The Wellingtoniad', from the pen of the young Thomas Babington Macaulay. A twelve-book epic with that title would, he predicted, be written in 2824. In it, the narrator 'with a laudable zeal for the glory of his country' ignores the allied contribution to the war. 'England and France, Wellington and Napoleon, almost exclusively occupy his attention.' The gods and armies look on as the two titans clash in a duel at Waterloo: the Duke's pistol shot strikes Napoleon, who thereupon flies. 'The arrival of the Prussians, from a motive of patriotism, the poet completely passes over.' Whilst Macaulay's distaste for the nationalist and great-man-of-history approach to Waterloo might commend itself to a modern readership, this satirical take was decidedly untypical of the 1820s. Far more representative was the Brontë family. In June 1826 the Reverend Patrick Brontë bought his son, Branwell, a dozen toy soldiers in Leeds. The models inspired all his children to participate in the creation of an imaginary literary world of their own. The 10-year-old Charlotte commandeered 'the prettiest of the whole' to be Wellington; her hero-worship of the Duke persisted into adulthood. From the parsonage at Haworth the whole family could see the monument to Wellington's wars on the top of Stoodley Pike.[307]

Wellington's version of the Waterloo story thus remained, as it would for decades yet, the orthodox British one. He could rely on the bulk of the media to continue to endorse it. The British press treated conflicting versions, especially ones from French sources, with no less contempt than he did.

Even press organs that cared little for his politics leapt to his defence. *The Times*, for example, was incensed that General Foy should allege that many British officers 'have nothing to say for the resources of his under-standing or the productions of his genius' and that Waterloo was a triumph for 'the force of inert resistance'.[308] Sir Walter Scott provided the fullest case for the defence during the 1820s in his multi-volume life of Napoleon. The final chapters are less biography than popular history. Waterloo, they conclude, was not, as Napoleon and his proxies alleged, 'lost by a combina-tion of extraordinary fatalities' which alone allowed the 'incapacity of the British General' to prevail. Neither was it the Prussians, for they had not 'made any physical impression by their weapons, or excited any moral dread by their appearance' by the time Wellington ordered the general advance. Wellington's repulsing the Imperial Guard was the 'decisive movement'. The Duke, considering that it read like a novel, did not rate the work. Possibly he objected to the author's limited admission that, 'The laurels of Waterloo must be divided – the British won the battle, the Prussians achieved and made available the victory.'[309] If so, Scott was only saying in so many words what Wellington had himself conceded in the Waterloo Despatch. Wellington's prejudices had conspired to make him uncharitable; the author had performed him a useful service.

Artists too could be useful, for they, no less than writers, remained enthusi-astic to treat Wellington and Waterloo as subjects. It was also a genre towards which the Duke was much more favourably disposed. He visited the Royal Academy in 1819 for an early viewing of James Ward's allegorical picture, *The Triumph of Great Britain after the Battle of Waterloo*, commissioned for the hall of Chelsea Hospital. He must also have seen Jan Pieneman's painting of Waterloo commissioned by King William of the Netherlands, which depicted himself about to order the general advance. Exhibited in Hyde Park in 1825, 18 June would have been the ideal opportunity since Waterloo veterans were admitted gratis.[310] But perhaps he was otherwise engaged, sit-ting for Sir Thomas Lawrence who was commissioned to paint him at least seven times between 1814 and 1829. So frequent were the Duke's visits to Lawrence's studio that in January 1830, shortly after the artist's death, he paid a final visit to retrieve the sword that he had carried at Waterloo.[311]

Wellington himself commissioned what turned out to be the most success-ful of all Waterloo paintings. His original 1816 instruction to Sir David Wilkie was that 'the subject should be a parcel of old soldiers assembled […] at the door of a public-house, chewing tobacco and talking over their old stories'.

Wilkie only began work on the commission in 1820. It was he who gave it a Waterloo theme by suggesting that Wellington's idea 'wanted some […] principal incident to connect the figures together'. The result was the *Chelsea Pensioners receiving the London Gazette Extraordinary, announcing the Battle of Waterloo.* When it was exhibited at the Royal Academy in May 1822, it proved so popular that it had to be protected by a rail from the crowds that thronged to view it. The figure reading the newspaper, Wilkie's notes informed visitors, had been with Wolfe at the taking of Quebec. Behind the black man, who had witnessed Louis XVI's execution, was a man who had served with Granby in the Seven Years' War and another who had served with Eliott at the Siege of Gibraltar. Even the dog, known as Old Duke, had been in the Peninsula and sat at the feet of a corporal of the Oxford Blues who had fought at Vitoria. Wilkie was consciously linking celebrated episodes in Britain's military past to the even more glorious achievement of 1815. *The Examiner*, no fan of Waterloo, declared that the painting was:

so congenial to the tastes of all spectators, so unhesitatingly and potently awakening to the mind, so expressive of curiosity, surprise, joy, in their over-flowing of heart, that if ever it could be pronounced with certainty of a performance that it would go down to an admiring posterity, this is one of which such a prophecy may unerringly be made.[312]

As Hamish Miles says, 'It is, in effect, a history picture with an invisible hero, the popular joy being in the victory of the nation rather than of a commander.'[313] But it did the commander's reputation no harm. If it was not quite what he originally had in mind when he commissioned it, he must have been more than pleased with the result.

It has been suggested that Wilkie's painting was also a response to Wellington's contemporary political unpopularity. This is plausible, for political controversy was rarely far from Waterloo episodes. General Gourgaud, living for a while in London, is a case in point. The German press presumed that his arrest and deportation at the end of 1818 were directly attributable to Wellington's pique at being characterised as essentially lucky in Gourgaud's account of the 1815 campaign. The British press doubted whether the Duke would stoop so low, though it did believe that Sidmouth, the Home Secretary, might. Members of the Opposition sensed enough political mileage in the story to present a petition on Gourgaud's behalf the following April.[314] More mundanely, Tories regularly sought to appropriate

Waterloo for themselves. In 1827, the Stockport Loyal Wellington Club dined to celebrate Waterloo Day in a room adorned with laurel, flags and military banners. Its chairman, William Hulton, told those present that they met at a time when people should be ready to come forward and support the throne and 'the preservation of the rights of the Church and Constitution'. Similarly, the Liberal press was concerned that William IV's attending Wellington's 1831 Waterloo dinner would be taken advantage of by their opponents to suggest that it was somehow a mark of royal approbation for the Duke's stance against Reform.[315]

The latter two incidents illustrate well how, after a quieter period during the mid-1820s, Wellington found himself once more at the forefront of partisan controversies. Those controversies were catalysed by the stroke that debilitated Lord Liverpool in February 1827, leading George Canning to succeed him in Downing Street on 10 April. Wellington, who loathed Canning, and was presumed to oppose his support for the granting of civil equality to Roman Catholics, resigned from the cabinet. His decision confirmed him as a leader of the 'Protestants'. It also brought the charge that he was behaving factiously, for he also chose to resign the bipartisan post of Commander-in-Chief, in which he had only succeeded the Duke of York the previous January.[316]

The perception that Wellington was activated by a mixture of personal animosity and party spirit was reinforced in early June. He moved an amendment that succeeded in torpedoing the government's attempt to liberalise the 1815 Corn Laws – substantially the same measure he had supported just months before as a member of Liverpool's cabinet. Both in and out of Parliament the fallout was considerable, for the emotive Corn Laws, whose rationale was to protect British farmers by prohibiting foreign grain imports until domestic prices reached 80 shillings a quarter, were understandably viewed by many as a tax on bread. Mrs Arbuthnot recorded that, 'Sir Rt Wilson says we have had Wellington boots and now we will have a Wellington loaf and make him odious all over the country.' So it partly proved. In Nottingham, on Waterloo Day, an effigy of the Duke with a small loaf pendant in its buttonhole was paraded and burnt. But Wellington's amendment had also made him the farmers' friend: the Holderness Agricultural Society duly made him an honorary member.[317] Argument over the question inside Parliament was further fuelled when some of the strongest criticism of Wellington's amendment fell on 18 June, prompting the Ultra, Sir Edward Knatchbull, to suggest that 'he thought he should be deemed immaculate on the anniversary of the Battle of Waterloo'. Many disagreed. It was an organ of the Canningite press, motivated by the political present, that wrote of the military past on the twelfth anniversary of Waterloo that, 'As Englishmen we feel no gratification of being reminded of a momentous crisis, at which our commander-in-chief was surprised by his vigilant enemy, dancing at a ball,(!) and of a conflict in which the timely intervention of the Prussian hordes, alone rescued our brave but overmatched troops from utter defeat and destruction.'[318]

Wellington was clearly more a hero of rural than urban and industrial England. He was also more a southern than a northern one. A tour of the north-east in early autumn 1827 was seen by some as a successful attempt to redress this. *The Times* reported that he was as well received as if his victories had just taken place. His official visits included York, Durham, Ripon and Newcastle. An estimated 20,000 turned out to see him in Sunderland. In the church porch at Kirby, near Tadcaster, a Waterloo veteran was given a sovereign.[319] In reality, though, Wellington's northern progress was primarily an attempt by his host, Lord Londonderry (Castlereagh's half brother, who, in an earlier incarnation as Charles Stewart had served with Wellington in the Peninsula), to underscore Wellington's ties to the Ultras and his distance from Canning's administration. Plenty saw through the ruse. When Londonderry appeared with Wellington at Stockton-on-Tees, the local press rightly doubted that Wellington's presence 'was intended to celebrate the battle of Waterloo, but the battle with the Corn Bill, and the cause of the Londonderries'.[320]

Circumstances would soon expose the differences between Wellington and the Ultras. Canning died in August. When his successor, the hapless Goderich, resigned in January 1828, George IV asked the Duke to form an administration. His cabinet was an uneasy combination of Protestants and Catholics. Lord John Russell cautioned Wellington's supporters against appealing to past military glories 'whenever the duke should propose any very objectionable measure'. He predicted failure because 'those very habits of command which had been most befitting the noble duke in his military station [...] were likely to prove most objectionable and dangerous in the situation of first minister of a free country'. In his *Political Register*, Cobbett agreed: Wellington 'must now stand or fall in the eyes of posterity by your actions in this new line of life'.[321] The events of the following weeks appeared to substantiate their forebodings. Palmerston, the Canningite Secretary at War, referred to the Premier as the 'Dictator' and wrote that,

'The Duke brings little to his extensive duties but narrow prejudices & an obstinate will to act upon them, but that forms a slender capital upon which to govern a nation.' Wellington, for his part, was not disappointed when the Canningites resigned en masse in May. Their replacements included Sir George Murray and Sir Henry Hardinge, both of whom had served under him in the Peninsula. They were comparative political lightweights but they were immeasurably more congenial colleagues. The *Dumfries Courier* was right in its estimation that Wellington would prefer to re-fight the battles of 1815 over again than deal with cabinet in-fighting.[322]

The great battle of Wellington's administration was that to grant Roman Catholic Emancipation. Although he had hitherto opposed it, Wellington's approach to the question was essentially pragmatic.[323] In July 1828, the election of the nationalist leader, Daniel O'Connell, as MP for County Clare, his Catholicism notwithstanding, threatened the spectre of widespread disorder in Ireland if the nettle were not finally grasped. Having convinced a highly reluctant George IV that the measure was essential, Wellington's cabinet thrashed out the minutiae of a Bill. By mid-April 1829 it was law. The Canningite, Charles Grant, welcomed it as 'a greater victory than the battle of Waterloo'. Radical critics conceded that only the Duke could have carried the measure in face of royal and political opposition. *The Times*, hitherto lukewarm at best towards Wellington's premiership, marked the anniversary of Waterloo by declaring that 'the greatest warrior of his time was the most zealous tranquillizer of domestic discord'.[324]

Not everybody concurred. *The Globe*, in an imperfect analogy, pointed out that it was the Whigs, not Wellington, who had played the part of Blücher in sustaining the long struggle against religious intolerance: 'they have maintained the position which was essential to make the efforts of reinforcements essential'. But this was as nothing compared to the vitriol hurled at Wellington by the Tory press. His staunchest press ally, *The Standard*, reflected that Waterloo Day 1829 was the first 'in which the people of England have felt as a painful burthen their obligation of gratitude to the hero of that day'. Passions ran high. At a parish vestry meeting in The Red Lion near Aylesbury, argument descended into disorder leading to seven arrests for assault, 'some denouncing his Grace the Duke of Wellington as the assassin of the constitution, and others as its friend and saviour'.[325] Most famously, though in the event neither man was hurt, the Earl of Winchilsea fought a duel with Wellington on Battersea Fields on 21 March. The Duke's attendants were the ever-faithful Dr Hume and Sir Henry Hardinge.[326]

A sub-plot of the Emancipation story was the falling out between Wellington and Anglesey. The latter was confirmed as Lord Lieutenant of Ireland in Wellington's administration but infuriated his chief by making public his support for Emancipation in the summer of 1828. Wellington ordered his recall in December. Anglesey in turn vented his anger at the Duke for his dismissal by clashing with him in the Lords. According to Mrs Arbuthnot, he also wrote to the Swedish minister and 'complained of the Duke most bitterly, said he had conferred the greatest obligations!!! On the Duke, that by his charges of cavalry he had gained for him the battle of Waterloo!!!' Mrs Arbuthnot was nearer the mark in judging that 'if anything could have lost the battle of Waterloo, it wd have been Ld Anglesey's management of our cavalry'. Anglesey was also seen as having had the worst of their parliamentary encounter, leading to the inevitable joke that, 'At the clubs they say that he has no longer a leg to stand upon, for that he lost one at Waterloo & the other in the H. of Lords.'[327]

Outside Parliament during 1829, as some struggling Waterloo veterans could have testified, bread-and-butter issues replaced constitutional ones. In February 1829 the journeyman weavers of Waterloo Town in Bethnal Green had met to petition Wellington about the fact that 7,000 looms lay idle. Cobbett told Wellington that 'there are great numbers of your admirers upon the point of starvation, and they cannot eat and drink the word "Waterloo"'. Wellington did not deny that distress existed, but on 4 February 1830 both doubted its extent and the ability of the legislature to remedy it. His remarks were not well received. Cobbett observed that he needed some Waterloo luck now. Luck, as it turned out, was in short supply. George IV's death in June triggered a general election that marginally weakened Wellington's parliamentary position. News of revolution abroad, particularly the fall of the Bourbons in July, added to rising popular excitement. As one irreverent individual added a pipe to the Achilles statue, 'Reform' became the watchword of the day.[328]

Beleaguered but defiant, the Prime Minister used the occasion of the debate on the King's Speech on 2 November to tell their Lordships in unambiguous terms 'that the Legislature and system of representation possessed the full and entire confidence of the country'. Not only would he not introduce Reform but 'he should always feel it his duty to resist such measures when proposed by others'. His comments surpassed in ineptitude those about county meetings in 1821. As Greville put it, Wellington's speech 'at once destroyed what little popularity the Duke had left, and lowered

him in public estimation'.[329] Popular excitement reached new heights. Even
Wellington conceded that the threat to public order made it politic to
cancel the Lord Mayor's procession and banquet scheduled for 9 November
at the Guildhall, something he later improbably described as the 'crisis in
my military life [that] cost me [...] the most anxious consideration'. It was
to little avail. His government lost a vote on 15 November and resigned the
next day. Many professed to believe that only this averted a popular uprising
and that 'his defeat is a greater triumph for the country than was the battle
of Waterloo'.[330]

Wellington compared his 1829 struggle to carry Emancipation to
Waterloo. The analogy would have been more apt for his rearguard over
Parliamentary Reform during 1831–1832. Grey's Whig-dominated government, formed in November 1830, staked its existence on the passage of the
Reform proposals it introduced in March 1831. This placed the Duke in the
not unfamiliar position of conducting a defence of what he conceived as
the forces of order against those of revolution. He genuinely believed that
the popular pressure for Reform was transitory; consequently confident
that he could defeat the measure by marshalling the Lords to hold out long
enough for the people to come to their senses.[331] In the event he was not
even to monopolise the Waterloo metaphor, let alone win the battle of the
Reform Bill.

As with Waterloo, so the battle of 1831–1832 is best narrated in stages.
The Reform Bill having passed the Commons by a whisker on 22 March,
Grey secured the dissolution of Parliament. During the ensuing election
campaign of April–May, at least one pro-Reform pamphlet argued that a
Reformed Parliament would have rendered Waterloo unnecessary, since
abler and more responsive ministers would have been in office during the
Peninsular War. Thus it was contended, 'can any one doubt that the Duke of
Wellington would have been enabled to take much more decided steps for
the expulsion of the French from the Peninsula, and that the contest might
have been brought to a much earlier termination?' This was debatable logic;
the Reformers nevertheless won a landslide. The Bill, now guaranteed a
majority in the Commons, went to the Lords. Their Lordships duly rejected
it in October by 199–158, not least, it was noted, because 21 bishops had
voted with the majority. Popular uproar ensued. Apsley House was stoned
by a mob on 12 October.[332] Meanwhile, at a county meeting in Hampshire,
Sir James MacDonald MP likened the bishops to Blücher's forces reach-
ing Mont St Jean. 'The arrival of the Prussians at the close of the battle of

Waterloo was not less looked for by the enemy than was the array of prelates, who thought fit to take the Government in the flank and thus lose them the day.'[333]

In the months that followed, sufficient peers were persuaded to compromise that a revised Reform Bill passed the Lords in April 1832. But Wellington had continued to speak and vote against it. The battle was not yet quite lost. On 7 May the government was unexpectedly defeated in the Lords on an amendment to postpone consideration of the disfranchisement of small boroughs. Grey resigned on 9 May; Wellington accepted William IV's commission to replace him. It was an unequal struggle. In Edinburgh alone, 38,000 signed a petition for the Reform Bill; in London, Daniel Wakefield warned that a Wellington government would mean 'an attempt would be instantly made to coerce the people, and establish a military government in support of the aristocracy'. Unable to construct a viable ministry, Wellington resigned on 15 May. Creevey reflected that what came to be known as the May Days had been the critical moment: 'The conqueror of Waterloo had great luck on that day […] but at last comes his own false move, which has destroyed himself and his Tory high-flying association for ever.'[334]

Against this backdrop, Waterloo Day 1832 proved to be the most memorable of Wellington's lifetime. Local celebrations took place as usual. Detachments of the Scots Greys, for example, celebrated in Birmingham, which had been at the heart of the provincial struggle for Reform. Upwards of seventy attended Wellington's Waterloo banquet. Earlier that day, however, the Duke had returned home from the Tower only to be assailed by a mob, at first verbally and then by various missiles. In Fenchurch Street, attempts were made to drag him from his horse before police intervened to rescue him. He had to be escorted all the way to Apsley House. On arriving there, he simply touched his hat 'and quietly said, "An odd day to choose! [Waterloo day] Good morning."'[335]

Thomas Carlyle thought that Wellington had become the most unpopular man in England by spring 1832: his effigy was being burnt in all market towns. In Edinburgh, a figure of 'Dukey' bearing the legend 'So perish all tyrants' suffered the further indignity of being grabbed by policemen 'who reached the Duke's unmentionables, and these they captured nobly, while his upper parts were drawn up by some boys into an office'.[336] The popular celebrations that followed the Reform Act's passage on 7 June brought Wellington renewed abuse. In his native Hampshire, a prominent Radical,

Richard Hinxman, even went so far as to suggest that the country had nothing whatsoever to thank him for. This was untypical but there was something approaching a consensus that his career was over. In London, Lord Yarborough was reported as having said that 'Wellington had ceased politically to exist' – and in circumstances that had irreparably damaged his previous reputation. As *The Times* put it, 'Under any contingency, the Duke of Wellington has earned for himself a load of distrust, which we apprehend – and it is not without regret we say so, "that enough of life scarcely remains to enable His Grace to shake off."'[337] Time would prove otherwise.

5

Wellington and Waterloo
(Despatched 1832–1852)

As he left the House of Lords on 30 April 1839, the eve of his 70th birthday, Wellington 'was grossly insulted by a blackguard in the crowd'. A coal-heaver:

> seized hold of the ruffian, shook him almost to death, and hurled him to the ground amid the cheers of the spectators who surrounded the Duke and followed him all the way to Apsley House. He was advised to mount his horse; 'no,' said he 'I'll lead them on foot,' and away they went, he at their head, and the crowds increasing at every corner.[338]

News of Wellington's political death in 1832 had clearly been grossly exaggerated. Whilst his earlier shortcomings were never forgotten, they were to some extent forgiven. This owed something to his continued service to the State. But it owed more to the memory of services rendered in 1815. Wellington the politician of 1832 had become disconnected from the Wellington of Waterloo. The story of his final two decades was one of how the two Wellingtons became reconnected.[339] Along the way, he played his part in ensuring that it was his vision of Waterloo that remained intact and largely undiminished in the national consciousness.

The revival of Wellington's stock was partly a reflection of the inevitable swing of the political pendulum. Reduced to a paltry 185 seats in the general election of 1832, the Tory party, increasingly labelled Conservative and now led by Sir Robert Peel, recovered to 279 seats in 1835 and 314 in 1837, a parliamentary minority of only 30. Following the 1841 election it returned to office with a majority of 76. Those who cheered Wellington home on 30 April 1839 also cried out, 'Down with the Whigs and up with the Tories.' The newspaper that reported it concluded, with evident satisfaction, that, 'England is herself again.'

But Wellington's popular rehabilitation was more personal and began considerably earlier. It can plausibly be dated to Waterloo Day 1832 when, or rather because, he had been ignominiously jostled. To abuse former prime ministers was one thing; to treat the national hero so, on 18 June, quite another. One of the Duke's sharpest political critics, *The Times*, expressed deep unease over the episode, concluding that, 'No political obstinacy or error could provoke reasonable men to such infamous ingratitude – no sophistry can palliate it.' Less than a year later, when riding with him in St James's Park, Charles Greville was:

> marvellously struck [...] with the profound respect with which the Duke was treated, everybody we met taking off their hats to him, everybody in the park rising as he went by, and every appearance of his inspiring great rever-ence [...] it is the more remarkable because it is not popularity, but a much higher feeling towards him. He has forfeited his popularity more than once [but] when the excitement subsides there is always a returning sentiment of admiration and respect for him, kept alive by the recollection of his splendid actions, such as no one else ever inspired.[340]

Traditional accounts of the Tory revival in the 1830s emphasise the impor-tance of the appeal of Peel's progressive Conservatism to the post-1832 electorate. In doing so, they miss the significance of Wellington's name and the memory of Waterloo. The 150 'youthful patriots' (Conservatives under 35), who met at Edinburgh's British Hotel in 1832 chose Waterloo Day for their dinner. A letter from 'A Tory', dated Waterloo Day 1833, urged those of like mind to stand firm against the Whigs.[341] And when Wellington appeared in person, even for ostensibly apolitical occasions, there was often a political subtext. Greville described his installation as Chancellor of Oxford in June 1834 – the University was, amongst other things, a bastion of Toryism – as 'on the whole a very disgraceful exhibition of bigotry and party spirit'. More than one Tory present deemed the event 'one from which I think the rally of Conservatism may be dated'. The following October, on Trafalgar

Day, it was alleged that all the guests at a public dinner in Ramsgate to fete Wellington as Lord Warden of the Cinque Ports were Conservatives. It was 'a trick to consolidate the scattered fragments of Toryism'.[342]

Within weeks of the Ramsgate dinner, William IV, objecting to the Irish Church policy of Melbourne's Whig government, dismissed it, and turned to the Tories. Since Peel was on holiday in Italy, Wellington was temporarily vested, on 17 November, with all the major offices of state. He subsequently referred, laughingly, to his brief dictatorship. But it was poor politics, reviving memories of 1832, alienating moderates, and allowing his opponents to say that, 'With unparalleled foolhardiness, the Duke of Wellington still continues to hold, alone, the reins of Government. He is himself the Cabinet.'[343] Though Peel's minority government gained seats in the January 1835 election, it was ousted in April. But the episode did not damage Wellington's reputation with the faithful. Lieutenant-Colonel George Gawler was fresh from controversy in arguing the case for the decisive intervention of his beloved 52nd in 1815. He told South Derbyshire Conservatives during the election that the Duke had been unfairly maligned and that, 'Englishmen at Waterloo defended the cause of Established Constitutions against the attacks of French democracy. You are now doing the same.'[344]

The events of 1834–1835 galvanised, if only for a while, the organisation of constituency associations. In these too, unsurprisingly, the rhetoric of Wellington and Waterloo was abundant. Somerset Tories, in particular, could hardly be accused of subtlety: they staged a grand gathering on 18 June 1835 in Wellington. Four years later, as their cause gained strength, they assembled again in Bridgwater's Royal Clarence Hotel to reward their agent, Ruscombe Poole, for his efforts on behalf of Peel's Conservative Party: Mr Poole was presented with a silver statue of Wellington on Copenhagen at Waterloo. Some 2,500 attended a dinner of the London Conservative Association in June 1837 where Sir Henry Hardinge, Wellington's liaison officer with the Prussians in 1815, was amongst the speakers. Their Glasgow counterparts established a Wellington Society in 1839.[345]

The Wellington and Waterloo rhetoric persisted down to the election of 1841. Rumours that Parliament would be dissolved on Waterloo Day [in the event, 23 June], were seen as 'an omen of victory for the Duke of Wellington's party'. Sir J. Hamilton, standing for Marylebone, told a meeting called on 18 June that, 'He might attribute much of the reception which he and his colleague had met with to their proffering those principles which were cherished by the illustrious Wellington.' And in a speech at a

celebratory dinner to Peel as incoming prime minister in his own Tamworth
constituency, W. S. Dugdale MP chose to reflect over the previous decade
with a suitably Wellingtonian metaphor:

> [The] conduct of his right honourable friend in his political tactics assimi-
> lated, in a great degree to the tactics of the duke [...] in his Peninsula
> campaigns. (Cheers.) Their right hon. friend commenced as commander
> of a very small company. (Cheers.) He entrenched himself, however, in the
> lines of the British Constitution. (Cheers.) That small company by degrees
> increased under his fostering care. (Cheers.) He sallied forth from his outposts
> – gained victory after victory (cheers), and, at length, attacked the enemy
> with his whole line (cheers) as did the Duke of Wellington at the close of the
> battle of Waterloo.[346]

The foregoing examples provide ample evidence that the Duke was seen
as a partisan figure; too many historians have been inclined to accept
Greville's – and Wellington's own – assessment that 'with reference to mere
party tactics, it is to his praise that he is generally "too fond of the right to
pursue the expedient"'. In truth, the Wellington of the 1830s was a complex
character finding his way in a new political landscape. Before 1830 he had
never been a member of, what was for him an alien concept, His Majesty's
Opposition. But he knew that he was anti-Whig. He also disliked Grey, a
critic of his from Peninsular War days, and Whig Prime Minister from 1830.
When Grey retired in 1834, the Duke paid him an indifferent parliamentary tribute 'and some one observed that "he would not have made so bad
and so heartless a speech even to gain a battle of Waterloo"'.[347] Grey's car-
dinal sin had been to preside over, what Wellington never really ceased to
believe, was a revolution in the shape of the Reform Act.[348] His successor,
Melbourne, was personally more acceptable to the Duke, but his party was
not. In September 1839 Wellington:

> spoke of his great alarm and anxiety at the danger from the present Ministry,
> leagued as they are with the worst enemies of the State. He compared them
> to the case of a servant left in charge of a house, but in confederacy with the
> gang that wished to rob and burn it.

He thus stayed silent when the government was assailed over the New Poor
Law in 1836, even though he had backed 'the original measure very frankly'.

And he was foremost in leading the attack on the ministry in July 1839 following riots in Birmingham, 'an outrage such as never happened, to my knowledge, in any siege that I have been present at'.[349] The disturbances, he asserted, were the consequence of the government's having sanctioned the appointment of unfit persons to act as magistrates in the town. He used his own position as Lord Lieutenant of Hampshire to ensure that Conservatives enjoyed an overwhelming preponderance on the county's bench. It prompted a letter to the *Morning Chronicle*, accusing him, with some reason, of 'political epicurism' and 'unjustifiable partiality'.[350]

But Wellington's reputation for being more than simply a party politician did have substance to it. He persuaded Conservatives to support the government on a range of domestic and foreign policy issues. In the later 1830s he was being referred to, albeit with suitably ambivalent Cromwellian overtones by some, as the 'Lord Protector of the Government'. Such a course was usually interpreted as being actuated by noble self-sacrifice on his part. As Anglesey put it, somewhat out of place at the 1838 Waterloo dinner, he supported 'a Government in which it was well known he placed no confidence, because he thought that the national honour and interest required that they should be supported'. The Whig-supporting *Caledonian Mercury* judged, in 1838, that Wellington's 'character at this moment stands higher among his political opponents than among those who profess to be his supporters'.[351]

In reality, Wellington was motivated more by self-interest than altruism. Since he did not think that the Conservatives could win the support of a majority of the post-1832 electorate, he discounted the possibility of a Conservative government. But neither did he want to see a constitutional showdown between the Reformer-controlled Commons and the Tory-dominated Lords. For both reasons, Conservatives needed sometimes to be restrained. In so doing, Aberdeen believed, in 1840, that Wellington had never 'rendered greater service in his whole life than he had done this session in moderating violence and keeping his own party together and in order'.[352] Coming from the elder brother of the Colonel Alexander Gordon killed at Waterloo, this was no small compliment. To Wellington, though, his course was pragmatic common sense. He did not like the Whigs, but as the lesser of evils they needed to be saved from themselves. The alternative was more Radical legislation, anarchy and ultimately, as the long shadow of French history informed him, dictatorship. The 1830s might be seen as a rearguard in defence of the hegemony of the old order no less successful than that which he had conducted in 1815.

Wellington suffered a serious stroke at Walmer Castle in November 1839. It was widely presumed that this marked the end of his active life. He was after all, 70, what the *Morning Post* described delicately as 'the date assigned by Heaven'. Less delicately, sensing that this might be a good time to publish, at least six new lives of Wellington appeared in 1840. The cabinet discussed plans for his funeral. Had the Duke died at this time, he would have done so with his reputation safely restored. In 1838, some 2,000 people had attended his ball in celebration of Queen Victoria's coronation. They included his political opponents and an erstwhile military one, Marshal Soult. No other Briton could even begin to have thought about holding such an event.[353] But it was not simply the combination of Wellington's age and ill-health that prompted the media to be so notably fascinated and deferential towards him at this juncture. There was also increased interest in Wellington the man. He was revealed as a generous paternal landlord, distributing food and clothing to the poor on his Stratfield Saye estate. There was mention, too, of the iron bedstead he had had with him during the Peninsular War, and which he still used when staying at Walmer Castle. The year of 1840 also prompted reflection because it marked a quarter century since Waterloo, the more poignant because the same year brought fears that war with France might erupt once more, this time over the Eastern Question. As in 1832, however, the obituarists were premature, for as was ruefully remarked, 'the brave Duke, by unexpected renovation of health and activity, so unreasonably deluded the speculation of our bibliophist neighbours'.[354]

One further reason why interest in Wellington increased during the late 1830s, to the advantage of his reputation, was the appearance in print of his despatches. The driving force behind this was John Gurwood, who had distinguished himself at Ciudad Rodrigo in 1812. Already, in 1832–1833, with the Duke's blessing, he had edited two well-received volumes, *General Orders, 1809–15*.[355] The prospect of editing his hero's despatches was a logical grand sequel. Gurwood was also keen to correct what he saw as the untruths in Sir William Napier's monumental *History of the War in the Peninsula*, the first volume of which had appeared in 1828. In January 1833, he duly proposed 'the project of making His Grace write his own history, in the publication of his letters and dispatches, by which the present age and posterity would be enabled to form a less erroneous judgement of his wonderful career'.[356]

Wellington was initially unconvinced. It was not usual for official papers to appear as printed editions. He was against the inclusion of any previously unpublished material. For fear they would prove tendentious, he likewise vetoed Gurwood's planned commentaries. He also insisted that 'some proper names [...] must be suppressed'. What appeared would be a simple compilation of his memoranda, despatches, and correspondence. These, however, must be uncensored. As he explained to Chad, when reviewing a letter he had written about wanting French prisoners to be well-treated, 'my only motive was the hope of reciprocity – I ought to have said, my only motive besides humanity [...] but I won't put it in – I won't alter a word – as they were written, so let them be printed'.[357] The first volume duly appeared in July 1834. The thirteenth and last, an index, was published in 1839. A revised eight-volume edition appeared from 1844–1847. There were also two volumes of *Selections* in 1841. They, at least, became a staple of many early-Victorian libraries.

The *Despatches* were not received without criticism: cost (£12 10s), the scarcity of notes and the Duke's imperfect French being the more salient. There was also substance in the *Morning Chronicle*'s complaint that, 'We cannot say that they are always very sublime or vastly amusing.' The volumes also provided plenty of ammunition to those looking for evidence that Wellington was ungenerous, critical no less of his officers and men than of his political masters. Radical critics seized particularly on a letter of 1 August 1800. In it he related how, when in India, 'I have taken and destroyed Doondiah's baggage and six guns, and driven into the Malpurba (where they were drowned) about five thousand people.' The *Chartist Circular* called him, in consequence, 'the cold-blooded unfeeling monster'.[358] In general, however, the critical reception afforded the *Despatches* was overwhelmingly favourable. The *Blackburn Standard* declared that 'it is impossible not to be struck with the extraordinary vigour of mind and energy of expression by which they are characterised'. What made them unique were the insights they provided into the reality of command. They:

first made the public acquainted with the enormous amount of labour thrown upon the hands of a general commanding an army in the field. The popular notion was, that he had but to fight the enemy, whereas, it would seem, that in comparison with the multitudinous details of organisation, means of transport, the supply of provisions, the necessity of continually stimulating the home Government to exertion, and checking its ardour for jobbing and patronage, and the preserving good will among the officers and discipline in the army itself, the mere winning of victories was an easy matter.[359]

Gurwood's endeavours finally gave the lie to Wellington's private complaint that 'it had always been his fate to be considered an ignorant fellow'.
A long-standing antagonist, Lord Grey, admitted, if only in private, that, 'I
have no hesitation in expressing my conviction, that in every circumstance
of public life the Duke of Wellington is the greatest man that ever lived.'[360]

It was, inevitably, the twelfth volume of *Despatches*, covering the Waterloo
campaign, published in 1838, which occasioned greatest public interest. The
period from Wellington's writing on 12 March in Vienna about Napoleon's
escape from Elba to the eve of Waterloo alone occupied over 200 pages.
From those, any reader could divine that he was initially unhappy with
some of the senior appointments foisted upon him and with the quality of
his army, but also that he remained reasonably confident that allied forces
would ultimately prevail. Most people, however, presumably read only
those letters that were reproduced in the press. These were highly untypical of the *Despatches* as a whole, since they tended to be drawn from the
few items of the Duke's personal correspondence which appeared in the
volumes. By far the most common letters drawn upon by newspapers were
those Wellington wrote reflecting on the titanic nature of the battle and his
feelings of revulsion at its horror. His letters to FitzRoy Somerset's father
expressing distress at his having lost an arm and to Lord Aberdeen on the
loss of his brother, Colonel Gordon, were also frequently quoted. They were
hardly, except possibly to a new generation of readers, unfamiliar. This was
not so true of another letter much cited, that of 28 June 1815 to Sir Charles
Stuart, in which Wellington emphatically disassociated himself from any
attempt to have Napoleon summarily executed. As commentators pointed
out, this was in stark contrast to Napoleon's bequeathing 10,000 francs in
his will to Cantillon, Wellington's would-be assassin of 1818.[361]

Wellington's despatches down to 1815 had been seminal in creating his
reputation. Published in full during the 1830s, they played their part in bur-
nishing it anew. The Waterloo material, especially, suggested, as had been
claimed by his parliamentary advocates during the Peninsular War, that the
great and apparently austere commander was also a humane man. Thomas
Raikes was not alone in thinking that Gurwood's work would 'place his
name above all conception in public opinion, not only as a great captain,
which was known before, but as a statesman, a gentleman, and a man of
humanity and kindness'.[362]

Publication of the *Despatches* also provided a fillip to writers: they were
immediately hailed as the indispensable source for anybody aspiring to

write authoritatively on the subjects of Wellington and Waterloo. And the market for such works remained undiminished. 'The battle of Waterloo,' wrote *The Times*, towards the end of Wellington's life, 'is still a story of this present generation, and whether its details are reproduced in a narrative or a model, in a circus or a puppet show, they still command the lively attention of everybody.'[363] One person alive to the fact was William Hamilton Maxwell. His 1829 *Stories from Waterloo* had been an early and successful example of rollicking military fiction. The third volume of his life of Wellington, which appeared in 1841, completing a project of nearly 2,000 pages, received both popular and critical acclaim. His own claim to have fought in both the Peninsula and at Waterloo was almost certainly erroneous. For those wanting something more manageable, drawing unashamedly on the *Despatches* and the Duke's speeches in Parliament, the 1845 volume, *Maxims and Opinions of the Duke of Wellington*, edited by G. H. Francis, was highly recommended.[364]

More commercially successful was Archibald Alison's ten-volume *History of Europe from the French Revolution to Waterloo*. The volume covering the 1815 campaign appeared in 1843. Alison was a Tory (he was satirised by Disraeli in *Coningsby* as Mr Wordy, who wrote a history to demonstrate that God was a fellow traveller), who admired Wellington, instancing his superior judgement, devotion to duty, perseverance and fidelity when comparing him to Napoleon. At Waterloo, Napoleon succumbed to the Duke's superior military skill and 'the fortitude of the troops which he attacked'. In an 1842 review, however, Alison had written that Wellington and Blücher 'were surprised, outmanoeuvred, and out-generalled'. Though he was referring only to the opening hours of the campaign on 15 June, this unwelcome reminder of reality, re-stated in his 1843 volume, earned him the lasting hostility of the Duke and his disciples.[365]

To modern historians, however, one name stands pre-eminent in this period. William Siborne served with the army of occupation in France until 1817. During the 1820s he made a name for himself as a military topographer. This led, in 1830, to his being commissioned by Wellington's government to make a model of the Waterloo battlefield. Siborne spent eight months surveying the Waterloo terrain. He also circularised surviving officers. The problem, so far as Wellington and his friends was concerned, was that Siborne decided to depict the action on the field at the moment when the Imperial Guard reached the crest of the allied ridge at about 7 p.m. By that time, Siborne's researches suggested that roughly half of the

men engaging French forces were Prussians. This was not what Wellington
had believed at the time, certainly not what he had written. Privately, Sir
James Willoughby Gordon voiced his concern that Siborne's model 'must
in great measure tend to weaken the high authority of the Duke's despatch'. If Siborne wanted to attain the accuracy he craved, it was suggested
to him that an earlier and more static point in the action would better serve
his objective, ideally its opening. The point was a fair, but hardly entirely
honest, one. Almost certainly with Wellington's connivance, the British military establishment's understandable preference for such an option would,
in depicting an earlier truth, have the advantage of excluding the Prussians
from the model altogether. FitzRoy Somerset, however, was unambiguous
when he told Siborne in March 1837:

> The position you have given to the Prussian Troops is not the correct one
> [...] those who see the work will deduce from it that result of the Battle was
> not so much owing to British Valour, and the great Generalship of the Chief
> of the English Army, as to the flank Movements of the Prussians.[366]

Siborne resisted the pressure. He was more preoccupied with practicalities:
ironically, the Whig government had withdrawn funding for the project in
1833, doubtless in part because they did not want to finance the glorification
in lead of the Tory chief in the House of Lords. Only loans and donations
allowed Siborne to cover the £3,000 he spent on the model before it went
on display at the Egyptian Hall in Piccadilly in October 1838.

In retrospect, the machinations over the model were, in a contemporary phrase which never quite caught on, 'a battle of Waterloo in a teapot'.
Its opening to the public was partially eclipsed by the publication of the
Waterloo volume of the *Despatches*. Numbers visiting it were relatively disappointing; its London run had ended by 1840. Many visitors, even veterans
of the battle, were simply overwhelmed by the detail. Consequently, the
press did not, as Wellington's supporters had feared, see anything untoward
in the presence of so many Prussians. Reviewers saw what they believed to
have happened in 1815: their focus was squarely on the model's portrayal
of Wellington and the British Army. *The Standard*, for example, informed
its readers that the model showed 'when the French imperial guard was
attacked and defeated on the Anglo-allied position by the British guards
and the light infantry brigade'. The *Morning Post* urged its readers 'all who
love and feel proud of their country to do as we have done' and go and

see it. Such perceptions were evidently blind to the facts as depicted by Siborne. Neither would Siborne have appreciated the irony of one review making the partisan aside that Wellington's Tory government had sponsored the enterprise whilst Liberal ones had not. The Duke, however, steadfastly refused to visit the model, in the apparently genuine belief that to do so would be to condone inaccuracy.[367]

Siborne's greatest contribution to Waterloo studies, in any case, was the archive of nearly 1,000 items that he built up from Waterloo officers over twelve years. He used them to further his surely naïvely optimistic presumption that 'by fairly weighing and comparing the data thus afforded me, I shall be enabled to deduce a most faithful and authentic record of the Battle'. His *History of the War in France and Belgium in 1815* appeared, to positive reviews, in March 1844.[368] Extending to well over 800 pages, its most significant revelation came in the preface. He had, he announced, since completing the model, reviewed his evidence in light of 'some objections [...] raised against the position thereon assigned to a portion of Prussian troops'. This led him to the 'conviction that an error of some importance [...] as regards time and situation did exist'. To be precise, Wellington had defeated the Imperial Guard at least twelve minutes before the Prussians launched their final decisive assault on Plancenoit. 'It is undeniably true,' he now concluded, 'that the blow which decided the victory was that given by Wellington, when, after having completely defeated the grand attack by the French Imperial Guard, he instantly followed up that defeat by boldly attacking and penetrating the Centre of the Enemy's Lines, and sustaining this movement by the General Advance of his whole Army.'[369] Whether in now endorsing Wellington's analysis of the climax of Waterloo, Siborne really had changed his mind, or was compromising his academic integrity in an attempt to secure much-needed funding from Peel's Conservative government, is unclear. Like Alison, however, he would discover that once decided against him, the Duke was immovable.

Siborne's more pressing concern by the mid-1840s was the discovery that he had a rival. G. R. Gleig's *The Story of the Battle of Waterloo* was published by John Murray on Waterloo Day 1847. Gleig had fought in the Peninsula, had known Wellington personally since 1829, and was to serve as Rector of Stratfield Turgis on the Duke's Stratfield Saye estate. This must surely confer upon his work something of a semi-official authority. He tells us that the *Despatches* were 'always [...] before me' as he wrote. He certainly follows the Wellington line very closely, even accepting as fact the Duke's

one-time claim that he had met Blücher after Waterloo at Genappe, not La
Belle Alliance. He also warmly acknowledges Siborne's signal contribution
in amassing first-hand testimony that 'has saved all who may be curious in
these matters, a great deal of trouble'. But Siborne was incandescently angry.
Gleig, in his view, both caricatured and rubbished his approach when he
(Gleig) wrote that 'my recollections of war lead me somewhat to undervalue
– perhaps in a measure to distrust – the stories told in perfectly good faith by
parties who happen to be the heroes of them. Modern battles are not won by
feats of individual heroism'.[370] Worse, as Siborne demonstrated in a lengthy
preface to the 1848 third edition of his *History*, Gleig had then proceeded to
plagiarise him. Compounding Siborne's frustration too, must have been the
realisation that Gleig had beaten him to the popular market: Siborne's first
edition cost 2 guineas; Gleig's 300-page account retailing at 6 shillings was
priced so that 'almost all classes could afford it'.[371] The latter consequently
won the literary Battle of Waterloo. Painstaking researcher and cartographer
he undoubtedly was, but Siborne was also unfortunate and lacking in business sense. Only 51, he died of an intestinal disease in January 1849.

The seemingly unending appearance of Waterloo material, not least the
Despatches, inevitably prompted those who visited Wellington to ask their
host for his recollection of events. Entirely typical was the after-dinner
gathering at Walmer Castle in October 1838 at which 'Lord Strangford
alluded to Gurwood's twelfth volume, which is just coming out; and this
led the conversation to Waterloo'. Most of the recorded material from these
occasions consists of familiar anecdote, for example that La Haye Sainte
should not have been allowed to fall and that Napoleon's tactics at Waterloo
had been no more than 'bullying with much noise and smoke'.[372] Doubtless,
however, with impaired health, advancing years, an expectant audience, and
in the wake of a good dinner, the tendency for Wellington and old comrades to embroider proved irresistible. That would seem the best explanation
for Wellington's otherwise curious claim that he could, as Lady Salisbury
recorded in 1836, 'distinctly see' the Prussian reverse at Ligny on 16 June
from Quatre Bras. In May 1845 he reiterated in writing that 'with a glass
from Quatre Bras, I positively saw the principal events on the field of Ligny'.
These included 'Blücher's personal situation, and the retreat of the Prussians
from the field of battle'. Gleig's account of Waterloo accepted Wellington's
claims uncritically. They could not, however, as well-placed contemporaries
with no particular axe to grind pointed out, literally be true. Neither had
they been made at the time.[373]

Another new story about the campaign, which became public during the 1830s, is that the Duke rode over to see Blücher on the night of 17 June. Wellington apparently relayed the episode to his daughter-in-law's father, Henry Pierrepoint, in 1833, and more fully to Mr Justice Coltman at Stratfield Saye in 1838. This is most probably a simple case of confusion on the part of those recording the anecdote. The Pierrepoint version was written down only third hand, whilst the Coltman one is surely that which appears to have originated in the *Dover Chronicle*. In this version, moreover, it is not 17 June but 15 June – when Wellington was actually at the Duchess of Richmond's ball – that his lone mission was reported as having taken place. It is inconceivable that the contemporary record would not confirm a journey on either of the dates: the confusion was with the well-documented visit Wellington paid Blücher on the morning of 16 June.[374]

Less doubt seems to attach to an episode concerning Hougoumont's role in the battle. In his table talk, Wellington occasionally expressed contradictory views about the importance of the château. In 1837, however, he was visited by the executors of a man who had left £500 for the bravest soldier in the British Army. The Duke plumped for Sir James Macdonell on the basis that he commanded the defenders at Hougoumont, 'the key to his entire position' at Waterloo, which was in turn 'the last, the greatest and most important action of the war'. Macdonell insisted on sharing the legacy with Sergeant Ralph Fraser of the Coldstream Guards, who had helped him close the north gates 'by dint of sheer physical strength'. The story was widely circulated in the press, thereby further consummating Hougoumont in Waterloo mythology.[375]

Of far more consequence was the lengthy memorandum Wellington penned on Waterloo in 1842, by far his fullest statement in writing on the subject since 1815. Why he should have been stirred into writing it is intriguing: controversy on the subject was hardly new! Perhaps he was simply more conscious of his own mortality? Gurwood had warned him in 1835 that unless he spoke, 'the truth will never be known; and posterity will be led into error by the imagination of historians whose narratives will otherwise become hallowed by time as uncontradicted authorities'. There is certainly no doubt that the Duke was irritated by the flurry of Waterloo accounts that had appeared in the wake of the publication of the *Despatches*: they were meant to help end the controversies over Waterloo, not fuel them. 'Surely,' he wrote, not entirely ingenuously, 'the details of the battle might have been left as in the original official Reports. The battle, possibly the most important single military event of modern times, was attended by advantages sufficient for the glory of many such armies as the two great allied armies engaged.' In particular, his memorandum reveals that he had been riled by the critique of his 1815 strategy contained in Clausewitz's *History of the Campaign*, a manuscript translation copy of which had been sent to him. He had also been provoked by Alison's con-tention that Napoleon had surprised and out-generalled him, reference to which he had inadvertently come across when reading the *Spectator*, and which he believed, wrongly, to have been political in motivation. Whatever the truth, when Lord Francis Egerton informed Wellington that he was writing a piece for the September 1842 number of the *Quarterly Review* about a life of Blücher, the Duke broke with past habit and offered to provide material to assist him. Charles Arbuthnot informed Egerton that Wellington had sought out volume twelve of the *Despatches* and read out portions to him from pp. 375–476 'with high delight'. This would be the raw material from which to 'write his Memorandum, and make out Alison to be a d-d rascally Frenchman'. The task was substantially completed between 22–25 July.[376]

Wellington was insistent that what he wrote was not for publication under his name. As he told Gurwood, 'I don't propose to give mine enemy the gratification of writing a book!' Egerton nevertheless drew heavily on Wellington's memorandum for his 1842 article. So, at least indirectly, did Sir Francis Head in a piece he wrote for the *Quarterly* in October 1843 defending Wellington's strategy. Egerton inevitably returned to it again for an article in the June 1845 number of the *Quarterly* on Marmont, Siborne and Alison. He sent Wellington the proofs; the Duke perused and annotated them on Waterloo Day. Together, the *Quarterly* articles constitute the clear-est and most detailed examples during his lifetime of what he called getting somebody to answer for him.[377]

Unsurprisingly, neither Wellington's 1842 memorandum, nor the subse-quent notes and annotations he provided for Egerton, reveal any significant new insights on Waterloo. The memorandum, in particular, as Arbuthnot's letter makes clear, was more or less a précis of the Waterloo material in the *Despatches*. Familiar charges were denied and rebutted: that he had taken a poor position before the campaign opened; that he had been surprised and was slow to react on 15 June; that he had not given the Prussians the credit they merited.[378] He was especially severe in his 1845 annotations on Egerton's review of Siborne's *History*: even Egerton thought the Duke guilty of unreasonable harshness towards the latter, either through confusing him with Alison or misinterpreting his language. But it was more than this. Wellington seized, for example, on details such as Siborne's statement that Uxbridge had been wounded before the general advance; the Duke was emphatic that it was afterwards. Wellington's fundamental objection to Siborne, as Egerton perhaps insufficiently grasped, was one of methodology. Siborne's *History*, after all, had reached favourable conclusions about Wellington. But, as the Duke explained, in words that anticipated Gleig's criticism of Siborne, he had reached them in the wrong way. It was the historian's duty:

> to seek with diligence for the most authentic details of the subject on which he writes, to peruse with care and attention all that has been published; to prefer that which has been officially recorded and published by responsible public authorities; next, to attend to that which proceeds from Official Authority, although not contemporaneously published, and to pay least attention to the statements of private individuals, whether communicated in writing or verbally; particularly the latter, if at a period distant from the date of the operation itself; and, above all, such statements as relate to the conduct of the Individual himself communicating or making the statement.[379]

In writing this, Wellington was simply being consistent. He had objected to all accounts since 1815, whether favourable or unfavourable, if they were not based squarely on the proper – namely, his – authority. This explains a largely overlooked and otherwise inexplicable paradox. Wellington was happy to sanction the publication of his *Despatches*, containing as they did his criticism and abuse of individuals, even countries – material clearly damaging to his own reputation and character. He did so because the *Despatches* were a true record. With so many Waterloo accounts, it was different. Whether they differed from his version of events through misperception, misinformation or through malice was immaterial. They could never be condoned; they must either be ignored or corrected. In old age, Wellington was as adamant in the belief that his version of the truth was the right one, no less than he had been in 1815!

The Duke's logic inclined him to dismiss all accounts of the 1815 campaign as either fiction or poetry. Such contempt did not deter practitioners of the latter two genres from continuing to treat either him or his battle as subjects. Waterloo-inspired poetry, often little better than doggerel, remained most likely to appear in newspapers on 18 June. More crafted was the English Prize poem read at Wellington's installation as Chancellor of Oxford in which Napoleon 'Bowed to thy Genius, Chief of Waterloo'. In 1846, Edward Bulwer-Lytton's 'The New Timon' referred in similar terms to Wellington as 'Our Man of men; the Prince of Waterloo'. Half a century later, Sir William Fraser presumed the lines would be familiar to everybody.[380]

It was, however, the novel that increasingly found favour with the mid-nineteenth-century reading public. Charlotte Brontë's Mr Rochester in *Jane Eyre*, published in 1847, is generally assumed to have been based upon her hero, the Duke. Dickens visited Waterloo as part of his first continental tour in July 1837, probably in search of ideas, for he was accompanied by his illustrator, H. K. Browne, as well as Mrs Dickens. Though his novels contain Waterloo allusions (Inspector Bucket in *Bleak House* refers to Life Guardsman Shaw as 'a model of the whole British Army in himself'), Dickens never engaged the subject directly. He found the emotions it aroused too powerful, being much moved on reading Lady Magdalene De Lancey's *A Week at Waterloo* whilst writing *Barnaby Rudge* in 1841.[381] Only Defoe, in his estimation, had possessed the genius required to do justice to it. But Dickens did not ignore the battlefield entirely. His now relatively neglected 1846 story, *The Battle of Life*, purporting to be set centuries before, begins when 'a fierce battle was fought. It was fought upon a long summer day'. Countless thousands had been killed. The farmers' ploughs, where 'every furrow that was turned, revealed some fragments of the fight', could leave no reader in any doubt as to where his inspiration had come from.[382]

William Makepeace Thackeray had no such qualms about treating Waterloo in fiction. The first number of *Vanity Fair*, his famous 'novel without a hero' appeared in January 1847. Thackeray was barely 3 when Waterloo was fought. As a young man, he was ambivalent about Wellington the politician. He professed also to having been bored mindless by countless after-dinner armchair analyses of the battle. When he visited the Low Countries in 1840, he determined to visit Brussels without the obligatory detour to Waterloo. He succumbed and was duly inspired. That, at least, is the claim of a letter he wrote under the alias of Mr M. A. Titmarsh, one of a series entitled *Little Travels and Roadside Sketches*. In his masterpiece, later that decade, Thackeray made explicit reference to Gleig's *Story of the*

Battle of Waterloo, though it surely appeared just too late to have been of more than incidental use to him. His impressions were probably formed more from the time he spent poring over contemporary newspapers. He exhorted his readers to do likewise in order that they might recreate for themselves the enormity of the titanic struggle against France: 'think of the condition of Europe for twenty years before, where people were fighting, not by thousands but by millions'.[383] A generation before, this would have been so obvious as to have needed no explanation.

Presumably because many veterans and painful memories still lived, Sir William Fraser was unhappy about Thackeray's blending of fact and fiction. But he was in a minority: *Vanity Fair* was the most popular nineteenth-century treatment of the Waterloo campaign. As such, it was surely important in both forming and reinforcing public perceptions of those events. Thackeray's account of the Duchess of Richmond's ball, in particular, confirmed its iconic status in the popular imagination, completing what Byron had begun in *Childe Harold's Pilgrimage*. Though he keeps the fighting in the background – Thackeray chooses to focus on some of his main characters in a Brussels church as the guns start to boom on 18 June – he cannot resist providing a brief snapshot as events unfold, for the 'tale is in every Englishman's mouth: and you and I, who were children when the great battle was won and lost, are never tired of hearing and recounting the history of that famous action'. In doing so, he is unashamedly patriotic. The references to the Duke are laudatory: he is 'the genius of the immortal Wellington!' He has, apart from a 'raw militia' of Germans and disaffected Belgians, only 20,000 British troops with which to confront 150,000 Frenchmen, a wild distortion even by contemporary standards of hyperbole. And reference to the Prussians is as brief as it is oblique: the reader is simply told that the French 'had other foes besides the British to engage'. It is emphatically the British who prevail: 'Then at last [with the Imperial Guard repulsed] the English troops rushed from the post from which no enemy had been able to dislodge them, and the Guard turned and fled.' The pursuit, it is implied, is effected by the British. Thackeray even ridicules General Cambronne, 'a commanding-officer of the Guard, who having sworn that "the Guard died, but never surrendered", was taken prisoner the next minute by a private soldier'. He must have known that Cambronne had been apprehended by Colonel Hew Halkett but delighted in maximising the ignominy of the episode.[384] Unlike Siborne, Thackeray was concerned with pleasing his public, not salving his historian's conscience.

Dickens and Thackeray were not the only literary luminaries of a new generation to see the battlefield in this period. John Ruskin made his second visit in 1833, aged only 14. Dante Gabriel Rossetti, who went there with William Holman Hunt in October 1849, was born in the year that Wellington became prime minister. Reflecting afterwards, in *A Trip to Paris and Belgium*, he dared to ask whether Waterloo:

> the name which travels side by side
> With English life from childhood

really was so unique? This was highly untypical. Thackeray spoke for the vast majority when he wrote of 'the little secret admission that one must make after seeing it. Let an Englishman go and see that field and he never forgets it. The sight is an event in his life [...] I will wager that there is not one of them but feels a glow as he looks at the place, and remembers that he too, is an Englishman.'[385]

The literati did not have the field to themselves. Tipu Sultan's son visited during the 1830s, but not to venerate Wellington. He is reported to have said, 'Ah, I hate the English; they killed my father!' Almost certainly he encountered some, for Henry Addison, retired dragoon guard turned battlefield guide, estimated there to be some 4,000–5,000 British visitors a year by the end of that decade. By then, John Murray had filled the void created by the absence of a good guidebook. Thackeray's complaint that it was a hack job which 'must have gutted many hundreds of guide-books' sounds suspiciously like sour grapes: it anticipated his own project for something similar. As he conceded, 'Every English party I saw had this infallible red book in their hands, and gained a vast deal of historical and general information from it.'[386]

Letters in the British press describing the battlefield become noticeably sparser after 1830. Those that did get published comment on how it was changing. In 1836 it was reported that there had 'recently been erected several manufactories of sugar from beet root, or, as it may on this occasion more appropriately be called, *mangel worzel*'. More noticeable still was the rapid decline of woodland as landowners of the forest of Soignes converted tracts of it to arable land. On the battlefield proper, by the end of the 1840s, the orchard and wood at Hougoumont had virtually disappeared with only a few trees and hedges left to delineate the boundaries of 1815.[387]

Anybody travelling to the battlefield in 1840 would have discovered that Wellington's Waterloo headquarters was no longer an inn. It had become the town's post house and post office. Further disregard of the past was apparent in the form of a new flight of stairs to the organ loft in Waterloo church: they obscured one of the regimental memorials. But at least the willow over Anglesey's leg was doing well. For travellers who wanted to stay or stop at Mont St Jean, there was either the Hôtel de la Couronne or the Hôtel des Colonnes. They reputedly sold poor maps; one even had no beer. As you approached the field itself, 'women and children sally out, with maps and charts, and relics' – the latter still readily to be found. A sceptical officer preferred to take a piece of charcoal from Hougoumont: 'This I value the more, as I feel sure it was not manufactured for the occasion.' On the south-eastern side of the field, the 1819 memorial to the Prussians, wantonly vandalised by French forces in 1832 en route to helping the Belgians against the Dutch, had been repaired and railings added to it.[388]

Visitors invariably recalled the Lion's Mound as the salient feature of the battlefield: its original clay steps were visibly crumbling under the weight of the tourist traffic. For all that it was an incomparable vantage point, however, it continued to prove annoying. French troops had damaged the lion's teeth and tail in 1832. In December that year, there had been an abortive attempt by a Belgian deputy to have it replaced with a 'funeral monument'. Still smarting from memories of their unwanted union with the Dutch, some of his compatriots hoisted a black flag at the summit on Waterloo Day 1843. As for the British, Thackeray reported that 'military men regard [it] as a kind of sacrilege, which they will not soon forget or forgive'. Ample proof of what he meant was provided by an 1839 officer's account fulminating that it disfigured 'the most interesting quarter of the field [...] thus not only disabling posterity from appreciating the refined military skill, the matured judgement, and the happy combinations of the veteran who won the day, but actually altering the bearing of positions so as to present to the eye of the spectator "the thing which was not" in matters of vital moment.'[389]

The Lion's Mound also appears in Wellington's two artistic 'visits' to the battlefield during this period. In 1849 Sir Edwin Landseer went to the battlefield as preparation for his *Dialogue at Waterloo*, exhibited in 1850. Supposedly set around 1833, it depicts an imagined scene in which the Duke conducts Lady Douro over the field. It was not generally well-received. Part of the problem was that his canvas had been anticipated by Benjamin Robert Haydon. Haydon had wanted to paint Wellington at Waterloo to mark the battle's twentieth anniversary. But Wellington initially rejected Haydon's request for a sitting, lecturing him portentously that 'a painter should be a historian, a philosopher, a politician, as well as a poet and a man of taste'. The proposed subject, he assured him, would accomplish none of this. Haydon conceded that it would, of course, be unhistorical but that 'imagining a great general visiting the field of his greatest battle after many years is both natural and poetical; that the musings that must occur to him there would be philosophical [...] I glory in placing you there, and think the public and the army will glory in seeing you there'. Haydon was subsequently granted access to his subject in May 1839 when a group of Liverpool gentlemen approached Wellington for a portrait from the artist. On this occasion he expressed complete indifference as to the subject matter. The canvas was completed later that year.[390] The episode is yet another illustration of the Duke's ambivalence towards the memorialising of Waterloo; Haydon's image was one of the most potent commemorations. Wordsworth, now Poet Laureate, explained its message for the public the following year.

> By Art's bold privilege Warrior and Warhorse stand
> On ground yet strewn with their last battle's wreck ...
> But by the Chieftain's look, though at his side
> Hangs that day's reassured sword, how firm a check
> Is given to triumph and all human pride!
> Yon trophied Mound shrinks to a shadowy speck
> In his calm presence! Him the mighty deed
> Elates not.[391]

In the absence of the Duke as a battlefield guide, British tourists found a worthy replacement in Edward Cotton. Born in 1792 on the Isle of Wight, Cotton served with the 7th Hussars at Waterloo, where he distinguished himself by rescuing a comrade pinned to the ground by a wounded horse. When he left the army in 1835, Sergeant-Major Cotton settled at Mont St Jean and quickly earned a reputation as 'an excellent and intelligent guide'. His home also served as a museum for the various artefacts found, bought and donated to him. Such was his success that during the 1840s he was able to relocate the enterprise to the newly-built Hôtel du Musée near the base of the Lion's Mound. By 1846 he felt confident enough to produce his own battlefield guide. Within a year it was sufficiently well-known –

especially for its section of Waterloo anecdotes – that it was being widely quoted in the British press. This helped persuade him to use a London pub-lisher for the third edition of February 1849. By then, *A Voice from Waterloo* was, in truth, less a guide than a history of the campaign, drawing heavily on the *Despatches* and Siborne. Running to over 300 pages, the mid-century tourist needed capacious pockets. Cotton continued guiding until two days before his death shortly after Waterloo Day 1849. He was buried in the grounds of Hougoumont.[392]

Cotton is a good example of a Waterloo veteran who prospered. Others were noticeable for their longevity. In 1835, Old Bustler, a dog who had supposedly been at the battle, died aged 22. Reference to horses was under-standably more common. The most famous of all, Copenhagen, who had carried Wellington throughout 18 June, died on 12 February 1836. The Duke ordered his burial at Stratfield Saye with full military honours. He fared far better than Jack, the last surviving Waterloo horse at the Knightsbridge Barracks. He was bedecked in laurel, as usual, on 18 June 1836, but infirmities led to him being unceremoniously shot a few days later.[393]

There was outcry in some quarters at Jack's fate: were not Wellington's Waterloo heroes – even the non-human ones – deserving better of the nation in their later years? One who believed they were was Mr Boxer of Southwark. He cited the case of a Waterloo widow with five children whose husband had served twenty-one years in the 52nd Light Infantry, but who was now confined to the workhouse, because of 'the enactments of this inhuman law'. Another who believed that Waterloo veterans were cases apart was a magistrate called Cottingham. In 1843 he 'declared that he never will punish any man who was present at the battle of Waterloo for any offence short of felony'.[394] His remarks caused a furore. But there is no real evidence that they had a basis in fact. In September 1845, Joseph Laycock was charged with hawking calico without a licence. He pleaded unfair arrest and 'added, as if to touch the sympathy of the court, that he was at the battle of Waterloo'. He was fined £10 and, being unable to pay, was sent to the house of correction for three months.[395]

For others, fortunes were inevitably mixed. James Thompson, the 6-foot-9-inch Scottish giant, who had been a circus attraction in the 1820s, appeared as a plaintiff at the Surrey sessions in 1838, accusing two of his fellow lodgers of stealing clothes to the value of £1. One thing at least was certain: they could not have been stolen to order for his landlord, George Strutt, for he was 'a mere dwarf'. The case excited much amusement.

Less funny was the fate of Dr John Gordon Smith. He spent the last fifteen months of his life in the Fleet Prison for debt, dying suddenly at the age of 41 in 1833. As surgeon to the 12th Lancers, he had saved the life of Lieutenant-Colonel Frederick Ponsonby, commanding officer of the 12th Light Dragoons, the account of whose horrific wounding was one of the best known personal stories from 1815. Also no respecters of reputation were the Rebecca rioters who completely destroyed the tollhouse at Penygarn in 1843. The keeper was a Waterloo pensioner; his medal was stolen.[396] And notoriety, rather than sympathy, was the fate of Joel Fisher, capitally convicted in 1844. After twenty-three years of exemplary service in the 11th Hussars, he murdered his wife with brutal ferocity. When he was hanged at Wilton Jail in Somerset, over 5,000 turned up to watch. One presumes this was at least partly due to his Waterloo association. So also, the fact that 'several applications were made to the governor of the prison by persons afflicted with the king's evil and rheumatism for permission for the hand of the dead man to be rubbed over the parts affected with idea that they would be cured'. The requests were declined.[397]

Mid-nineteenth-century society was clearly more comfortable with murder than insanity. A striking number of Waterloo men who appear in the columns of the press were said to be suffering from the latter affliction, though whether their number proportionately was greater than that for society as a whole is impossible to say. One such was 42-year-old Captain William Henry Rowlls, erstwhile of the 14th Light Dragoons. He was prone to periods of blindness, a belief that he was the MP for Surrey, and a propensity to undress in public. Such details are suggestive of what we would now call post-traumatic-stress disorder. This is surely more plausible than the contemporary verdict that his symptoms were the consequence of his 'leading a very idle and luxurious life'. Far less ambiguously, the jury in an 1838 lunacy commission on William Bartlett of Chelsea, an ensign in the 69th Foot at Waterloo, was instructed to 'find that the delusions under which Mr Bartlett laboured were strongly tinged with the events of that day and the characters who took a prominent part in it'.[398] And madness was inextricably linked in the contemporary mind with suicide: the latter almost invariably attracted a verdict of temporary insanity. At least ten Waterloo veterans took their own lives between 1839 and 1845, most famously John Gurwood, editor of the *Despatches*, who cut his throat with a razor on Christmas Day 1845.[399] His suicide was ascribed to depression, but the battle, a generation on, was still claiming its victims.

Wellington's dictum that not every man in uniform was a hero thus remained as true as ever. One obvious exception was Charles Ewart of the Scots Greys. He had generally chosen to shun the limelight that followed his capture of the Eagle of the 45th. Walter Scott had prevailed upon him to appear at an 1816 celebration dinner in Edinburgh, but Ewart had told his audience that he would rather fight the battle again than make a speech. He retired, after thirty-two years' service, with his wife to Salford, where he became a fencing master. Proof that he had succeeded in lying low is suggested by the fact that some newspapers referred to him, phonetically, as 'Hewitt' in 1837. The occasion was the presentation to him of a silver cup by some of his erstwhile comrades on Waterloo Day that year. The cup was stolen three months later by Ewart's neighbour, John Reddish. It was never recovered. Ewart died, aged 77, on 23 March 1846. His grave would be virtually forgotten. But his exploits were kept alive and consummated in oils by Richard Ansdell's 1848 *Battle for the Standard*. The painting was on display in Regent Street in 1852.[400] Partly because of it, almost alone of the rank and file who fought at Waterloo, Ewart's name would survive into the next century.

Ewart's name was presumably unknown to the boy, who, according to the great Radical apostle of free trade, Richard Cobden, had asked his father, when taken to see Siborne's model of Waterloo, what the battle was about. This was partly the result, with the passage of time, of the ignorance of youth. The *Worcester Journal*, in 1838, deemed it necessary to explain to 'our younger readers' that Wellington's annual rent for Stratfield Saye consisted of a tricolour flag. For their parents, the fact had long been common knowledge.[401] But there is some evidence that the public was losing its appetite for celebrating Waterloo. As early as 1833, in Stockport, it was claimed that the battle's anniversary had 'entirely lost its attraction'. Only eighteen tickets were sold for a Waterloo dinner at Nottingham in 1840, whilst the bells of York Minster, in full peal each 18 June since 1815, were not rung in 1849.[402] Most such objections to marking the date appear to have been grounded in the seeming glorification of war in general, as opposed to Waterloo in particular. In Leicester, Mr West, a Quaker, protested about the 10 shillings paid to the local bell-ringers each year. 'It struck him as being a most inconsistent thing that this should be done; and he trusted that, as Christians, they would not retain this celebration.'[403] And in 1849, 'Philo Junius' maintained that:

the intelligent people of this country 'want no boast of Waterloo' – no public commemoration of any such unchristian atrocity. It is by peaceful arts that

society advances; and as succeeding generations learn more justly to appreciate achievements that really tend to benefit mankind, the anniversaries
celebrated by the country will be those which refer to great discoveries, or
inventions, or exertions tending to promote the permanent prosperity and
freedom, and the moral and religious welfare of mankind.

The London Peace Society, which had been established in June 1816, enjoyed
some popularity during the 1840s: Cobden was a prominent supporter.[404]

However laudable the sentiments of 'Philo Junius', they represented,
overwhelmingly, a minority viewpoint. Even organs of the Radical press
sympathetic to it had to concede that 'every Briton's heart throbs as a feeling of patriotism thrills through it' at the remembrance of 1815.[405] Whilst
Wellington lived, British society continued to celebrate Waterloo with him
and his veterans. Events ranged from the modest dinner prepared by Mr
Tubb at East Tytherley's Star Inn to the huge fetes at Vauxhall and grand
military reviews in London's St James's Park or Dublin's Phoenix Park. By
the mid-1830s, it had become an unwritten convention that no new parliamentary business would be transacted on Waterloo Day. In 1836, William
Lynn, who owned the Waterloo Hotel in Liverpool, inaugurated a three-day
hare coursing event at Great Altcar in Lancashire known as the Waterloo
Cup.[406] Messrs Rundell and Bridge struck a commemorative medal for the
battle's twenty-fifth anniversary. In 1842 Robert Burford opened a new
Waterloo panorama in Leicester Square based on Henry Barker's original
drawings from 1815. In 1844 Wellington himself was amongst those who
went to see General Tom Thumb's impersonation of Napoleon at St Helena
in P. T. Barnum's circus at the Egyptian Hall.[407] Musical and dramatic per-
formances about 1815 were common throughout the nation, and staged
with a pleasing disregard for health and safety. Early in November 1846,
the Garrick Theatre was totally destroyed by a fire started by wadding fired
from cannon during a performance of *The Battle of Waterloo*.[408]

Thackeray was another who was uneasy at the motivation for Waterloo
celebrations: 'It is a wrong, egotistical, savage, unchristian feeling, and that's
the truth of it.' Doubtless many base emotions were stirred, but Wellington's
generation, inured to war, was also genuine in its gratitude that Waterloo
was followed by a prolonged era of relative peace. In 1836, the *Essex Standard*
claimed that the years since 1815 marked the longest period without war
between European states since 1066. A 'Birmingham Reformer' reflected
approvingly upon the nature of that peace: in 1815 it had seemed as if the

forces of reactionary Toryism had prevailed; instead, a new spirit of reform and Liberalism was abroad. And to those who thought likewise, progress was increasingly linked to prosperity. In 1840, the *Morning Post* estimated that the wealth and industry of Britain had increased by a half.[409] It was not coincidental that the first iron ship built on the Clyde was the *Iron Duke*, with a figurehead of the great man. Railway entrepreneurs, overseeing the greatest revolution in transport during the period, were the most prominent in perceiving a connection between 1815 and the present. Lines frequently opened on Waterloo Day: the 61-mile Newcastle to Carlisle line officially opened on 18 June 1838. One engine, inevitably, was named *Wellington*. Exactly six years later, the final link in the 303-mile London to Newcastle line was opened. The Duke was toasted at a celebration feast in Newcastle, hosted by the line's chairman, George Hudson, 'the railway king'. Thanks to Waterloo, declared the Reverend G. Townsend, over dinner, railways would spread peace, prosperity and civilisation. From 1848, these virtuous expresses would be able to set off from London's Waterloo Bridge station.[410]

Waterloo veterans, of course, kept 18 June as a day to look backwards rather than forwards. In Bury St Edmunds the preparations were overseen by William Middleditch, formerly of the First Foot Guards, latterly landlord of the Ram Inn. When he died in 1834, six of his former comrades bore him to the grave. The annual veterans' gathering at the Ram outlived him.[411] The grandest dinner outside London was hosted by the civic authorities in Preston. It was rejuvenated in 1846 by the expedient of including Peninsular, not just Waterloo, veterans. 'There had,' explained Mr Vallet, 'naturally been hitherto a little feeling that ought not to exist, and which this would put aside, and shew that the country appreciated both.' Some ninety-eight Peninsular veterans and fifty-one Waterloo men – some could claim to be both – took part in a two-hour march around the town accompanied by flags and a band before proceeding to dine at the Bull Hotel.[412]

Preston's initiative was presumably related to the 5th Duke of Richmond's campaign to gain greater reward for all soldiers who had fought in the wars since 1793. As Earl of March, he had served as an aide-de-camp at Waterloo before marrying Uxbridge's daughter, Caroline, in 1817, and succeeding to the title in 1819. His efforts bore fruit in 1847 with the authorisation of the Military General Services Medal. Richmond was not alone in being indignant that society insufficiently recognised its veterans. Thackeray, though impressed by the memorials to officers that he had seen at Waterloo in 1840:

felt very much disappointed at not seeing the names of all the men as well as
the officers. Are they to be counted for nought? A few more inches of marble
to each monument would have given space for all the names of the men; and
the men of that day were the winners of the battle. We have a right to be as
grateful individually to any private as to any given officer.[413]

His sentiments were given added force by the fact that British soldiers were
soon to be engaged in both the first Anglo-Afghan war (1839–1842) and
two Anglo-Sikh wars (1845–1846, 1848–1849). Some Waterloo veterans, for
example Major Baldwin of the 31st Foot, were to fall in these later conflicts. News of these new fatalities prompted MPs once more to consider
properly recording the names of all British service personnel who fell in
battle. Mr Williams Wynn, the Member who had proposed doing so in 1815,
recalled the earlier occasion, and added his amen to the idea. Again it came
to naught, let alone the suggestion that, 'if glorious battles are worth commemorating, the orphans and widows of soldiers and sailors ought to be
prominently, if not permanently assisted'.[414]

Parliament's inaction was hardly a matter of cost (Thackeray reckoned
£500 would suffice for the marble to memorialise the Waterloo fallen by
name); it was one of class. One reason why disquiet at the lack of memorials
to the common soldier was being voiced in the 1840s was that the decade
witnessed the working-class phenomenon that was Chartism. Its press
organ, the *Northern Star*, claimed to have seen a Chelsea Pensioner wearing
his Waterloo medal being totally ignored by the crowds gathering to see
the comings and goings at Apsley House on Waterloo Day 1845: 'This is
the gratitude of the aristocracy! – we turned away with disgust.' Thackeray
agreed that, 'English glory is too genteel to meddle with those humble fellows. She does not condescend to ask the names of the poor devils whom
she kills in her service.' Thus, whilst the common soldier, 'when shot down
shall be shovelled into a hole [...] and so forgotten', his officer 'is knighted
because the men fought so well'. Mid-nineteenth-century Britain remained
overwhelmingly deferential in character.[415]

The occasion for the *Northern Star's* revulsion was, of course, the annual
dinner Wellington hosted at Apsley House for his surviving senior officers from the 1815 campaign. This, above all other commemorative events
after 1832, was pre-eminent. It was reported in greater detail with each
passing year. From the mid-1830s, the nobility were admitted by ticket to
view preparations in the Waterloo Gallery. By 1840, the crowds gathering

outside were said to be 'immense'; it was an occasion of European interest. And not just for the masses: at least seven peers were listed amongst the 'vast number' who gathered to watch those arriving in 1843. The crowds cheered the arrival of those more easily recognised, Lord Anglesey in particular.[416]

Royal patronage, not that it needed it, bolstered the event: William IV was a particular devotee of the occasion. As he lay dying on 17 June 1837, he told his physician, Dr Chambers, that, 'If you do not keep me alive for another day the Duke of Wellington will not be able to hold his annual festival in celebration of the battle of Waterloo.' For some things, even royalty and the Grim Reaper had to defer. The King died on 20 June and subsequently lay in state in the Waterloo Gallery at Windsor. Prince Albert was privately censured for declining to attend the 1841 dinner, 'for the invitation was a great compliment, and this is a sort of national commemoration at which he might have felt a pride at being present'.[417] He was assiduous in his attendance thereafter.

The dinner, lasting two to three hours, had a well-established format by the 1830s. There were toasts to the Crown, the Duke, the memory of the fallen, and the constituent parts of the British Army, each interspersed by an appropriate piece from the band engaged for the occasion. Depending upon which foreign dignitaries were present, a glass might be raised to them as well. In 1845, for example, Wellington alluded to 'the bravery of the allied forces who assisted at Waterloo'. This was not, as might be supposed, a reference to the Prussians, but chiefly to the Hanoverians, whose minister was present.[418] The Prussians, indeed, do not seem to have been represented at the banquet. In his last years, however, Wellington was in the habit of referring to them, though chiefly in the context of thanking Sir Henry Hardinge, his liaison officer with them in 1815. This was particularly the case from 1849 when Hardinge (since 1846 Lord Hardinge) was present in person, having returned from his posting as Governor-General of India. In consequence the Prussian Army was toasted directly that year. The following year, Wellington's longest speech of the evening was 'mainly in praise of the Prussian army, and the great service it proved at Waterloo'. Frustratingly, his comments were not recorded. But they are unlikely to have been any more revealing than those he made in 1852 when 'he always at these meetings was proud to acknowledge the great services rendered by the Prussian army at Waterloo. Indeed, he could not speak too highly of the advantages which followed upon their operations.'[419] It was his last public reference to them. But he no more defined the precise nature of the services than he had in his 1815 despatch.

The dinner was, anyway, emphatically a celebration of living British legends. In 1844 the *Spectator* reflected that half the country's population had been born since Waterloo and that 'these old fighting men have almost come to belong to a past generation'. They were 'relics of a fighting era preserved in an era of peace'.[420] And above all, the dinner was an annual reminder of one particular legend, Wellington. It took place in his home, specifically in his Waterloo Gallery, which at 200 feet long and 85 feet wide extended the whole length of Apsley House, 'the finest specimen of modern taste within the metropolis'. His guests ate off Dresden porcelain depicting scenes of his victories from India to Waterloo. Around them, as the press delighted in describing, the room contained a cornucopia of gold and silver plate, a silver gilt shield from the allied monarchs, three gold candelabra from the corporation of London and a solid gold vase from the English nobility.[421] It was the supreme example of how the Duke and a willing media colluded in the twin processes of Wellington's self-fashioning and Waterloo commemoration.

More substantially, Wellington was also being commemorated in statues. A crowd of 20,000 turned up in October 1844 to witness the inauguration of Carlo Marochetti's equestrian bronze in front of Glasgow's Royal Exchange. Its success quickly confounded the opposition of *The Times*, which held that awarding the commission to an Italian would be 'quite out of keeping with the character of the nation; one with a British name and a foreign spirit, a sort of military harlequin, all start and stare with his clothes in a flutter, and his horse mad. They will obtain this at the expense of patriotism and justice.'[422] Less controversial were those executed by Francis Chantrey for the City of London, inaugurated on Waterloo Day the same year, and Sir John Steell's in front of Edinburgh's Register House. The latter was officially unveiled on 18 June 1852 with the irresistible billing of 'the Iron Duke in bronze by Steell'.[423]

Huge controversy, however, surrounded what was meant to serve as the nation's official memorial statue of the Duke. Queen Victoria agreed to the project in May 1838; by Waterloo Day 1841, some 2,300 people had contributed over £25,000 towards realising it. But protracted arguments over aesthetics and location meant that it was September 1846 before Matthew Cotes Wyatt's 30-foot-high statue cast from 40 tons of Waterloo cannon was hoisted onto Decimus Burton's victory arch at Hyde Park Corner opposite

Apsley House. Lord Francis Egerton spoke for many in calling it 'a bad thing in a bad place'.[424] The arguments have obscured the rather more important point that a generation on, the nation was seeking to honour equally the Duke and Nelson and their most famous victories. Queen Victoria, symbolically, sent 500 guineas simultaneously in 1838 to the committees responsible for the two commemorative projects. The Duke himself contributed £200 to the latter enterprise and was in the chair at the London Tavern meeting of August 1838 that confirmed the sanctioning of the site for what would become Trafalgar Square.[425]

Wellington also remained involved in more consequential affairs. The Conservatives' return to power in 1841 saw him resume cabinet office as minister without portfolio; he also continued as leader of the party in the Lords. Much of the day-to-day burden of the latter role was shouldered by Lord Stanley from 1844. Before then, in August 1842, Wellington had returned to his old post at the Horse Guards as Commander-in-Chief. From there he was able to give voice to his concerns about the state of the nation's defences and, in April 1848, prepare for the possibility of popular unrest in the capital in the event of Chartist unrest. Neither invasion nor insurrection materialised.

Waterloo allusions, so common in political discourse during the 1830s, diminished in frequency as the Duke assumed a lower political profile. The one notable exception was the issue of free trade. The *Manchester Times* would facetiously dub its London namesake 'the Blücher of the press' for having converted to the cause only when the battle was 'well nigh won'. The Conservative Party, though, was popularly presumed to have pledged itself to upholding the Corn Laws at the 1841 election. Sir John Tyrell, MP for North Essex, told electors that he knew from private sources that Wellington was prouder of his part in framing the Corn Laws than he was of Waterloo.[426] His sources would fail him. Peel, in face of pressure from Cobden's Anti-Corn Law League and the humanitarian crisis triggered by the failure of the 1845 Irish potato crop, decided that the Corn Laws must go. Tyrell assured fellow Protectionists at Chelmsford in December 1845 that though Peel had deserted them, Wellington would not. They could have the same confidence in him that his men had when winning at Waterloo. Tyrell was not alone in calling on the Duke to lead. Wellington, it is true, was unconvinced by the merits of free trade. But he did admire Peel's determination to provide strong government and thus 'he set about doing his duty, and preparing for battle'. Without Wellington's support, the House of Lords may well have rejected the Repeal measure. Once more a constitutional clash was averted. It was a final political victory. When Peel's government fell in June 1846, Wellington effectively retired from politics.[427]

Wellington's part in helping resolve the crisis over the Corn Laws contributed to the ongoing 'softening' of his public image that is apparent from the late 1830s onwards. *Punch*, the satirical magazine that first appeared in 1841, also played a significant part in it. Gentler in the treatment of its subjects than political caricaturists of the previous generation, Wellington's hooked nose made him irresistible to that periodical's cartoonists. *Punch* was also responsible for popularising the 'Iron Duke' sobriquet, one of the many names he was being called by 1838.[428] Increasingly, it was meant respectfully, denoting the perceived Wellingtonian virtues of determination and resolution; not the competing connotations of a cold and uncaring figure. *Punch*, like others, further delighted in reproducing (and mimicking) the Duke's famously terse – and often amusing – replies to correspondents. For all that he complained about his voluminous postbag, Wellington seems to have been more or less addicted to answering the myriad of inquiries that reached him. In 1846 one newspaper included Wellington's ostensible views on marriage, corns and lotteries. On the latter:

> F. M. Duke of Wellington presents his compliments to Messrs. Heine, and in answer to their letter, never dabbles in lotteries. He thinks them a swindle upon the public, and begs they may send him no more letters. As for the prizes, he never won one, and never heard of anybody who did. They are a fiction – a snare – a take-in.

Greville was exactly right in noting that this idiosyncrasy was 'not only unprecedented, but quite unnecessary, and I think unwise, although certainly it contributes to his popularity'.[429]

The Duke was incontrovertibly popular, even revered, during his last years. He was at once infallible sage, benign elder statesman and national treasure. No friend of his politics, the *Scotch Reformers' Gazette* was aghast to learn that somebody had taken the reins from the Wellington statue in Glasgow in September 1845. The perpetrator, it thought, should be dragged through the streets on a hurdle and sentenced to hard labour interspersed by thrashings until the next 18 June. At the opening of the Great Exhibition in May 1851, Wellington's appearance was, said Palmerston, 'accompanied by an incessant running fire of applause from the men and waving of handkerchiefs and kissing of hands from the women'. When he joined arms with Lord Anglesey, there was virtually a stampede. Nobody seemed to mind that he was upstaging both the royal couple and the raison d'etre of the event: Victoria and Albert had happily christened their son, born on Wellington's 81st birthday, Arthur. A year before, Wellington's 80th birthday in 1849 was marked quite widely by public dinners.[430] The Duke's passing in September 1852 would therefore test the nation: how would it deal with Waterloo without Wellington?

6

Victorians Remember: Wellington and Waterloo Reassessed 1852–1901

'On this day Arthur, Duke of Wellington, perhaps the greatest man that ever drew breath, departed.' Thus ran the entry in Lady Shelley's diary for 14 September 1852. The Duke had died earlier that afternoon at Walmer Castle. His passing triggered a remarkable outpouring of eulogies and other assessments. For a few months, his reputation returned to levels not reached since 1815. Even Waterloo was eclipsed by the shadow of the man. In December 1852, Charles Dickens, who found the phenomenon unseemly, wrote that 'it strikes me that no topic ever considered since the earth was without form and void, has been so exhausted as the Death of the Duke of Wellington'.[431] The debate generated more heat than light, for Britons were already largely agreed who they felt Wellington was and what Waterloo represented. By the century's close, with more of the real Wellington having been revealed, he could be re-evaluated; and Waterloo would again loom larger than the man with whom it was synonymous. But Waterloo too, by dint of new memoirs and fresh histories, would slowly come to be viewed more dispassionately by Britons. The popular commemorations of 18 June would die with those of the Waterloo generation that outlived the Duke. Even so, the battle lived on in the national consciousness, and continued to inform the unfolding national story.

The Duke received the rare honour of a state funeral and burial in St Paul's Cathedral.[432] First, over 250,000 people filed past his coffin at the Royal

Military Hospital, where it lay in state for four days from 13 November. On the night of 17 November it was transferred to Horse Guards, from where the 10,000-strong funeral procession, headed by Prince Albert, set out at 7.15am the following morning. Wellington's body lay on a huge funeral carriage. Behind it walked his immediate family and closest friends. It was 2.40 p.m. before the service concluded and the coffin could be lowered into the crypt. Inclement weather notwithstanding, the day was judged a success. Even Dickens acknowledged 'the sincere and deep expression [...] of reverence' shown by the masses. Some 20,000 had crammed inside St Paul's, whilst 300,000 had secured vantage points in public buildings or on hastily erected stands. An estimated 1½ million were said to have witnessed the procession. This, facilitated by the rapid expansion of the railways, equated to roughly 7 per cent of the population. Queen Victoria's aspiration 'that the greatest possible number of her subjects should have an opportunity of joining in it' would seem to have been realised. For those who did not attend, there were memorial services up and down the country. In a link with the past, the sermon at Preston was preached by a Waterloo veteran, the Reverend Gilmour Robinson.[433]

Wellington's funeral was protean. Some have suggested that it was a deliberate attempt to outshine Napoleon's reburial in Les Invalides in 1840. There is greater force in the thesis that it served a more immediate diplomatic purpose. On 4 November 1852, the French Senate announced that a plebiscite would be held on the question of whether or not Louis Napoleon should be elevated to imperial status: Victoria was privately hopeful that a grand spectacle on 18 November might dissuade her Gallic neighbour against seeking to revive *la gloire*.[434] For ordinary Britons, however, the Duke's passing was seen more as a time to reflect upon the ending of an era. Thomas Cooper, the former Chartist, put it well when he wrote that Wellington:

> was an institution in himself. We all felt as if we lived, now he was dead, in a different England [...] I seemed myself to belong now to another generation of men; for my very childhood was passed amid the noise of Wellington's battles, and his name and existence seemed stamped on every year of our time.[435]

As such, the funeral was also an opportunity to reflect upon, and celebrate, Englishness: another of Victoria's aspirations was that the proceedings 'should be deprived of nothing which could invest it with a thoroughly national character'.

The latter theme was especially apposite since, as the *Glasgow Herald* put it, Wellington was 'the most perfect and illustrious impersonation of the English character'.[436] In the weeks that followed his death, commentators fell over each other in identifying what more precisely this was. Formal obituaries competed with selections of Wellington anecdotes, examples of his terse written style and citations from the *Despatches*. Particularly influential were a lecture on Wellington by the Earl of Ellesmere, and Henry Reeve's obituary of the Duke in *The Times*. At 47,000 words, more than twice the length of any other in the newspaper that century, it proved so popular that it was republished as a pamphlet.[437] But popularity did not equate to originality. The *Bristol Mercury* had needed no great prescience when it predicted in 1840 that 'it will be forgotten that the Duke of Wellington belonged to a party, and the nation will write his epitaph as that of a good, great, and honest man'. Specifically, in a speech at Carlisle on 18 September, his former cabinet colleague, Sir James Graham, maintained that 'devotion to his country, his never-ceasing patriotism, his self-denial, and his love of duty [...] were the qualities which made the Duke of Wellington what he was'. Former political opponents did not demur. Lord John Russell exhorted an audience in Stirling to emulate the Duke's personal qualities, 'that sincere and unceasing devotion to his country – that honest and proud determination to act for his country on all occasions [...] that vigilance in the constant performance of his duty [...] that unostentatious piety by which he was distinguished at all times in his life'.[438] In what might be termed this dutiful consensus, mention of Waterloo was not, at first, especially prominent. Reeve, for example, wrote soberly that it revealed no new military trait in his subject. He simply listed it as one of Wellington's great achievements, in the same sentence as crossing the Douro, entering Madrid and passing Catholic Emancipation.

But the Duke's funeral could never be simply a matter of what Disraeli termed the 'contemplation of his character'. Part of its purpose was to bring to a culmination the national commemoration of him as no less a hero than Nelson. Spencer Walpole, the Home Secretary, had even suggested that Nelson's tomb be moved in order that Wellington share centre stage with him beneath the dome of St Paul's. The point was fully understood by the Poet Laureate. Having already written *Morte d'Arthur* (there were plenty who saw resonances between the Duke and the legendary king in 1852), Tennyson opted for the more prosaic *Ode on the Death of the Duke of Wellington* as the title for his 1,900-word literary tribute. In the sixth stanza

he imagines Nelson asking what the commotion of 18 November means
and is told that,

> this is he
> Was great by land as thou by sea …
> Worthy of our gorgeous rites,
> And worthy to be laid by thee;
> For this is England's greatest son …
> If love of country move thee there at all,
> Be glad, because his bones are laid by thine!

The *Ode*, which first appeared on 16 November, quickly exhausted its first
print run of 10,000 copies.[439]

The comparison with Nelson – 'His foes were thine' wrote Tennyson
– inevitably took one back to the great struggle with Revolutionary
and Napoleonic France. And thus, for all the talk of commemorating a
virtuous servant of the State in peace and war, it was Wellington the warrior's achievements that were really being celebrated on 18 November
1852. And the latter were inexorably synonymous with Waterloo. The
most common criticism of the funeral was that it had been too martial
in character. Dickens thought it 'a grievous thing – a relapse into semi-
barbarous practices […] a pernicious corruption of the popular mind'.[440]
It was eighty-three Chelsea Pensioners, one for each year of the Duke's
life, not eighty-three Tory Lords, who took part in his funeral procession. That procession also included soldiers from every regiment in the
British Army, including over 3,000 infantrymen, eight squadrons of cavalry and three artillery batteries. Lord Anglesey carried Field-Marshal
Wellington's baton. And the most poignant image of the day for many
was Wellington's horse, led by his groom, with the eponymous boots
reversed in the stirrups.[441] The other memorable image of the day was
the 10-ton bronze funeral car. Prince Albert had instructed that it should
be 'a symbol of English military strength and statesmanship'. Cast from
cannon captured at Waterloo, with 'Waterloo' inscribed above its front
right wheel, it amply succeeded in the former without, perhaps, quite
conveying the latter. Count Walewski, the French ambassador, was understandably reluctant to attend.

French newspapers also took exception. The *Patrie* and the *Presse* declared
that the Duke would never be found in a pantheon of liberty. He was 'a

vestige of times which exist no more [...] the future owes him nothing; his name will only be for posterity a sonorous word'. The comments provoked a furore from their English counterparts. With the dead Duke yet unburied, the press refought Waterloo, except that this time the Prussians came to nobody's assistance. Indeed, the German *Augsburg Gazette* insisted that the British had been losing the battle until the Prussians arrived and 'expresses [...] wonder that Wellington, who was naturally magnanimous, should have uniformly claimed a monopoly of the victory of Waterloo, thus defrauding Blücher of his due share of merit'.[442] By way of reply, *The Standard* published a letter saying that Wellington had never presumed on any Prussian assistance and that the French had effectively been beaten by 5 p.m. The French press in turn denied the latter claim. It did so in such vehement terms that just four days before the funeral, *Lloyds Weekly Newspaper* included a piece with the ironic heading 'How the French won Waterloo'. The French, it added, 'have excited a feeling of hostility which it will take some time to abate'.[443]

There was no immediate sign, as the above exchange confirms, that Wellington's death would much alter Britons' desire to remember the events of 1815. Even before the Duke's funeral, Mr Burford revived his Waterloo panorama in Leicester Square after a nine-year absence 'in accordance with the feeling that pervades all classes of society at this moment'. The United Services Institution reopened out of season: Siborne's model was reported to be exciting much interest.[444] As 18 June 1853 approached, local events were scheduled to take place as normal. The Glasgow Wellington Club held its annual dinner; Manchester veterans held their annual banquet at Pomona Gardens. In the theatrical world, Astley's kept up the good fight by reviving its production of *The Battle of Waterloo*. Plans were announced for the grand annual military parade in Phoenix Park, Dublin.[445] And then, suddenly, these and many similar acts of popular celebration ended, never properly to revive.

The reason for the cessation of festivities was the developing international tension that would escalate into the Crimean War. In this, Britain found itself an ally of the French: the two nations' fleets rendezvoused in Besika Bay five days before Waterloo Day 1853. The Crown consequently let it be known that public acts of commemoration on 18 June would be unwelcome. Britons mostly deferred. The *York Herald* was delighted to report that the erstwhile common practice of ringing church bells had virtually ceased as well as 'other needless demonstrations, offensive to our French neighbours'. In Paris, 'The determination of the English Government not to celebrate the battle of Waterloo' was well received as proof of 'a disposition to cultivate the French alliance'.[446]

Neither was Queen Victoria's determination that her people should not be amused on 18 June a one-off gesture to diplomacy. The crowds who turned up in London and Dublin in 1854 anticipating military parades were disappointed. Britain and France had, after all, formally declared war on Russia in March 1854. More than Wellington's death even, the Crimean War underscored the belief that a former age had passed, that Waterloo was indeed history. Roger Fenton's images and William Howard Russell's even more famous despatches to *The Times* gave the new conflict an immediacy that eclipsed Waterloo. Who would want to read Tennyson's *Ode* when they would soon be able to read his *Charge of the Light Brigade*? Mindful of that sentiment, Sir John Colborne (now Lord Seaton), gave a gratuity of 5 shillings to all veterans in Dublin's Kilmainham Hospital on Waterloo Day 1855, to demonstrate that 'their services in days of yore have not been lost sight of in the attachment to ones more recent, but equally sanguinary'. There were others too who, with the war having ended by Waterloo Day 1856, dared question the official line by remarking that, 'It seems sad and strange that the grandest triumph of British arms should thus be so totally consigned to the silent keeping of history.'[447]

But Wellington and Waterloo could hardly be kept out of the national debate on the Crimean War; rather they informed it. *The Times* cautioned, as war loomed in 1853, that the carnage of the Napoleonic Wars offered a salutary reason as to why the country should not enter into conflict. After it did, a Berlin correspondent compared the assistance rendered to the British by the French at Inkerman in November 1854 to the Prussians at Waterloo. And the bloody experiences of both Balaclava and Inkerman, as the Reverend J. O. Daykene, rector of Wolverhampton, reminded his congregation, brought to mind Wellington's remarks about the tragedy of victory being eclipsed only by that of defeat.[448] A sombre House of Commons was presented with the report made by the Army Before Sebastopol Committee on the fortieth anniversary of Waterloo. That same day, with all combatants mindful of the totemic date, Anglo-French forces launched a costly and unsuccessful attack on the defences known as the Redan in front of Sebastopol.[449]

In the immediate short term, Wellington's reputation was enhanced by the Crimean War. There was certainly a popular belief that, had he lived, war would have been avoided. Sir William Fraser thought that 'the Prestige of his own name preserved the Peace of Europe for forty years. He was the Keystone of European Peace. No sooner was he gone than difficulties began; and developed into a bloody, and more or less useless, War.'[450] Raglan (formerly FitzRoy Somerset), commander of British forces in the Crimea, certainly appeared devoid of his former chief's genius. Longer term, one could take a different view. Wellington had, after all, been Commander-in-Chief himself for a decade until shortly before the war. He might, charged Field-Marshal Lord Roberts, have done more to espouse the cause of army reform, the need for which had been cruelly exposed by shortcomings in the Crimea. Instead, as even sympathetic biographers conceded, he was too preoccupied by economy. But even Wellington was only one man. The war was an indictment of the 'aristocratic system' in the army, one where officers bought and exchanged commissions irrespective of merit. Events in the Crimea accelerated its demise. Roberts, an example, if not the original, for Gilbert and Sullivan's model of a modern major-general, could reflect by the 1890s that, 'The Duke's objection to the special education of staff officers sounds almost heterodox in these days of intellectual activity and constantly recurring examinations.'[451]

With the war over by spring 1856, Waterloo commemorations made something of a comeback, if only because the press felt more at liberty to report them. The presentation of a French tricolour as annual rental for Stratfield Saye by the Wellesley family, for example, was noted in 1858. A few days later, the Queen viewed Siborne's Waterloo model when she visited the United Services Institution. In 1859 Astley's revived its Waterloo production for the first time since 1853.[452] But most events were a shadow of what they had once been. They consisted primarily of dwindling bands of ageing veterans meeting to dine with each other, in such places as Leicester, Worcester and Bury St Edmunds. Cavalié Mercer kept the day at his Devon home alone. He had been given a lance from a wounded Guardsman on the morrow of Waterloo. Each 18 June he stuck it in his lawn decked with roses and laurel. On his death in 1870, Mercer bequeathed it to a fellow veteran, Dr Hall, an almost literal case of passing on the torch of memory as the 1815 generation faded.[453]

The most concerted local attempt to defy time was in Preston. It owed everything to the largesse of John Cooper of The Oaks, Penwortham. Married to an officer's daughter and an obsessive visitor to battlefields ancient and modern, he determined to keep alive the annual parade and dinner to Waterloo and other veterans which had flourished in the town since the mid-1840s. He flouted the calls from on high to suspend celebrations in 1853. Some 150 attended the dinner where he demanded that the State provide a *6d* daily pension for all veterans. The following year he criticised the government for, in his view, providing inadequate support to British forces in the Crimea.[454] But even the indomitable Mr Cooper had, very reluctantly, to face reality. In 1861 only fifty-seven attended the dinner, and just thirty-eight had been able to parade around the town. Cooper admitted that the occasion had become more a chore than a pleasure for those attending. Given continuing improved relations with France – the Cobden-Chevalier trade treaty was signed in 1861 – he conceded that 18 June 'has lost much of the interest which used to be concentrated in it'. For the future, he offered veterans the option of either the dinner or half a crown. To his disappointment, three quarters opted for the latter. The 1861 Preston dinner was the last gathering of any size of Britain's Waterloo veterans.[455]

Wellington's memory had been invariably toasted at the Preston dinners. He was also the subject of more permanent memorials during the 1850s. In Manchester in August 1856, a crowd of 100,000 watched a procession by Waterloo veterans to mark the unveiling of a 13-feet bronze of him at the edge of Piccadilly Gardens. It depicted the Duke, controversially, not in familiar equestrian pose but in a frock coat speaking in the Lords.[456] The same year, the Queen laid the foundation stone for Wellington College at Crowthorne near Stratfield Saye, a school for the sons of deceased army officers. She returned for the official opening in January 1859. It was meant to serve as a national memorial to the Duke. Succeeding dukes, the Prince of Wales, Prince Arthur of Connaught and the Reverend G. R. Gleig were amongst the dignitaries at the College's Speech Day, which always fell on or around 18 June. The occasion was fully reported in the national press until well into the next century.[457]

Remembering the Duke in civilian guise and a Berkshire school was, perhaps, part of the wider attempt during the 1850s to avoid offending French sensibilities. That decade was also to give birth to one of the most famous of Wellington sayings, that 'the Battle of Waterloo had been won on the playing fields of Eton'. He never said it. The aphorism was probably coined by the Comte de Montalembert in 1855. Montalembert possibly interpolated it from Wellington's more general words to Brougham that 'The schoolmaster is abroad'. Brougham denied the precise wording, but the two had enjoyed a light-hearted encounter in the Lords in 1835 when

Brougham inadvertently proposed moving some educational clauses on 18 June. Realising his faux pas, 'he begged pardon; he would not let the schoolmaster come in competition with the hero on that day'. It matters little. The extraordinary fact is that the phrase embedded itself so rapidly in the national consciousness. It was being cited in a speech in Ireland early in 1857, from the election hustings in Yorkshire in 1865, and by the Archbishop of Canterbury in 1885. By 1900, only the Duke's assessment of Waterloo as a 'close run thing' was a more familiar piece of Wellingtoniana. It is most plausibly to be explained by British society's increasing preoccupation with the importance of education and a consequently understandable desire to give it the Duke's retrospective celebrity endorsement.[458]

Wellington College owed more to the Prince Consort than the Duke's supposed interest in education. Albert's Germanic hand is also evident in the choice of scene to adorn one wall of the Royal Gallery when Westminster Palace was rebuilt following the fire of 1834. The popular favourite amongst the submissions to adorn the prominent palatial thoroughfare was one by Sidney Cooper showing the repulse of the French cavalry at Waterloo. Instead, the Prince opted for two scenes by Daniel Maclise. One depicted Nelson's death at Trafalgar; the other, Wellington's greeting Blücher at La Belle Alliance. Had he still been alive, it is hard to believe that Wellington would have allowed this symbolic image to grace the mother of parliaments. Neither would he have appreciated the irony that the press reported it to have been finished on what would have been his 94th birthday. Nearly half a century after the battle, Prussia's perspective on Waterloo had at last been endorsed in Britain's corridors of power.[459]

One might have expected Waterloo's fiftieth anniversary to have been deemed worthy of celebration. Britain's 1815 allies certainly thought so. Eleven hundred people attended a dinner in Brunswick; 20,000 dollars was distributed between surviving veterans in Hanover; Rotterdam's programme of events lasted a fortnight. In Belgium, meanwhile, a committee was formed to invite representatives from all the allied nations to join with them in an international festival culminating with a grand procession to the Lion's Mound.[460] The British government declined the invitation. This was partly because its 18 June commemorations had generally always been more low-key than those of their former comrades-in-arms. There was also some resentment that those comrades did not afford the role of the British Army at Waterloo greater prominence in those celebrations. But it owed most to Britain's continuing entente with France. Just days before the fiftieth anniversary, Napoleon III suggested that the former adversaries' fleets make courtesy calls to each other's shores. More than one commentator compared the 'savage spirit' existing between the two powers in 1815 with the 'mild and brotherly feelings of 1865'. France was now 'the closest ally, the most reliable, and, at the same time, the most valuable one, England has'. *The Times* ridiculed events in the Low Countries where, 'The fiftieth anniversary of the Battle of Waterloo has been celebrated with an enthusiasm which, in many cases, approximated to patriotism run mad.'[461] Britain's celebrations were consequently scarcely different from those of any other recent year. They included fifteen veterans dining at the Crown Inn in Wainsgate, Yorkshire, with twenty-one veterans attending a similar event in Halifax. In Preston, true to his word since 1861, John Cooper distributed 31 half crowns from his office in Winckley Street and hoisted a Union flag there, as well as outside his home.[462]

The dearth of commemorative events in Britain on 18 June 1865 also reflected some unease about what should be celebrated. For many, the case for Waterloo was summed up for the enlightenment of his grandchildren by Frederick Hope Pattison, erstwhile of the 33rd Foot:

> That campaign, as you are aware, spread an imperishable lustre over the British army, dethroned Napoleon, and secured an uninterrupted peace to Europe for over forty years. During all the interval we have been reaping the fruits of it. Men have had time to solve those problems in science, and to make those discoveries in art, which have been of unparalleled importance to the human race. Distance has been almost annihilated; materials are transported from one place to another with as great rapidity almost as the flight of the bird; and thought is conveyed from continent to continent across land and sea with the speed of lightning. And thus all peoples and nations are fast becoming united in those bonds of social communion which forbid war, and prepare the way for the arrival of the happy time foretold in Scripture, when 'The righteous shall flourish, and abundance of peace so long as the moon endureth.'[463]

There had also been at least an undercurrent, however, that what was being remembered was a Tory victory. And Whig-Liberal governments were the norm in Britain after 1832. Amongst their supporters, it had never been entirely clear that the cause of 1815 was a good one, or even the right one. In a widely-reproduced editorial to mark Waterloo's fiftieth anniversary, *The Times* judged that whilst the battle might be said to have ended the French

Revolution, it had not proved politically decisive. As subsequent French history testified, it had neither saved the Bourbon monarchy nor ended the rule of a Bonaparte:

> Instead of stemming and turning a mighty current, it set up nothing but a little porous dam which was washed away by the stream before a dozen years were out [...] what we fought against then was simply what we regard without objection now [...] we think the celebration of Waterloo might as well be discontinued. The victory was a splendid military achievement, but the policy which the war expressed was no enduring or successful policy. The battle was a battle which soldiers may well remember, but it decided nothing which younger generations need be at the pains to commemorate.[464]

This, of course, was highly tendentious. It all rather depended upon one's view of Napoleon. If one saw him as a despot, the British cause was just enough. But not everyone did. 'We must read into Waterloo,' wrote Victor Hugo in *Les Misérables*, 'no more than it truly represented. There was no intention of liberty.' For him, Waterloo was a battle between the ideas of liberty and the divine right of kings; the French Revolution was essentially about 'progress'. If one accepted his thesis, there was much in the Emperor's cause with which British Liberals could find sympathy. *The Times'* editorial was tacitly acknowledging his case. What is remarkable is that the latter provoked far more agreement than controversy. That was surely in part because it fell short of endorsing Hugo, as champion of the oppressed, in taunting the English for still cherishing 'their feudal illusions. They believe in heredity and hierarchy. They are a people unsurpassed in power and glory, but they still think of themselves as a nation, not as people. As people they willingly subordinate themselves, accepting a lord as leader.'[465] To follow Hugo on this would have been an abnegation of patriotism and a denial both of the genius of Wellington and the fortitude of his troops. *The Times* was as vehement as any British newspaper in denouncing Hugo's analysis of the battle in strictly military terms.

The generation after 1865 witnessed the final passing of Wellington's Waterloo veterans. Of the best known senior figures who outlived the Duke, Anglesey had been reunited with his leg when he died in 1854; Raglan succumbed to dysentery in the Crimea in 1855; and Hardinge died shortly after resigning as Commander-in-Chief in 1856. But there were still 137 men above the rank of lieutenant alive on Waterloo Day 1864. By 1875 their numbers had thinned to seventy-four, which in turn had reduced further to sixteen in 1880 and seven by 1885.[466] They included Barton Parker Browne of the 11th Dragoons, who died at Bath, aged 92, two days before Waterloo Day 1889. Another was the 6th Earl of Albemarle, who as the 16-year-old Ensign George Thomas Keppel had carried the colours of the 14th Foot in 1815. The Prince of Wales visited him around Waterloo Day 1887, perhaps to partake in the tea he was in the habit of hosting each 18 June. Albemarle eventually died in February 1891. Lieutenant-Colonel William Hewett of the 14th Foot was the last British Waterloo officer to die when he passed away in Southampton in October 1891, aged 96.[467]

No similar attempt was made to follow the fortunes of surviving rank and file veterans in the decades following Wellington's death. Corporal Shaw of the Life Guards, who had died at Waterloo, remained the best known. In 1867, Liverpool's New Adelphi Theatre staged *The Battle of Waterloo and the Death of Shaw*; in 1885 he was the subject of a biography. Somehow, what purported to be his skull went first from Sir Walter Scott's library to public display at the Royal United Services Institute. It was returned to his native Nottinghamshire for burial on 21 June 1898. Twenty-one years before, several hundred had gathered to witness the unveiling of a memorial to him and two others from the small village of Cossall who had served in the campaign.[468]

By comparison, only months after the Duke's grand funeral, James Farnfield, discharged from the 95th after Waterloo and now aged 70, faced the prospect of having to enter the workhouse, 'from which melancholy abode the spirits of many of the gallant though humble companions in arms of the late Duke will take their flight. Should this be,' asked an anonymous officer's widow, 'when England is anxious to perpetuate the memory of his victories?' Another unfortunate was Samuel Brown, former Coldstream Guardsman and weaver. He died of heart failure in Leicester County Jail in June 1855, where he had been sent for unpaid debts of £2 8*d*. Amongst the more fortunate of those who survived the battle, the last Waterloo horse to die outlived the man who had ridden him in the battle, Sir Charles Colville. His steed was said to be at least 47 when he died in 1857.[469] Mr Stovey of Milborne Port's good fortune allied longevity with fecundity. He fought at Waterloo on his 25th birthday. Fifty-two years later he could boast having fathered ten children by each of his three wives and, even more remarkably, that all thirty of his offspring were still alive. What might be termed the last sensationalised story involving a Waterloo veteran (turned tailor), occurred in 1870. Joseph Constantine, aged 74, happily admitted to the attempted murder of his wife in Manchester. Twenty years his junior, he alleged that she was being unfaithful. More widely reported was the passing of the Reverend Henry Bellairs on 17 March 1872. He had joined the navy, aged 13, and was twice wounded at Trafalgar before serving with the 15th Hussars at Waterloo. He was the only Briton to see action in both engagements.[470]

Although the *Birmingham Daily News* estimated that only one person in a hundred would have been aware of the significance of the day by 18 June 1870, a few veterans still continued to gather. Triumvirates met in Sheffield and Leicester in 1872. In Preston the following year, 91-year-old Mark Myres of the 45th was still alive to claim John Cooper's annual half crown. In 1879 Cooper delegated a friend the task of paying the two widows who turned up at his office, whilst he paid his respects at Wellington's tomb in St Paul's. If Cooper judged the time for annual commemorations to be over, it probably was.[471]

A few veterans nevertheless continued to be active. William Williams, who served in the 44th at Waterloo, was, aged 84 and going blind, reported to be working on the roads at Monnington-on-Wye in 1871 at the rate of 3*d* per 14 yards 'and may amount to a daily 6*d* when fine weather and respite from rheumatism permit him to labour'. In 1874, James Jenner, an 80-year-old labourer at Wadhurst, had a Waterloo musket ball extracted from his hand. Another veteran, 'said to be 96 years old, in his stained uniform and quaint side-whiskers […] sat selling programmes' outside a new panorama of Waterloo, which opened in London in 1880. Ambrose Miller was repairing the roads near Newbury until 1882, a year before he died aged 87. He was trumped by John Scott. In 1889, aged 85, he was working in a forge at Elswick, albeit in the hardly arduous job of ringing a bell. His life thereby attained a sort of symmetry. Son of a father in the Black Watch, he had, as a boy at Waterloo, been stationed in an infantry square tasked with playing a triangle and shouting, 'Scotland for ever'.[472]

But the last bells duly tolled. The London Stereoscopic Company showed an awareness of a vanishing past when it published a photograph of the five surviving Waterloo veterans in Chelsea Hospital on the battle's sixty-fifth anniversary. Others, as the officer's widow had foretold, died in the workhouse. James Lambourn of the 14th Foot died, aged 94, in 1885 in the Nunhead workhouse. In death he was treated to four horses, a gun carriage and the Union flag. William Henson of the 16th Foot passed the last eight years of his life in the Barrow-on-Soar workhouse until his death in 1889, aged 93.[473] The fictional last survivor was Sergeant Gregory Brewster, a forgotten hero fallen on hard times, and subject of the 1894 play *A story of Waterloo* by Arthur Conan Doyle. In reality, though his claims cannot absolutely be verified, Britain's last Waterloo veteran was possibly John Hopwood of Whitchurch in Shropshire. He died in December 1900, aged 101.[474]

As Waterloo faded from living memory, some voiced concern that it might soon be forgotten altogether. Astley's revived its grand theatrical re-enactment of Waterloo in 1869 to coincide with the centenary of Wellington's birth, but it enjoyed only a short run. Siborne's models, it was suggested in 1872, were 'doomed to destruction'. Waterloo panoramas, once seemingly ubiquitous, certainly declined in number. Mr J. S. Laurie complained in 1884 that he knew of young adults who thought that it was Nelson who had won Waterloo.[475] But some of this is to be explained by changing popular tastes. *How Bill Adams won the Battle of Waterloo*, a music hall comic recitation by a garrulous and bragging soldier, remained sufficiently well-known that it was being alluded to on the floor of the House of Commons until well into the twentieth century.[476] Waterloo could still capture the imagination. Robert Alexander Hillingford produced a series of popular and acclaimed canvases with a Waterloo theme over more than three decades down to his death in 1904. Now better remembered, Lady Butler's *28th Regiment at Quatre Bras* (1875), captured in oils as well as anybody would the stoicism of the British soldier in defence. Six years later, in her most famous canvas, she would further consummate one of the most iconic moments of 18 June, the charge of the Scots Greys, in her *Scotland for Ever.*[477]

The battle's seventy-fifth anniversary, whilst hardly replicating the fervour of past celebrations, did not therefore go unnoticed. A new panorama opened behind the Army and Navy Stores in London's Victoria Street. G. A. Henty, prolific author of boys' action stories, doubtless mindful of the year, chose 1890 to tell the 1815 saga to a new generation in *One of the 28th: A Tale of Waterloo.* The most significant act, however, was the unveiling, on 26 August, of a British national memorial in Belgium at the *Cimetière de Bruxelles* in the municipality of Evere. Plans for it had been catalysed some years before by the announcement that it was intended to close two Brussels cemeteries and deposit their remains in a mass grave. These would have included Waterloo luminaries such as Sir William De Lancey and Sir Alexander Gordon. That this did not happen owed most to the efforts of Lord Vivian, British minister in Brussels and grandson of Sir Hussey Vivian,

who had commanded a brigade of light cavalry in 1815. By 1887 he had
secured a plot at Evere, which would serve as both mausoleum and memorial. There remained the issue of cost, for the British government would
provide only £500 of the £2,000 necessary to construct the figure of a
mournful Britannia. Vivian, rightly pointing out that 'England has hitherto done nothing to perpetuate the memory of her soldiers who fell in
1815, and [that] the breaking up of their last resting place offers a favourable
opportunity to repair this neglect', spearheaded an appeal for the short-
fall.[478] With endorsement and support from, among others, the Duke of
Cambridge (then Commander-in-Chief), and the 2nd Duke of Wellington,
the money was finally raised.

Reporting the inauguration of the Evere memorial, *The Times* said that
'continual bands of pilgrims' would flock to it. Evere certainly attracted
public interest in 1890. Hitherto, the closest approximation to a British
memorial in Belgium was the one in Waterloo church paid for by surviving officers in 1858. By contrast, the one at Evere is generally regarded
as the first major British war memorial anywhere to commemorate all
the dead of a campaign as opposed to ones lauding individuals or celebrating a victory. One must doubt, however, that this unprecedentedly
democratic act of remembrance would have happened, as and when it did,
had it not been for the imminent threat to some well-known graves. In
the event some sixteen sets of remains were to join those of Gordon and
De Lancey in the crypt of the new monument, with one exception those
of officers. They included 17-year-old Lord Hay, killed at Quatre Bras, and
Sergeant-Major Cotton, who was exhumed from his first resting place
in the garden at Hougoumont.[479] The modern observer cannot help but
conclude that it was too little too late. Contrary to what *The Times* predicted, the monument attracted little notice once the fanfare surrounding
its opening had died down. Despite the care now afforded it by the Royal
British Legion, it remains relatively unknown and little visited. Above all,
it was located in the wrong place. British soldiers fought and died to the
south of Brussels; their memorial lies, incongruously, in the north-eastern
part of the city.

Their monument should have joined that of other nationalities on the
Waterloo battlefield. For though Victor Hugo may have been right in 1861
that 'Each year the anniversary of the battle of Waterloo is being observed
less, even at Waterloo, and the English no longer come on that day bearing
laurels', there remained a good number of visitors. The first rail links from

Brussels to Waterloo were completed in 1854; Thomas Cook included the battlefield in his first continental tour of 1855. At that time there were still guides available who could remember 1815 at first hand: Matthew Arnold was thrilled to be shown the field by Byron's guide of 1816 when he visited in 1860. Hugo reckoned the going rate for such tours to be 3 francs. And even though fellow travellers would agree with him that 'The field of Waterloo today resembles any other stretch of country', he was still able to find 'the neck of an exploded bomb eaten with rust of forty-six years, and fragments of metal that broke like twigs in his hands'.[480]

Hugo's is amongst the best descriptions we have for the battlefield just after mid-century. The Hougoumont complex, in particular, is described in helpful detail. A 'shattered and gutted wing' is all that remained of the manor house, whilst a tree had grown up through what was the main staircase. Whitewashed in 1849, the chapel walls were again 'covered with graffiti'. The Lion's Mound ('that monumental hillock') was soon to be more easily scaled by virtue of the fact that some 226 stone steps and an iron rail had been added. Entry cost half a franc.[481]

Hugo's celebrity added the Hôtel des Colonnes in Mont St Jean, where he had completed *Les Misérables* in 1861, to the list of must-see attractions. It proudly boasted a letter from the novelist. Other notable visitors included the 13-year-old son of Napoleon III in September 1869. A decade later, the hopes of Bonapartists would die with him when he fell fighting with the British against the Zulus. Thomas Hardy paid his first visit to Waterloo in June 1876. He visited the Hôtel du Musée, still flourishing and run by one of Edward Cotton's nieces. It proved less memorable than the peasant woman who showed him a basket of skulls with perfect teeth. Hardy, understandably, did not probe the question of their provenance. The trade in original artefacts had, after all, long since dried up: you were most likely to be assailed with locals proffering walking sticks made from wood cut near La Haye Sainte. 'They must,' declared one guide irreverently, 'be the great-offshoots from the Holy Hedge of 1815.'[482]

Another to notice, indeed complain, about what he called beggars selling sticks, was Sir William Fraser. Born in 1826, he had first visited the battlefield in 1844. He was anxious to trace his father's footsteps, Sir James having been a colonel in the 7th Hussars as well as reputedly steadying Uxbridge as his leg was being amputated. Sir William was amazed to spy his father's sword amongst Cotton's exhibits and eventually managed to buy it for £25. His third visit of 1888 provides us with the best end-of-century account, not just of the Waterloo battlefield but of other 1815 campaign landmarks.[483] Le Caillou, where Napoleon passed the night of 17 June, was owned by an architect, Emile Coulon. He showed Fraser the tables on which the Emperor had both breakfasted and spread his maps on the morning of 18 June. At a more or less deserted Quatre Bras, he found the locals less helpful. They were gathered in an inn at the famous cross roads and 'repudiated all knowledge of the battle; in fact declared that there had been no battle there'. Fraser concluded: 'Such is Fame!' More likely, he was experiencing an example of what Rossetti remembered as 'how the English are victimized to a beastly extent everywhere' contrasted to most Belgians' 'servile aping of the French'. But Fraser's account is also suggestive, perhaps, of a past that was no longer relevant for locals who had once enthusiastically supplemented their income with tales of 1815.[484]

One way in which Waterloo was given new relevance in later-nineteenth-century Britain was through empire. When Tennyson's 1852 *Ode* opened with 'an empire's lamentation', it was the constituent parts of the British Isles that he had in mind. By the time he died in 1892, popular imperialism was nearing its height. Thus, to Waterloo's dividends, which at mid-century were seen chiefly to consist of peace and prosperity, could now be added the bonus of imperial expansion. The battle also set the standard for the soldiers of empire to emulate. The heroics performed at Rorke's Drift in January 1879 inevitably brought to mind those at Hougoumont and La Haye Sainte, all examples of how the few could defy the many and in so doing 'exert a strong influence over the fate of the day'. News that Germany and Britain had resolved their colonial frictions in East Africa and elsewhere was made public, surely not coincidentally, around Waterloo Day 1890.[485] During the Second Boer War of 1899–1902, the dowager Duchess of Wellington lent the 1850 Landseer painting, *Dialogue at Waterloo*, as well as what purported to be the Duke's Waterloo watch, for an exhibition at Weybridge to assist with the War Relief Fund. Six months later, on the eighty-fifth anniversary of the battle, hopes were voiced that this, of all dates, with the tide turning in South Africa, would be a good one to receive further good news from Lord Roberts, arguably Britain's most popular soldier since Wellington. Long since safely returned, the Field-Marshal was the distributor of prizes at Wellington College's speech day on Waterloo Day 1906. In his address, 'he trusted that the boys of Wellington would feel it was their bounden duty to defend the empire when called upon, no matter in what calling or situation in life they found themselves'.[486]

Late-nineteenth-century imperial history inevitably impacted upon wider foreign policy considerations. Colonial rivalries with France weakened the entente that had grown up since the Crimean War; it culminated with talk of war when the two nations clashed at Fashoda on the Nile in 1898. This was one reason why some in Britain sought a new understanding with their old ally from the Waterloo campaign. Though at the start of the Crimean War, reports from Berlin had proclaimed that 'What the Prussians did then they are ready to do again at our side', Prussia had remained neutral throughout that conflict. The fact that the British press subsequently condemned what it deemed excessive displays of commemoration on 18 June in Berlin and elsewhere, implied that France was Britain's preferred ally of the two.[487] But the memory of Waterloo, at least in the short term, was one reason why British public opinion generally welcomed the proclamation of the German Empire in 1871 following the Franco-Prussian War. As an 18-year-old, Kaiser Wilhelm I had been at Waterloo; his heir, Frederick, married Queen Victoria's eldest daughter. In 1889 the Duke of Cambridge was appointed to command a Prussian cavalry regiment of the Guard, 'a special compliment, intended to recall the brotherhood in arms of the English and Prussians at the battle of Waterloo'. The following year, in wake of news of the Anglo-German agreements, *The Times* told its readers 'to remember that on the 18th of June, 1890, as on the same day seventy–five years before, the bonds of union have been drawn closer between the two great Teutonic nations'. For Waterloo Day 1895, Kaiser Wilhelm II sent a wreath to the Royal Dragoons in Ireland in his capacity as their honorary colonel. Though there was some unease in Britain at Germany's rising population, its soaring industrial output, and its support for the Boers, the general presumption around 1900 was that the two nations would celebrate Waterloo's centenary together in grand style.[488]

By 1900, Britain's politicians were rightly preoccupied by French colonial ambitions and the Kaiser's *Weltpolitik*, not Napoleon and the Seventh Coalition. So too, the British public were more disposed to celebrate empire and its generals than Waterloo and Wellington. Even so, the half century after the Duke's passing would witness no real let up in the outpouring of works about him and the battle. Such change as there was included attempts to present a more dispassionate assessment of both.

Wellington's death triggered a flood of unofficial lives and related works such as J. Timbs' *Wellingtoniana* and the cumbrously titled *Characteristics of the Duke of Wellington, apart from his military talents*. Far more consequential was the decision by the second Duke to resume publication of his father's papers. The former, for all his eccentricities (he kept a small elephant to mow the grass at Stratfield Saye), proved a worthy keeper of the Wellington flame. In 1858 he began a series entitled *Supplementary Despatches*. Fifteen volumes, consisting mostly of items received by the Duke down to 1818, were published in the years to 1872. That covering Waterloo included Wellington's famous letter to Lady Frances Webster about the Finger of Providence having been upon him; he had withheld it from the original series of *Despatches* on the grounds that it contained nothing of public or military interest. The second Duke also took his father's story beyond 1818 with an eight-volume series of *Despatches, Correspondence and Memoranda* covering the years down to 1832. Disraeli considered the latter 'the best reading he had ever had'.[489]

The most significant new work about Waterloo, as even Britons conceded on the battle's fiftieth anniversary, was by Frenchmen. Two writers stood out. One was the literary statesman, Adolphe Thiers. He was reported to be visiting the battlefield in 1860 as part of his research for the concluding volume in his history of the French Consulate and Empire. It duly appeared in 1862. An apologist for Napoleon, Thiers ascribed the Emperor's defeat to Grouchy's treachery. For good measure though, he also belittled Wellington and his army. His thesis was widely ridiculed in Britain. *The Times*, typically, declared that his account 'is as thickly charged with error and bombast as the field was with its lurid war-clouds'.[490] It was the brilliance of Victor Hugo's pen, however, that really excited British passions. Hugo was the son of an ardently Bonapartist general. Having overcome a long-standing aversion to visit Waterloo, he became obsessed with explaining it. When not immersed in contemporary accounts and histories, he more or less lived on the battlefield between May and July 1861. *Les Misérables*, published in 1862, may primarily be fiction and only incidentally about Waterloo, but the novel contains a memorable account of the battle. Nineteen chapters are devoted to what he called his 'autopsy of the catastrophe'.[491]

Hugo's Waterloo did create or perpetuate some potent myths, including those of a defiant Cambronne refusing to surrender; and of the sunken lane along Wellington's defensive ridge, passable only when filled with the bodies of 1,500 Frenchmen and 2,000 horses.[492] The latter was an example of what offended British sensibilities, Hugo's thesis that Waterloo was decided by contingency: for example, the storm of 17 June that thwarted Napoleon's plans for an early start on 18 June, and the decisive fact that

it was Blücher, not Grouchy, who reached Mont St Jean. This marginalised Wellington's contribution to victory. Hugo was blunt in his conclusion
that Waterloo was 'the complete, absolute, shattering, incontestable, final,
supreme triumph of mediocrity over genius'. It was 'a battle of the first
importance won by a commander of the second rank'.[493]

Rees Gronow, erstwhile of the 1st Foot Guards, helped rally the forces
of patriotism in Wellington's defence. A volume of colourful, if unreliable,
reminiscences appeared in 1862, with a preface cheerfully admitting that his
timing owed not a little to the offence caused by the Gallic pair. Waterloo
was won, Gronow insisted, by 'the genius of Wellington, the energy of
Blücher, and the dauntless courage of the English and Prussian armies'.[494]
A more redoubtable champion was on hand in G. R. Gleig. From 1858–
1860, Gleig was working on an English version of a life of Wellington by
a Belgian military engineer, Henri Alexis Brialmont. A revised 700-page
single-volume second edition appeared in 1862 under Gleig's own name.
It is the nearest we have to an official life, based as it is on access to the
Duke's papers and help from his family and friends, not to mention Gleig's
own long-standing acquaintanceship with his subject. The third, 'people's
edition' of Gleig's *Life of Wellington*, which appeared in 1864, proved even
more successful than his *Story of the Battle of Waterloo*. Its hardly original
theme was that 'the guiding star of Duty through life' was the key to understanding the Duke. With cheap editions being reissued until well into the
twentieth century, Gleig amply succeeded in his aim of producing 'a book
which shall come within the reach and be level with the understandings
of the great body of my countrymen'.[495] Those countrymen were also
reminded, in language even more emphatic than the Duke ever used in
public, of what had happened at Waterloo:

> The French had delivered their last attack, and failed in it, before the pressure
> of the Prussians on their flank and rear was felt by either side […] The oppor-
> tune arrival of the Prussians, therefore, sufficed to convert defeat into rout;
> but it contributed in no degree to the preservation of the English army.[496]

This was going too far. Work prompted in part by Thiers, Hugo, and
Waterloo's fiftieth anniversary, said so. Published posthumously in 1865, Sir
James Shaw Kennedy's *Notes on the Battle of Waterloo* came from an author
who had served with the Third Division in 1815 and who was regarded as
one of the ablest soldiers in the service. Essentially a series of 171 extended

observations, Shaw Kennedy said something that the Duke's pride and honour had never allowed him to admit, that even great commanders made mistakes. Wellington's included risking battle on 16 June, keeping men at Hal on 18 June and inadequately defending La Haye Sainte. Even so, he judged that victory 'would have been eminently imperilled had the Duke of Wellington fallen at any period in the action previous to the last general attack'.[497] Three years later, Colonel Charles Cornwallis Chesney dared to go further in *The Waterloo Lectures: A Study of the Campaign of 1815*. Chesney was a hugely respected figure in military circles, writing and speaking with the authority of a former professor at Sandhurst and the incumbent one at the Staff College, Camberley. In his preface he declared that the idea that Waterloo had been won by British pluck was 'hardly less a romance' than Victor Hugo's colourful interpretation of events. He gave due weight to the Prussian contribution, insisting that as many as 50,000 were engaged at Waterloo by the time Wellington ordered the general advance. For all that Wellington performed well, he owed much to Napoleon's mistakes and his Prussian ally. Chesney had, said one reviewer, finally exploded national myths to which the younger generation in both France and Britain were still being subjected.[498] He was the first recognised British authority to really challenge the Wellington orthodoxy.

The next two decades would see no new British account of Waterloo of any great durability but they did witness the publication of some of the best known memoirs. They included Cavalié Mercer's incomparable *Journal of the Waterloo Campaign* (1870) and Magdalene De Lancey's heart-wrenching *A Week at Waterloo* (1888). Neither these, nor other works in the genre, have overly much to say about Wellington; still less do they offer any systematic analysis of the battle. An exception, at least in terms of providing raw material, was Major-General Herbert Siborne's decision, prompted by the seventy-fifth anniversary of Waterloo, to publish a selection from 200 of the officers' replies received by his father when constructing his model during the 1830s.[499] However, William Siborne's correspondents, given that their brief was to detail what was happening to them at 7 p.m., very often make no mention of Wellington. Reading them, one could easily reach the Duke's ironic conclusion that he had not been there.

For a new popular work that explicitly addressed both Wellington and Waterloo, readers of the later Victorian period turned to Sir William Fraser's *Words on Wellington*. In and out of Parliament for a generation after 1852, Fraser established a reputation as a collector of Waterloo memorabilia, an authority on the Duke and a lively raconteur. By 1889 he had sufficient material for a volume on his hero. Probably his most frequently cited anecdote is Wellington's answer to the question of how he was able to beat a succession of Napoleon's marshals in the Peninsula. The Duke memorably responded that, 'They planned their campaigns just as you might make a splendid set of harness. It looks very well; and answers very well; until it gets broken; and then you are done for. Now I made my campaigns of ropes. If anything went wrong, I tied a knot; and went on.' Historians have treated this, and much else in Fraser, uncritically. But Fraser rarely provides the reader with any provenance. The foregoing example, for instance, appears sandwiched between an anecdote about a sword concealed in an umbrella and Wellington's dictum that the best test of a great general was 'to know when to retreat; and to dare to do it'. And Fraser's broader judgements make Gleig read like a model of scholarly objectivity. He ranked only Shakespeare and Michelangelo as comparable to the Duke in the entirety of human history. Napoleon's downfall, he contends, was 'mainly owing to his utter incapability of comprehending the British Character', whilst at Waterloo, Wellington 'was fighting the true, honest cause of Civilization, and of Freedom [...] and he must have felt during the Greatest Battle that the World has ever known, that it was *his* guiding spirit that would give Europe half a century of peace'.[500] One can readily understand why Fraser's patriotically colourful portrayal was popular with the late-Victorian public. It should not continue to be so influential.

Much more reliable and revealing about Wellington the man, if not always about Waterloo, was a handful of memoirs, notes and diaries which appeared in the last quarter of the century. The catalyst, in a succession of volumes in the decade from 1874, was the publication of Charles Greville's memoirs covering the forty years down to 1860. As Clerk to the Privy Council from 1821, Greville was well placed to observe the great events of the day. Though he was never an intimate of the Duke (Mrs Arbuthnot called him 'the most unprincipled reprobate in the Kingdom'), his brother, Algy, acted as Wellington's private secretary and sometimes showed him his employer's private correspondence.[501] Never totally convinced by the Duke's persona of simplicity, he found him difficult to fathom. But for all that he thought Wellington politically misguided, Charles Greville could not help but like him. Even at the nadir of his unpopularity in May 1832 he records that, 'I never see and converse with him without reproaching myself for the sort of hostility I feel and express towards his political conduct, for there are a simplicity, a gaiety, and natural urbanity and good-humour in him, which are remarkably captivating in so great a man.' Greville's is the most comprehensive contemporary account we have of Wellington in the context of his political world after Waterloo. It is far less helpful about his military career. His only lengthy entry about Waterloo is his record of a conversation they had in 1820. However, Greville is the source for the popular version of the Duke's terse reply to Uxbridge on losing his leg.[502]

The earliest version of the Wellington-Uxbridge exchange was John Wilson Croker's. Greville's memoirs were still appearing when the three volumes of Croker's diaries and correspondence appeared in 1884–1885. He became Wellington's friend following his appointment as the Duke's deputy as Irish Chief Secretary in 1808; they last met on 2 September 1852. Staunchly Tory in his politics, Croker was best known as a writer, in particular for the *Quarterly Review*. His great fault was what Gleig called his 'excessive self-appreciation'. In 1836, for example, he was recorded laying 'down the law after dinner to the Duke of Wellington, and according to custom asserting the superiority of his own information on all subjects having even flatly contradicted the Duke, who had mentioned some incident that took place at the battle of Waterloo'. When he further insisted that the Duke was wrong about percussion cups, Wellington seized the moment for a memorable put-down: 'My dear Croker, I can yield to your superior information on most points, and you may perhaps know a great deal more of what passed at Waterloo than myself, but as a sportsman, I will maintain my point about the percussion cups.'[503]

Fortunately, Croker's overbearing ego was redeemed by his Irish charm. It also meant that he was rarely, as so many were, overawed by the great man. He is consequently a source for many of the best-known Wellington anecdotes and the first or sole source for some of them. These include Wellington's burning his violin as a young man, his view that Assaye was his finest achievement and his meeting with Nelson. Croker also secured from the Duke his version of one of the most celebrated Waterloo lines, 'Up, Guards, and at 'em!' The words were not his, Wellington assured him, a view confirmed by the son of the man to whom they were supposedly addressed, Sir Peregrine Maitland. They had already been too long part of Waterloo mythology, however, for such conclusive denials to make any difference.[504]

Books more explicitly about the Duke included Earl Stanhope's 1888 *Notes of Conversations with the Duke of Wellington 1831–1851*. Known as Viscount Mahon until 1855, Stanhope held minor political office under

Peel and later helped found the National Portrait Gallery. He first encountered Wellington in 1831 and their subsequent meetings owed much to the fact that the family home of Deal Castle was close to the Duke's favourite summer residence of Walmer Castle. From October 1831, Stanhope took it upon himself to record details of their conversations 'either on the same day or at the furthest the day after the conversation which they record; and I have never noted anything when not quite sure of remembering it exactly.'[505] Unlike Greville, Stanhope eschewed political gossip in favour of what he termed 'history'. For all this, the book is a little disappointing. He was markedly deferential to his subject and often relied on other guests such as FitzRoy Somerset and Hardinge to draw Wellington out. Moreover, approximately half of what he records covers a relatively short time span between May 1837 and the end of 1840. Much of this merely confirms what had already appeared in Greville and Croker, and of the fifteen references to Waterloo only two or three amount to anything substantial. Stanhope nevertheless records for us the authentic voice of Wellington. We hear his estimation of Napoleon's being equivalent to 30,000–40,000 soldiers in an army, as also his less-than-complimentary verdict that soldiers in the British Army were scum who enlisted for drink, and maxims such as, 'My rule always was to do the business of the day in the day.' Perhaps the most important detail for which we are indebted to Stanhope was Wellington's confirmation, in November 1840, both of the venue and the substance of his meeting with Blücher on the evening of 18 June near La Belle Alliance.[506]

The other great memorialist of Wellington's later years was Lord Francis Egerton, from 1846 Earl of Ellesmere. Earlier proof of his devotion to the Duke, whom he first met in 1818, was his marrying Charles Greville's daughter on Waterloo Day 1822.[507] Their daughter, who edited *Personal Reminiscences of the Duke of Wellington* in 1904, described it as a 'sort of Diary and Book of Reminiscences etc, etc'. It is, in fact, far more about Waterloo than its title suggests, though it did not reveal anything especially new. Rather, like Stanhope, it confirmed some of the Duke's comments about the battle that were already in the public domain, for example his contention that with his army from the Peninsular War he would have made short shrift of Napoleon. Also reproduced were Wellington's memoranda on Waterloo drawn up for Egerton's use in preparing his articles for the *Quarterly Review* in the 1840s. These had previously appeared out of context in the *Supplementary Despatches*. There was some original material in the form of table talk from the mid-1840s, though this needs to be treated with caution. In 1845, for instance, Egerton records that Wellington told him that, 'The French had not the ghost of a chance till they carried La Haye. It was their only success and came too late to be of consequence.'[508] This was a far cry indeed from the close run thing of 1815.

One of the original sources for the latter, the most famous of all Wellington's comments about Waterloo, is contained in *The Creevey Papers*. Creevey was an eccentric Foxite-Whig and gossip. Serendipitously, he had gone to Brussels for the sake of his wife's health in autumn 1814. He met Wellington there the following April. His account of the Hundred Days was written up in 1822. There is no doubt that in doing so, he was guilty of at least some embellishment: the account is assured; contemporaries recalled him as having been in a panic. But there is no reason to doubt the substance of what he says. Above all, he tells us how he enjoyed a personal meeting with the Duke at his Brussels headquarters on the early afternoon of 19 June. To him, therefore, posterity is indebted for confirmation of Wellington's conviction that Blücher had been 'damnably licked' at Ligny, the bravery of his men, especially the Guards defending Hougoumont, and the idiom that would become part of the English language:

> He made a variety of observations in his short, natural, blunt way, but with the greatest gravity all the time, and without the least approach to anything like triumph or joy – 'It has been a damned serious business,' he said. 'Blücher and I have lost 30,000 men. It has been a damned nice thing – the nearest run thing you ever saw in your life.'[509]

Though it was long known that Creevey had interesting papers, and even his incautious friend, Charles Greville, thought it premature to publish them before 1840, it is remarkable that they only appeared in 1903.

Such a cornucopia of new and original published material inevitably gave rise to a new generation of Wellington biographies and Waterloo histories as the century drew to a close. Amongst the former, the best was that by the Conservative MP, Sir Herbert Maxwell. It was made the more authoritative for his having been allowed access to Wellington's unpublished papers at Apsley House for the years after 1832. He devoted fewer than forty pages in his 1899 two-volume tome to Waterloo. They did not attempt to argue that the Duke was infallible and Maxwell cites without comment the Waterloo Despatch as proof that he 'made honourable acknowledgement of what he owed to his faithful ally'. The most original part was an appendix which transcribed Lady Salisbury's notes of her 1836 conversation with the Duke about Waterloo in which he denied feeling exultation and confirmed the truth of his improbable meeting with Creevey.[510] Distinguished amongst the histories was John Codman Ropes's 1893 *The Campaign of Waterloo: A Military History*. Ropes was an American lawyer who turned military historian when his brother was killed at Gettysburg. His main focus was Napoleon, 'to explain […] the complete defeat in a very brief campaign of the acknowledged master of modern warfare'. Ropes's conclusion was that the outcome was more to be explained by French errors than the merits of their opponents. Had Grouchy intercepted the Prussians 'Napoleon would have been able to employ his whole army against that of Wellington, and would have defeated it'. Wellington indeed was censured for delaying the order to concentrate at Quatre Bras: 'this […] was not only uncalled for, but […] gravely imperilled the success of the allies'.[511] Ropes was also amongst the first writers in English to take account of a short letter found in Prussian archives in 1876 from Wellington to Blücher. It was written south of Quatre Bras at Frasnes on 16 June at 10.30am. Not amongst Wellington's published papers, it suggested that his forces were sufficiently assembled as to be capable of providing imminent assistance at Ligny. Some Prussian writers saw this as a deliberate falsification on Wellington's part in order to ensure that his ally stood and fought. Ropes rejected the charge but did conclude that Wellington had been badly served by his subordinates as to the precise disposition of his army.[512]

One of Britain's most famous soldiers, Sir Garnet Wolseley, agreed with Ropes on the latter point – 'one that very closely concerns our national honour' – in his 1895 *The Decline and Fall of Napoleon*. He too though, was quite critical of Wellington's conduct, especially before 16 June, and concluded that 'the honest historian must admit that it was the splendid audacity of this Prussian move' born of Blücher's loyalty to Wellington, 'that determined the fate of Napoleon's army at Waterloo'. His Despatch, which he judged, contained 'an unusual number of mistakes' (albeit the result of incomplete information as opposed to anything more sinister), gave him 'abundant reasons for wishing his official account of the battle and of the operations which preceded it to be accepted as final and without question'.[513]

Perhaps perversely, it was another great late-Victorian soldier, Field-Marshal Lord Roberts, who saw fit to re-state the case for the Duke's infallibility. In *The Rise of Wellington* (1895), like Wolseley's book a series of essays which had first appeared in *Pall Mall Magazine*, Roberts asserted that during the Waterloo campaign, 'a feat almost unequalled in the annals of war', 'Napoleon made many mistakes, Wellington made none'. He had therefore been 'greatly underrated as a commander'. However, Roberts' book proved offensive to Wellington devotees by advancing the further suggestion that the Duke had been 'somewhat overrated as a man'. He ventured the astute observation that the accepted public image of Wellington as a slave to duty obscured the reality that 'there appears to be no instance in his military career of his adopting a course where his duty was opposed to his own interests, or of his being called upon to sacrifice the latter in order to carry out the former'. His root objection to him as a man, however, was that he 'did little or nothing to promote the welfare of his soldiers, or to make the nation understand what a debt of gratitude it owed them'.[514]

It was surely Roberts she had in mind when Lady Rose Weigall decided to publish Lady Burghersh's correspondence with the Duke in 1903. Lady Burghersh was both her mother and Wellington's niece. Her aim was clearly to rehabilitate her great uncle's character, which, she complained, had recently been unjustly represented 'as hard, stern, and unsympathetic'. For this reason, she also included a brief memoir of the Duke, written by Lady Burghersh soon after his death, which emphasised his kindness to servants, fondness for children and his generosity. Lady Rose was not concerned with his military reputation, which she felt to be intact: most of the letters date from after 1830 and include next to nothing on Waterloo.[515] The same motive, of wanting to defend Wellington from the old charge that he was cold and unfeeling, seems to have dictated the timing of the publication of the Reverend G. R. Gleig's reminiscences. Gleig had written them, clearly prompted by the likes of Croker and Stanhope, in the mid-1880s, but with the express instruction that they should not appear until well after his death (1888). His daughter published them in 1904 but only after having had the proofs sanctioned by the third Duke. They emphasised the first Duke's love of hunting, music, and his prodigious memory.[516] Twentieth-century writers would have much to draw upon and debate.

The *Weekly Dispatch* had written on Wellington's death that, 'Many among our readers will have to talk of the subject of this article to satisfy the interest of children's children; the best proof of the sincerity of present praises is our belief that his name will be spoken to children's children with increased reverence and affection.' Half a century later, there was some evidence that the paper's prediction had been borne out. Growing up near Walmer, a future Wellington biographer, Richard Aldington, recalled that elderly people regularly spoke deferentially of 'The Duke', 'The old Duke' and 'In the old Duke's time' without the need for further elaboration. Similarly, Harry Boland of the Inner Temple wrote that, 'It is undoubted that every fresh fact which comes to light about the Duke goes still further to establish the nobility of his character.' A retrospective in *The Times* on New Year's Eve 1900 judged Wellington the 'greatest of modern Englishmen'.[517]

The reality was that though still high, Wellington's personal reputation had inevitably fallen since his funeral. This was partly because Wellington the man, much as Lord Roberts insisted, was popularly believed to have been insensitive, particularly towards those who had served under him. Comparison to Nelson is instructive here. Immediately after Waterloo, the Duke's popular reputation had exceeded Nelson's; at the time of his death it was still at least comparable. In the second half of the century, however, the popular tide moved strongly in favour of the more charismatic admiral. The fate of their respective London memorials mirrored the pattern. Whilst Trafalgar Square with Nelson's column became a much-loved landmark, Wellington's statue at Hyde Park Corner remained controversial. In 1884, despite some opposition, Parliament sanctioned its removal as part of a scheme to ease traffic congestion. In August, Pickford's duly transported it to Aldershot; it was officially re-inaugurated at Round Hill near the Royal Garrison church on 19 August 1885.[518] Perhaps even more telling was a Sotheby's auction of 1904. Wellington's letter of 19 June 1815 to Sir Charles Flint in which he first referred to Waterloo as a battle of giants sold for an impressive £101. The same anonymous buyer paid a world record £1,030 for Nelson's last complete letter to Lady Hamilton.[519]

The dent in Wellington's reputation between 1852 and 1900 was also partly the product of a reaction to his politics. These were largely, because controversial, conveniently ignored at the time of his funeral. Wellington left no obvious political legacy. The more able Peelites, such as Gladstone, whose careers survived the 1846 Corn Law split, morphed into what became the Liberal Party during the 1850s. They could hardly claim the Duke as their political inspiration. Neither could Derby and Disraeli, the Conservative Party's leaders down to 1880, for they had broken with Peel and Wellington in defence to Protection. The generation after Wellington's death, moreover, was to be dominated by Liberal governments and two fresh extensions of the franchise. Wellington's name politically was, above all else, popularly identified with opposition to Reform. Even the Duke's strongest advocates in the half century after his death found his political career problematic. Sir William Fraser asserted quite openly that he had been wrong to pursue it. Many biographers consequently either stopped in 1815 or devoted relatively little attention to it. It was unfortunate in this respect that the *Supplementary Despatches* stopped at 1832 for the Duke's best political service was rendered after that date. A few scholarly writers, such as Sir Charles Parker and Sir Herbert Maxwell, pointed out this fact, the former noting how Wellington had helped avoid a constitutional clash between the two houses of Parliament, the latter that 'it was his influence in Opposition which mainly operated to prevent sweeping political change becoming a vast and destructive convulsion'. But their arguments simply did not percolate into a popular consciousness ingrained with Wellington as anti-Reformer.[520]

Wellington's reputation as a warrior indelibly associated with Waterloo fared better. Though new conflicts intervened, the memory of what he and his men had achieved may have dimmed but it still shone. Whilst Wellington may not have been comfortable with the fact that the battle was now more fully appreciated as an allied victory, it was still remembered as a predominantly British one. As such, it remained the point of reference for any subsequent British military engagement down to 1900. And though popular celebrations of Waterloo Day had ceased by the 1870s they still had echoes in the great end-of-century celebrations of monarchy and empire in 1887 and 1897. Mementoes of the Duke were not uncommon in Diamond Jubilee exhibitions, whilst a parade of veterans in Boston the same year was headed by someone who had acted as a boy-assistant to surgeons in the 14th Dragoons at Waterloo.[521] Rightly or wrongly, the inference was that without Wellington and Waterloo there might have been neither empire nor monarchy.

As the new century dawned, however, there was a clear recognition that warfare was changing. Speaking at the United Services Institute in 1901, Major-General C. E. Webster estimated that modern weaponry would necessitate armies of Waterloo size fighting in an area nine times as large. Britain's position in the world was changing too. In 1900, with the Second Boer War ongoing, the Bishop of Southwark said that, 'It was a hackneyed saying that the battle of Waterloo was won in the playing fields of Eton.' He thought that race and character would determine the fate of twentieth century conflicts. A fortnight later a Mr Verney thought that the Battle of

A sketch by George Jones of Wellington, ordering the general advance at Waterloo. (Author's collection)

A sketch of Life Guardsman Shaw by George Jones. (Author's collection)

1819 aquatint, published by Edward Orme, showing Anglesey wounded. (Courtesy of Albion Prints)

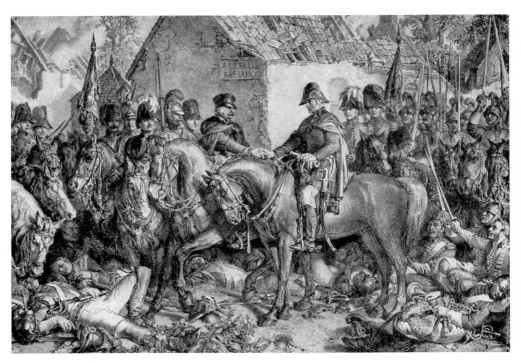

Detail from Daniel Maclise's mural for the rebuilt Westminster Palace, showing Wellington meeting Blücher at La Belle Alliance. (Author's collection)

Wellington
Waterloo, June 19 1815

Wellington writing the Waterloo Despatch. Sketch in the *Illustrated London News* of 29 November 1852, based on the painting by Lady Burghersh. (Author's collection)

Drawing from 1815 showing La Haye Sainte from the south soon after Waterloo. (Author's collection)

Hougoumont, from an 1815 drawing. (Author's collection)

The 175ft Wellington Monument on Somerset's Blackdown Hills, overlooking Wellington. (Author's collection)

FIELD-MARSHAL ARTHUR WELLESLEY
DUKE OF WELLINGTON

Wellington in Waterloo attire. A painting by Sir Thomas Lawrence (1824) commissioned for Peel. Lawrence followed the Duke's instruction to show him with telescope – not watch – in hand. (Author's collection)

Wilkie's 1822 *Chelsea Pensioners receiving the London Gazette Extraordinary; announcing the Battle of Waterloo.* (Author's collection)

Wellington shows
George IV over the
field in the early
1820s. Sketch from the
Illustrated London News of
9 September 1858, based
on the original painting
by B. R. Haydon.
(Author's collection)

Wellington, the
politician, with Sir
Robert Peel, by Franz
Winterhalter (1844).
(Author's collection)

La Haye Sainte from the *Pictorial Times*, 1845. (Author's collection)

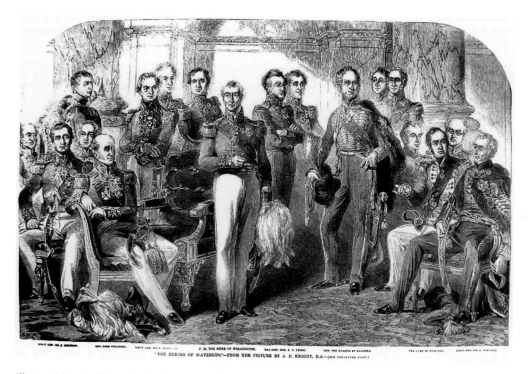

Illustrated London News sketch from 1852 of John Prescott Knight's painting of Wellington and thirty-one officers assembled for the 1842 Waterloo Banquet. (Author's collection)

Carlo Marochetti's 1844 equestrian statue of Wellington in Glasgow; current Glaswegian tradition/humour is to cap it with a traffic cone. (Courtesy of Susanna Foster)

SEPTEMBER XIV. MDCCCLII.

Punch's ground-breaking cartoon tribute to Wellington, 2 October 1852. (Author's collection)

An 1853 lithograph, after Louis Haghe's painting, of Wellington's controversial funeral car passing his Apsley House home and Benjamin Wyatt's no less contentious Wellington statue. (Author's collection)

THE FUNERAL OF THE DUKE OF WELLINGTON.
THE PROCESSION LEAVING APSLEY HOUSE.

Waterloo village showing Wellington's 1815 headquarters as it appeared in the 1845 *Pictorial Times*. (Author's collection)

The 1858 memorial to the fallen of the 1815 campaign in St Joseph's Church, Waterloo. (Author's collection)

Front page from a late-Victorian toy theatre game by Benjamin Pollock utilising an 1842 original, which was, in turn, based on *The Battle of Waterloo*, staged by Astley's Theatre. (Author's collection)

THE FIGHT FOR THE STANDARD.

A Victorian trade card for Ayer's Pills, based on Richard Ansdell's *Battle for the Standard*, depicting Charles Ewart capturing the Eagle of the 45th at Waterloo. (Author's collection)

The Waterloo campaign memorial of 1890 in Brussels' Evere cemetery, now maintained by the Royal British Legion. (Courtesy of the Royal British Legion, Brussels)

Picture of John Hopwood, published in *The Sphere*, January 1901 – possibly Britain's last Waterloo veteran. (Author's collection)

"ARS (BRITANNICA) LONGA."

Paris—Hôtel des Invalides, 1840. London—St. Paul's, Nineteen hundred and——?

SHADE OF F.-M. THE DUKE OF WELLINGTON. "BEGAD, SIR, HERE'S NEWS! THEY'RE GOING TO FINISH MY MEMORIAL IN ST. PAUL'S!"   SHADE OF NAPOLEON. "DÉJÀ?"

Punch cartoon of 4 February 1903 commenting on the protracted completion of Alfred Stevens' memorial to Wellington in St Paul's Cathedral. (Author's collection)

Postcard from around 1900 showing the cluttered Mont St Jean crossroads from the Lion's Mound. (Author's collection)

Reverse of the £5 note in circulation between 1971 and 1991, based on Sir Thomas Lawrence's portrait of Wellington, painted shortly after Waterloo. (By permission of the Bank of England)

Ticket for the 18 June 1983 Wellington seminar, based on Paul Pry's caricature *A Wellington Boot*. (Author's collection)

La Belle Alliance, today. (Author's collection)

La Haye Sainte, today. (Author's collection)

Hougoumont, today, showing the entrance to the north gate. (Author's collection)

The Waterloo battlefield as it is today from the Lion's Mound, looking west. (Author's collection)

Colenso had been lost there and that professionalism must replace amateurism in the army.[522] Within a decade or so, with the battle's centenary approaching, a new conflict would prompt contemporaries to reassess once more Wellington and Waterloo.

7

Battling into Posterity: Wellington and Waterloo 1901–2015

*I*n December 1903 Queen Victoria's grandson, Kaiser Wilhelm II, attended a dinner to mark the centenary of the raising of three Hanoverian regiments. Wellington, he claimed, would have been lost without them. It was they who, 'in conjunction with Blücher and the Prussians at Waterloo, saved the British army from destruction'. His remarks were very widely reported in the British press. *The Times* called them 'unfortunate [...] an absurd over-statement'. It cited Wellington's Waterloo Despatch as proof that the British Army had not been as imperilled as the Kaiser maintained. The German press responded by accusing the British of being hypersensitive.[523] In terms of wider contemporary Anglo-German relations, it was a trivial incident; it was nevertheless indicative of a developing trend of hostility that would reach its tragic conclusion in 1914.

In the short term, the outbreak of war made improper and impractical any plans to celebrate the centenary of the 1815 campaign. More importantly, the First World War would finally eclipse Waterloo as the national reference point for collective endeavour, military achievement – and horror. In the age of mass democracy, the common man would be duly commemorated. This did not bode well for the reputation of Wellington, a man popularly presumed to consider the common man the scum of the earth and universal suffrage as anathema. Conversely, the Duke's generalship, part of which was the careful husbanding of the human resources at his disposal, was likely to compare well set alongside the record of his Great War counterparts.

Ambivalences about his proper place in history, in academic circles at least, were therefore set to persist. This would be even truer of the Waterloo campaign. The First World War destroyed the last vestiges of the European order created at Vienna in 1815. In 1919, the peacemakers who met at Versailles forged a Europe whose succeeding century would be characterised principally by further conflict and division. Those seeking greater European unity and stability could be forgiven for looking to the earlier period for inspiration. Much later, as the 200th anniversary of Waterloo loomed, it was not just historians who found it of continuing relevance.

In the minor Waterloo controversy unleashed by Wilhelm II in 1903, it was, in a significant irony, the French who came to Britain's aid. In a leading article, the *Débats* described the Kaiser as 'a little grasping. The heavier side of the scale, although only by little, is incontestably that in which is thrown the unconquerable tenacity of the Iron Duke'. Its comments were amplified by the heavy artillery that was Henry Houssaye. His view was that prior to the arrival of the Prussians, both the Anglo-Allied and French armies were exhausted. 'But it was the British who up to that moment had kept the victory in suspense. The result is due to the Prussians, but the glory remains with the English.' Without the Prussians, they would have been beaten and 'probably annihilated'. But it was not true that the German troops in Wellington's army alone saved it from destruction.[524]

Houssaye (1848–1911) had pursued a career as a classical scholar before his fascination with Bonaparte led to his becoming better known for his work on the Napoleonic period. His 1899 account of Waterloo had made him the greatest living authority on the battle. He was quite prepared to admit that Napoleon had made errors in 1815: he should have forced the allies farther apart on 15 June; he should have ensured that the Prussians were destroyed at Ligny; Wellington should never have been allowed to retreat from Quatre Bras during 17 June. At Waterloo the next day, an early start would have won the battle by 1 p.m. Even as matters unfolded, 'had not the approach of the Prussians paralysed a portion of the army, it is probable that the plateau of Mont-Saint-Jean would have been carried by them about five o'clock'.[525] Events determined otherwise. In reading Houssaye's account of them, British readers would discover greatest vindication in the detail of his extensive endnotes. For though Houssaye wrote, with respect to whether it was the British or the Prussians who caused the French to be routed, that 'both manoeuvres took place almost simultaneously, the discussion might be carried on for ever', he judged that British actions alone were responsible for bringing about the disintegration of two-thirds of the French line.[526]

Houssaye thereby contributed his own small part to the making of the Entente Cordiale, the series of agreements concluded by Britain and France in April 1904. They reflected the new orthodoxy at the Foreign Office that Germany was now regarded as the main threat to the British Empire. Winston Churchill, newly in cabinet, told an audience in Manchester in May 1909 that:

> The wonderful century which followed the battle of Waterloo and the down-fall of the Napoleonic domination, which secured to this small island so long and so resplendent a reign has come to an end. We have arrived at a war time [...] strange methods, huge forces, larger combinations – a Titanic world – have sprung up around us. The foundations of our power are changing.[527]

When the Lord Mayor of London, Sir William Treloar, visited Berlin in June 1907, Sir Edward Grey cautioned him that 'the Foreign Office had heard that the Germans intended to call attention to the fact that June was the anniversary of the Battle of Waterloo in order to annoy France, and, if possible, to create bitterness between the English and the French'. If they did, it was unsuccessful; the Kaiser was the new Napoleon.[528]

Even so, deteriorating relations notwithstanding, when members of the British and German chambers of commerce met together in January 1906 it was pointed out that, 'Both countries would in nine years be fraternally celebrating the centenary of the battle of Waterloo.' On the eve of the event, *The Times* reflected wistfully on the 'wide public celebration' that was to have taken place. Recent historians, too, have asserted that, had it not been for the outbreak of war in August 1914, the 100th anniversary of Waterloo would have been celebrated in grand fashion.[529] In Britain, at least, it is by no means clear that this would, in fact, have been the case. As late as October 1912, in a parliamentary question, Sir Hildred Carlile MP asked what national celebrations the government was planning, 'particularly in view of the fact that there was no memorial to the nation's arms as a whole on the field of Waterloo'. Replying for the War Office, Colonel Seely stated that there was nothing official planned; nor was the government endorsing any private venture. His admission prompted the perhaps mischievous, though not untruthful observation, from an Irish Nationalist MP, Mr J.G. Swift MacNeill, that 'the celebration of Waterloo was discontinued many years ago in deference to the wishes of the highest authority in order to promote feelings of peace and to let bygones be bygones'. German observers might have done well to note this evidence of the strength of the Anglo-French Entente.[530]

But the centenary would not have gone completely unmarked. In November 1910, it was agreed that a British Dominions Exhibition would be held at the Crystal Palace in 1915. Plans were well advanced by the end of 1913. These would at once have neatly marked the year, whilst linking back to the Great Exhibition of 1851 and the themes of Waterloo as a harbinger of progress and empire without explicitly offending French sensibilities. The lead for commemorating Waterloo per se was taken by a centenary committee established in Belgium by 1911. Its approach was in marked contrast to the national chauvinism that had characterised Europe's fiftieth anniversary events. Representatives from Holland, Britain, Germany and France were invited to join them. The main project was an international memorial. It would 'consist of a mass of dark porphyry on which the principal group, carved in white marble, will stand out in relief, with bronze figures round it representing the various nations'. Remarkably, for bones were 'daily unearthed by the plough [...] the victims of a scandalous trade with tourists', it would also need to serve as a mausoleum. Both symbolically and practically, it would 'in a measure become the tomb of all who fell at Waterloo'.[531]

Britons taking an interest in the Waterloo battlefield were generally more inclined to see it preserved unaltered than blight it through the addition of new structures. Edward Moon, a former MP who reconnoitred it on 4 June 1914, voiced concern at what he termed the 'outbreak' of monuments. These included the Wounded Eagle monument to the French, dedicated in 1904, and a large column to Victor Hugo, just over 200 yards south of La Belle Alliance, still under construction as Moon toured. Interestingly, he did not take exception to the Lion's Mound, which 'serves at once as a memorial, a trophy and a tomb': age, as it would for the contemporary monuments he complained about, presumably conferred legitimacy. He reserved his special ire, however, for the hotels and refreshment outlets at its base and along Wellington's ridge, 'hopelessly interfering with the dignity and quiet of the place'. One of them even displayed a giant advertisement for Blackpool. Also near the mound, he objected to what he could only describe as the gasometer housing a panorama of the battle, over a hundred yards in length, by the Swiss artist, Francois Dumoulin, completed in 1912. Walter Guinness put it more politely in writing that, 'The painting is stated to be lifelike and animated, but regret is expressed that some other site has not been selected.'[532] He did not, however, dissent from Moon's view that the best act of commemoration for the centenary would be a 'clean sweep' of buildings.

A law to stop any development likely to interfere with the characteristics of the battlefield was passed in Belgium on 26 March 1914. Just a few days previously, a meeting of the committee of the 'Fund for the preservation of the Battlefield of Waterloo' took place in the Waterloo Gallery at Apsley House. The 4th Duke of Wellington presided with Field-Marshal Lord Roberts as treasurer. Representatives from the Belgian Waterloo centenary committee were also in attendance. Presumably unpersuaded that the new law would be a failsafe, those present voiced concern that speculators would build on the battlefield for 1915. To prevent it, they hoped to raise £10,000 to buy the building rights to 1,347 of its acres. A public appeal for the money was launched in April. The intention was that any surplus would be diverted to the preservation of Hougoumont and the planned international memorial. By May, however, the fund had raised less than £4,800. This was judged a poor response, one which ran the risk that 'the ground on which heroes fought and died and in which they lie buried should be desecrated by the erection of shoddy buildings'. Edward Moon suggested that if government declined to help, MPs, who since 1911 had been paid £400 per annum, might like to surrender 25 per cent of their salary 'to some really national object'.[533]

Days later, all talk of parliamentarians' altruism and acts of international commemoration was rendered irrelevant by the outbreak of war. By 18 June 1915, the campaign fields of a century before were in the German sector of the Western Front. In Brussels, Blücher's heirs celebrated alone. In a speech near Wellington's 1815 residence, Belgium's new German Governor-General, General Moritz von Bissing, declared that 'we are the conquerors. It is thanks to the strength of our arms that we stand here.' Sixty miles away, near Ypres, Sir John French, commander of the British Expeditionary Force, made no public reference to Waterloo, but spent part of the day reviewing units from the 3rd Cavalry Division, praising their recent endeavours in face of 'dastardly gas attacks'. Back in Britain, in a tone reminiscent of that struck at the time of the Crimean War, *The Times* declared that the landmark date 'must necessarily pass very quietly'. The nation's French allies must not be affronted. Thus, although Leicester Galleries continued with its exhibition of Lady Butler's pictures of the Waterloo campaign on behalf of the

Officers' Families Fund, annual regimental dinners were cancelled. A projected Waterloo display at the Royal United Services Institute was similarly abandoned. Wellington College decided to replace its annual speech day with one commemorating the nearly 200 former pupils who had already fallen in the new war. Part of it involved the 4th Duke planting an acorn from the oak tree planted beside the grave of Copenhagen at Stratfield Saye. Another involved the College's army corps parading across its playing fields. How many of them were amongst the 707 former Wellingtonians who would perish in the war by 1918?[534]

Elsewhere, recorded acts of centenary commemoration were relatively few and far between. They included bouquets adorned with tricolours left by a French lady at the figures of both Wellington and Napoleon at Madame Tussauds. Someone placed a wreath on the Wellington statue outside Apsley House, unveiled in 1888 to replace the one ignominiously removed to Aldershot. The Royal Artillery commemorated their forebears by placing a wreath on the grave of Cavalié Mercer in Devon. Amongst the living, the most notable celebrant was the Reverend W. T. Kingsley. The eighteenth of June marked his 100th birthday; his father had been an army surgeon at Waterloo.[535]

As it had in 1865, *The Times* offered its readers a substantial article on the campaign of 1815.[536] 'A hundred years ago today,' it began, 'the fate of the world was decided on the field of Waterloo. Today, after the lapse of a hundred years, the Low Countries are the scene of a mightier struggle, and once more the fate of the world hangs upon the issue; but the foes of a hundred years ago are brothers-in-arms against a common enemy.' Claiming, unconvincingly, that, 'It is very long since Englishmen thought of the Battle of Waterloo primarily, if at all, as a national victory,' it was on surer ground in saying that it had enduring appeal as an epic romantic drama in which circumstance had brought down Napoleon. The thesis that it wished to advance, however, was one of Waterloo launching a hundred years of Anglo-French amity, the two nations bound together by their common belief in allowing ordered liberty to develop. Wellington was praised less for his military genius, therefore, than for his statesmanship. He had waged neither a war of conquest, nor saddled France with a vindictive peace. His approach contrasted sharply, it was argued, with the brutal approach to both war and diplomacy preferred by the Prussians in 1815, one that had been given substance when France was forced to cede its provinces of Alsace and Lorraine to Germany in 1871 at the close of the Franco-Prussian war.

Though not entirely bad history, the article was clearly better propaganda, a nice example of how Waterloo continued to be reinterpreted to inform the present. It was, unsurprisingly, neither the first nor the last Waterloo allusion during the First World War. In apologising for an attack by Berliners on the British Embassy following Britain's declaration of war in August 1914, the Kaiser's emissary told the British ambassador 'how deeply the people felt the action of England in ranging herself against Germany and forgetting how we had fought shoulder to shoulder at Waterloo'. As the Germans advanced into Belgium, Douglas Haig recorded in his diary that 'another great battle' might be imminent in the fields between Waterloo and Charleroi.[537] In September 1914, news of the Scots Greys in action near St Quentin prompted the inevitable headline 'Waterloo Recalled'. It was later claimed that the 70-year-old son of an ensign in the 28th, who had carried the regiment's colours at Quatre Bras, tried to get himself sent to Flanders when he heard that the Gloucester Regiment, its descendant, was near Waterloo. In 1915, Sir John French's wife was presented with a pistol supposedly carried by Wellington in the battle. Later that year, the Prussian standard that hung on the walls of St Paul's near the Duke's tomb was removed.[538]

As the war deepened, and casualties mounted – Lord Richard Wellesley, son of the 4th Duke, was amongst many descendants of Waterloo fathers to be killed – the memory of Waterloo was enlisted in new ways. The 'Anglesey leg', for example, patented by a John Potts of Chelsea and advertised in 1914, would soon be needed in tragically large numbers. The Red Cross, which held auctions to raise money for those with wounds of any description, included original editions of 1815 newspapers in its catalogues. With the flood of volunteers failing to keep pace with the demands of Total War, Captain Cecil Battine recommended 'conscription as our best method of celebrating the anniversary of Waterloo'.[539] Most salient, however, were the reminders of Prussian brutality from the 1815 campaign. The 1,500 German soldiers in Belgium in 1915 reported to be making plans to demolish the Lion's Mound were the uncivilised descendants of those who Wellington had prevented from blowing up the Jena Bridge in Paris a century before. The story was pure propaganda, one implying that vileness was part of the Hun's genetic make-up. But it played well. In 1916, the press reproduced extracts from a July 1815 letter written by the publisher, John Murray, describing Prussian excesses in Paris. As the war was entering its final weeks, Henry Lucy was reminding people of a Robert Southey letter from October 1815 on the same theme. 'The Prussian,' Lucy added with ironic superfluity, 'is the same, whether trained under "that abominable Frederick" or living under the pious Kaiser Wilhelm.'[540]

The end of the war, too, prompted Waterloo associations. In November 1918, the 1st Royal Dragoons and 10th Royal Hussars, both regiments whose forebears had participated in the 1815 campaign, were reported to have ridden over the battlefield in their advance towards Germany. The armistice saw George V address MPs in the Royal Gallery flanked by Maclise's picture of Wellington greeting Blücher. For one well-read individual, James Simpson's once popular account of the earlier conflict, specifically his description of everybody shaking hands with everybody in Edinburgh when the news of Waterloo arrived, was reminiscent of 'a touch of the hilarity of Armistice Day'.[541] The First World War, however, as for so much else, drew a final line under the Waterloo century. For all that comparisons were made between the 1815 and 1914–1918 campaigns, there were enormous differences, most obviously the human cost. In 1815 this had, rightly, been judged to be horrendous. But when the Prince of Wales unveiled a cross in Exeter to the men of the Devons in 1921, it was remarked that they alone had sent about twice the number of men to the 1914–1918 war as there were Britons in Wellington's 1815 army; they had also incurred roughly twice the casualties. And in the new democratic age of mass citizen armies, the ordinary British soldier received individual burial. Not for him the large pits of 1815 or his remains suffering the gross indignity of being traded to tourists. Where those remains were unidentifiable or lost, his name at least, as Charles Williams-Wynn and William Thackeray would have approved, was inscribed on memorials such as the Menin Gate at Ypres or the memorial to the missing of the Somme at Thiepval.[542] It was indicative of how the 1914–1918 conflict would thenceforth supplant that of 1793–1815 as a reference point in the national consciousness that it should even appropriate its moniker of the Great War.

Like its earlier namesake, the end to the Great War of the twentieth century would spawn a literature commensurate with its subject. Before that deluge broke, and following their late-nineteenth-century flourish, studies of Wellington and Waterloo went through a relative hiatus. The influential professional historian, Sir Charles Oman, wrote the entry on the Hundred Days for the *Cambridge Modern History* (1906), but its salient note was its focus on the 'amazing delay' of the Prussians on 18 June. Best known for his magisterial history of the Peninsular War, Oman, like Napier and Roberts before him, admired Wellington the soldier but not Wellington the man ('this hard and unsympathetic figure'). Major A.F. Becke published the most durable early-twentieth-century account of the battle, *Napoleon and Waterloo*, in 1914, but he was hardly original in his conclusion that, 'Wellington's skill and leadership combined with the admirable tenacity displayed by his troops enabled the Anglo-Dutch Army to hold its position and wear down the *Armée du Nord*. Blücher's arrival and wholehearted cooperation then enabled the Allies to overwhelm the last of the Grand Armies'.[543] Easily the most original new work was by Thomas Hardy. As a young man, he had known 'many Waterloo men'. In middle age he spoke to some of the last surviving veterans at Chelsea. He also visited the battlefield in 1876 and again in 1896. In between whiles, Hardy's plan for a novel set around the campaign evolved into something far grander. He began serious research and writing in 1897, but it was a decade later before the third and final part of *The Dynasts* was completed. The single-volume edition of 1910 runs to over 500 pages.[544] It was, as its subtitle proclaimed, 'an epic-drama of the War with Napoleon, in three Parts, nineteen Acts and one hundred and thirty Scenes'.

Hardy wanted *The Dynasts* to be regarded as his masterpiece. He was particularly proud of his account of the pre-battle fauna. It allowed him to offer, literally, a new perspective on events. On the eve of Waterloo:

> The mole's tunnelled chambers are crushed by wheels,
> The lark's eggs scattered, their owners fled;
> And the hedgehog's household the sapper unseals.
>
> The snail draws in at the terrible tread,
> But in vain; he is crushed by the felloe-rim;
> The worm asks what can be overheard,
>
> And wriggles deep from a scene so grim,
> And guesses him safe; for he does not know
> What a foul red flood will be soaking him!

In 1919, Walter de la Mare wrote of *The Dynasts* that, 'We are as close to actual experience as words can bring us.' The Waterloo sections, roughly a tenth of the whole, remain impressive. Though Hardy has Napoleon say that it is England who has 'thumbed me by the throat, And made herself the means of mangling me!', he devotes several scenes to the movement of the Prussians on 18 June, and more than once has Wellington saying that he needs them to arrive. Hardy's main conclusion, however, evident both from his private correspondence and in *The Dynasts*, is that Waterloo was decided, as it was for Hugo, by fate. He ends the work on a note of optimism ('a stirring thrills the air [...] till It fashion all things fair!'), something the experience of the Great War caused him to regret by 1918. That, perhaps as much as anything else, explains why the work never enjoyed great popular success and quickly fell out of fashion after Hardy's death in 1928.[545]

Those who wrote about Waterloo soon after 1918 found it difficult to resist prejudice engendered by the conflict just ended. Sir John Fortescue, the historian of the British Army, reached his volume covering the Waterloo campaign in 1920. Though he was admiring of Blücher and the ordinary Prussian soldier, his anti-German feelings are at times palpable, as for example when he relates the fate of the French cannon after Waterloo, 'which with characteristic arrogance and dishonesty the Prussians promptly appropriated to themselves'. His particular bête noire was Gneisenau, whom he unreasonably held to account for the Prussians not having reached Waterloo earlier. 'If the Prussian staff, with Gneisenau at its head, did not foresee these complications and their inevitable results,' he wrote, 'it stands convicted of gross incompetence; if it did foresee them, and of deliberate design contrived them, it cannot be acquitted of despicable disloyalty to the Allies of Prussia and to the common cause of Europe.' Not least of Gneisenau's crimes was his suspicion of Fortescue's cynosure, Wellington. The Duke may have made the 'unfathomable' decision to leave 18,000 men at Hal, but he more than compensated for it, for, 'wherever weakness was, there by magic appeared Wellington, perfectly calm and collected, inspiring all with confidence and fortitude. He said himself that he personally saved the battle four times, and, if he had said forty times, he would not have overstated the truth.'[546] It was the most adulatory assessment of the Duke's handling of the campaign since Roberts a quarter of a century before. In some ways, a better inter-war account of the battle was provided by Georgette Heyer's 1937 historical romance, *An Infamous Army*. Based on extensive reading of the printed sources, it remained a staple of university history department reading lists for many years.

The most important new material relating to Wellington published before the First World War for Heyer and others to draw upon was Frances, Lady Shelley's diary. Lady Shelley (1787–1873) first became acquainted with the Duke in 1814 and met him regularly in Paris in the summer of 1815. She happily pleaded guilty to the charge of hero-worship. Though her account of the Waterloo campaign is disappointing – it is garbled and appears to have been set down several weeks after the event – she is second only to

Creevey as a source of anecdote for June 1815. Lady Shelley provides us with the fullest version of Wellington's already well-known sentiment that he considered a battle won the worst misfortune apart from a defeat, and his consequent hope that Waterloo was his last engagement. She also secured the service of the Duke of Richmond as her personal guide to the battlefield in September 1815, on which occasion he repeated to her what he had earlier told Captain Bowles at the fabled ball, that in his map room Wellington had said, 'If the Prussians are beat, which I think is very probable, we shall be obliged to retreat. If we do, that is the spot [Mont St Jean] where we must lick those fellows.'[547]

Debate as to Wellington's true character nevertheless continued. Whilst conceding his military abilities, a hostile interpretation of the man was presented by C. R. M. F. Cruttwell in 1936. Lady Shelley was one of several women he insinuated had become the Duke's lover. This was the more incomprehensible to Cruttwell because he judged the Duke:

> aloof, bleak and cold to his subordinates, that he was on the worst terms with his eldest [sic] son, that he never had a friend, that the Creeveys, Crokers and Arbuthnots were only agreeable parasites and that he had an unpleasing reputation for the pursuit of pleasure without passion prolonged until late in life.[548]

Though far less comprehensive in their condemnation, British labour historians, for example J. L. and Barbara Hammond, were also clear that Wellington entertained no sympathy for the common man. They ascribed the draconian sentences handed down in Hampshire following the 1830 agricultural labourers' disturbances (the 'Captain Swing' riots), in part to his being present throughout the special commission held in Winchester to try them. Some 101 of the 285 cases heard had resulted in capital convictions.[549]

The best and most sympathetic inter-war life of Wellington was Philip Guedalla's *The Duke* (1931). Written in his allusively epigrammatic style, Guedalla reflected that Wellington's 'memory [...] seems a trifle faded. He cast so large a shadow once [...] he survives to later memory as little more than the instrument of a single victory and the gruff hero of a dozen anecdotes.' Wellington, he suggested, had been militarily far too successful for British tastes. He had fallen victim also, to the cult of Napoleon, and even more so to his post-Waterloo reputation as an anti-Reform Tory. Since, Guedalla reasoned, the political history had been written predominantly by Whigs such as Macaulay, 'the Nineteenth Century tended to belittle his entire achievement'. He might have added the early-twentieth-century too. George Kitson Clark's 1929 tome on the Conservative Party after 1832 concluded that Wellington's reputation sank 'behind his military glory […] it was Peel's achievement and character, and not the Duke's, that were to dominate the next eleven years of Conservatism'. Guedalla duly set himself the task of explaining for a new generation why Wellington's 'portrait richly deserves to hang in the great gallery of English prose'.[550] Though he regarded the Duke, at times, as an anachronistic and anomalous figure, it was largely thanks to Guedalla's biography that a Wellington of substance was restored to the reading public.

The story of Waterloo during the inter-war years, initially at least, was one more of completion than restoration. In a belated centenary act in 1921, the Royal Artillery Barracks at Aldershot were renamed the Waterloo Barracks. Another piece of deferred business was the British Empire Exhibition, originally scheduled for 1915. It finally opened on St George's Day 1924, not, as had been planned, at Crystal Palace but at the newly-constructed Wembley Stadium. On Waterloo Day 1924, *The Times* wondered how many children attending the exhibition would be able to explain the significance of the date. Presumably some, if only because the newspaper was selling copies of its 22 June 1815 edition at its stall in the exhibition pavilion. A year later, in a further consciously retrospective centenary act, the Club Anglo-Belge laid a wreath at the Evere memorial in Brussels.[551]

For some, the memory of Waterloo was kept alive by personal connections. In a notable coincidence, the 4th Duke of Wellington, a grandson of the first, died on Waterloo Day 1934. The passing of descendants of lesser Mont St Jean alumni also attracted newspaper coverage. A son of William Leeke, who as a 17-year-old had carried the colours of the 52nd at Waterloo and subsequently wrote a celebrated history of the regiment, died in 1925. This prompted inquiries as to how many siblings of Waterloo men were still alive. The answer was reckoned at about forty. One of the last, Kate Cam (still alive in 1936), was the daughter of George Erving Scott. He had been an 18-year-old ensign with the 62nd in 1815 and subsequently went up to Trinity Hall, Cambridge where his poem on Waterloo beat Macaulay to the Chancellor's Medal for English Verse. Perhaps the past was not so very far distant? In 1930, the Minister of Health, Arthur Greenwood, claimed that he knew of a case where an 18-year-old who had fought at Waterloo had married a young woman when he was over 60. As the widow was still alive in 1930, she would qualify for the new Widows' and Orphans' pension.[552]

Greenwood's story may have been contrived, but society was at last awakening to its responsibilities for its veterans.

One celebrated veteran, who had lapsed into relative obscurity since Ansdell's mid-nineteenth-century painting of his capturing the Eagle of the 45th, was Charles Ewart. Ansdell had wanted the painting to go to Chelsea Hospital, but it was sold for 900 guineas in 1874. When it reappeared on the market in 1910, Ansdell's son bought it and presented to the Hospital, where it was hung alongside the Eagle, resident since 1835. The attendant publicity brought Ewart's story to a new audience, including the detail that his sword had been acquired by W. H. Lever, founder of Lever Brothers, who displayed it in Port Sunlight Museum. Ewart himself, meanwhile, lay forgotten in his Salford grave, which had become part of a contractor's yard. In 1936, following a twelve-year search by a veteran of his regiment, it was rediscovered. Ewart's remains were re-interred in a grand ceremony on the esplanade of Edinburgh Castle in 1938.[553]

There was a less seemly response to what should be done about Waterloo Bridge. Cracks, caused by subsidence, were reported in 1923. More than a decade of wrangling then ensued over whether Rennie's structure should be reconditioned or demolished and rebuilt. It involved debates in Parliament and a royal commission; a young John Betjeman devoted a radio broadcast to the subject in 1932. Though the majority viewpoint moved in favour of a new bridge, some concern remained that the only national memorial to the battle should disappear. This was scotched by Lord Ponsonby of Shulbrede who said that, 'In this vulgar and utilitarian age I am afraid the word Waterloo conveys to most people not a battle but a station or a cup, and the idea that people reverence this bridge because it is a war memorial, I think must be dismissed as an exaggeration of sentimentality.' In truth, the arguments were primarily ones about aesthetics, cost and the practicalities of dealing with the capital's burgeoning road traffic problems. London County Council eventually voted for a rebuild in 1934. Designed by Sir Giles Gilbert Scott, the replacement Waterloo Bridge was not officially opened by Herbert Morrison, erstwhile leader of the Council, until December 1945. A plaque commemorating the fact boasts, scandalously, neither the name of Wellington nor his soldiers, but those of Morrison and his former colleagues.[554]

In the same year that Waterloo Bridge was reported to be subsiding, General Sir William Robertson bemoaned the fact that few homes now displayed military pictures: when he was young, there were scenes of Waterloo 'hung in every cottage in the land'. Waterloo was, in fact, contrary to what he and Lord Ponsonby thought, still popularly remembered, albeit in new art forms perhaps unfamiliar to them. In July 1913, a film of Waterloo premiered at the London Palladium to widespread acclaim, apparent proof that Britain's fledgling film industry could compete with its American counterpart. The cast of 1,000 horses and 2,000 people included local shoe workers, as well as 500 unemployed men, who each received 2 shillings for two days' filming. Shot at Irthlingborough in Northamptonshire, with Jack Brighton as Wellington, the hour-long film was completed in three days at a cost of £6,000.[555] It spawned an eight-minute comedy, written by, directed and starring Fred and Joe Evans. The first in what became known as the Pimple parodies, part of the joke was its cheap production. With echoes of Macaulay's *Wellingtoniad* and anticipating *Blackadder*, the Evans brothers had Napoleon assaulted by a suffragette before he arrived at Waterloo station, where he flipped a coin with Wellington for the right to take first shot. He was finally charged by Boy Scouts. The battle provided the subject matter for further films in 1923 – minus any reference to the Prussians – and 1929, when the 2,000 extras were accused of having no idea of what they were doing. A short film version of Conan Doyle's *A Story of Waterloo* was released in 1933; George Arliss portrayed Wellington in *The Iron Duke*, which premiered before the Prince of Wales in November 1934 and raised £7,300 for Great Ormond Street Hospital. On the stage, the actor Stanley Holloway won acclaim for his comic monologue, 'Sam and his Musket' (presumably an updated version of the Victorian 'Bill Adams'), the story of a Lancashire guardsman on the eve of Waterloo; whilst the newly-chartered BBC broadcast radio concerts on Waterloo Day.[556]

The popular depiction of Waterloo through new media may have encouraged some to visit the battlefield for themselves. This occasioned surprise in some quarters:

> because of the Great War it was thought Waterloo and its memories might no longer attract. This belief has been proved to be wrong. The number of visitors to Waterloo is still as great as in pre-war days; and is even said to have increased. Cars full of foreign visitors can be seen every day making the trip from Brussels to Waterloo.[557]

A combination of visitor numbers and the apparent indifference of the Belgian authorities to take preservation of the site sufficiently seriously led

to some depressing, even alarming developments. By 1930, the memorial to
Colonel Gordon had become so unsightly and inaccessible that £100 was
needed for its refurbishment. Mont St Jean farm, which had served as the
main field hospital for Wellington's army in 1815, was sold in 1930; La Belle
Alliance was sold for £820 in 1937.[558] In 1933 a Bill to allow building on
the battlefield was introduced in the Belgian Parliament. The novelist, John
Buchan, was amongst those who protested and got the British government
to lobby against it. Though the Bill lapsed, four years later the provincial
authorities wanted to widen a stretch of Wellington's famous sunken road;
they showed little inclination to address the problems of decay occasioned
by damp at Hougoumont, where the kitchen gable was said to be in danger
of imminent collapse. They had, perversely, acted to save the Lion's Mound
from a similar fate in 1923. Well might Philip Pilditch, as the 1930s drew to
a close, enter the plea that:

> it is true the magnitude of operations in the Great War has reduced the Battle
> of Waterloo to the dimensions of a skirmish, but there is something in that
> campaign of a few days, culminating in a clash of as many hours, that still holds
> the imagination of the world, when the genius of the Captain leading the army
> of one of our Allies in the World War failed in his aim by very little, owing to
> the loyalty of the leader of the forces of our recent great enemy and the stub-
> born valour of the Allied soldiers under our own Chief. If the alignment of the
> nations presents a different picture today it must not be forgotten that the battle
> profoundly affected the course of history for several generations.[559]

At the end of the Great War, the Belgian government was asked to turn
round the lion on its eponymous mound so as to acknowledge France's
contribution to Belgium's liberation. It was just as well that the idea was
rejected, for it would presumably have been reorientated once more in
1940. The Second World War, even more than the First, would indeed make
Waterloo seem like a skirmish. Among its 55 million or more casualties was
the 6th Duke of Wellington, great-grandson of the first, killed by a German
officer shortly after the Salerno landings in Italy in September 1943. It was
a reminder, not that it was needed, of the Finger of Providence.[560] A few
weeks later, it was calculated that 36,700 tons of bombs had been dropped
on Germany between April and June, compared to the 37 tons of shells
fired at Waterloo. Small wonder, as early as the 'Phoney War' of 1939–1940,
which preceded the Nazi Blitzkrieg of May 1940, that there was something

of a wistful nostalgia for black-powder warfare. 'This is not like any other war,' declared an editorial, 'The Battle of Waterloo was easy; you shot once; if you died you were buried; if you lived you came home; that was the end, quickly. The Americans say this is a cock-eyed war. It is true, also.' From the other side of the Channel, the Nazi take on Waterloo was nothing, if not predictable. In 1940, Propaganda Minister Joseph Goebbels approved the release of *Die Rothschilds*. The film included a scene in which the Jewish financier, Nathan Rothschild, is seen bribing a French general to ensure Wellington's victory.[561]

The Wehrmacht's victory of June 1940 ensured that there would be no international events commemorating the 125th anniversary of Waterloo. Instead, de Gaulle chose the day to broadcast his famous *L'Appel du 18 Juin* from London, a speech popularly credited with being the origin of the national resistance to the Nazi occupiers. Though, characteristically, he did not mention the events of 1815, his timing was surely an attempt to abrogate them by rallying the French to a more subliminal purpose. The British were, of course, more comfortable and explicit in comparing the Napoleonic Wars and the Second World War as ones of national survival against tyrannical aggression. The Cambridge historian, G. M. Trevelyan, a great-nephew of Macaulay, published his hugely popular *English Social History* in 1942. Written in 1941, it concludes with a footnote comparing Waterloo being won on the playing fields of Eton (actually, in his view England's village greens), to RAF pilots who 'could not be the product of rural simplicity. If we win this war, it will have been won in the primary and secondary schools'.[562] Comparison was most blatantly apparent, however, in the oeuvre of Arthur Bryant, who morphed from appeaser to celebrant of British patriotism following the fall of France. His *English Saga 1840–1940* (1940) contained a cameo of the Duke as the embodiment of all that was best about old England. It was followed by *The Years of Endurance 1793–1802* (1942), and *Years of Victory 1802–1812* (1944), celebrating his achievements whilst openly equating Napoleon with Hitler. Even a modern critic has conceded that Bryant 'did a superb job in helping to stiffen the people's resolve by putting their sacrifices in historical context'.[563] Both Churchill and Attlee admired his work.

Bryant would extend his story beyond Waterloo, as well as writing a biography of Wellington, after the war. But the popular press did not have to wait for him to make the analogies. Following the Normandy landings of June 1944, the *Nottingham Evening Post* wrote that, 'On June 18th, 1815, the brilliant

Napoleon met his fate on the field of Waterloo. He aspired to be world dictator. Today, side-by-side with French patriots, we are overthrowing another dictator.' As the allies advanced that autumn, General Montgomery found time to see the Waterloo battlefield, including Hougoumont. He inevitably climbed the Lion's Mound, viewed the panorama at its base and even sent some musket balls to a Mrs Reynolds.[564] Montgomery was, in fact, relatively critical of the Duke as a commander. When he lectured at the University of St Andrews on the subject of military leadership towards the end of 1945, he chose Napoleon (as well as Moses and Cromwell), to illustrate his theme that the very greatest possessed an inner conviction transcending reason, 'which enabled them at a certain point – the right one – to take a short cut which took them straight to their objective more swiftly and surely than equally careful but less inspired commanders'. Wellington, by comparison, 'sometimes lost part of the fruits of victory through an inability to soar from the known to seize the unknown'. Perhaps Montgomery was piqued by rumours that the sword Wellington wore at Waterloo had recently been presented to Eisenhower.[565]

The 7th Duke, who succeeded to the title in 1943, denied the Eisenhower story. Over the next thirty years, nobody would do more than he to advance Wellington studies. He also took a keen interest in his ancestor's battlefield. In 1955, for example, he provided documentary material to assist in the creation of the Musée Wellington in the building where he had slept after Waterloo. The 7th Duke also facilitated greater access to his great-grandfather's papers by depositing his correspondence as Lord Lieutenant of Hampshire with the county's record office in 1961, and his more voluminous general correspondence from 1833 with the Historical Manuscripts Commission in 1967. Unhappy with how the 1st Duke had been portrayed in Richard Aldington's biography, first published in Britain in 1946, and even more so by Cruttwell's 1936 life, he also devoted considerable time to his own literary endeavours. This included a slight volume, *The Conversations of the First Duke of Wellington with George William Chad*, chiefly important for its account of 13 August 1821 when Chad, a minor diplomat, was one of three people who accompanied the Duke to Mont St Jean, where he 'rode over the field to explain the action'.[566] He also published a selection of letters, mostly from the Duke's female confidantes, under the title *Wellington and his Friends*.

The 7th Duke's most important contribution to Wellington studies was his co-editorship of the journals of the most famous of those confidantes,

Harriet Arbuthnot. Harriet Fane (1793–1834), a granddaughter of the Earl of Westmorland, became the second wife of Charles Arbuthnot (1767–1850), twenty-six years her senior, in 1814. It was widely presumed, even by his cabinet colleagues, that she was the Duke's mistress: shortly after her death, the *Brighton Patriot* risked the thinly disguised suggestion that she knew all about the great man's virtues. Her journals offer no corroboration for the imputation; the case remains unproven. Wellington knew that she was keeping a journal for he asked her curiously about it in February 1822 and on being denied a look at it 'said he was afraid of a person who kept a journal [...] He was very anxious to know if it treated of politics or only where I dined, & c.' Had he seen it, he would have discovered, as their later editors intended, a Wellington 'in daily contact with people who neither disliked him nor cringed to him, and they should make him a better understood, though, to some of his admirers, not necessarily a greater man'. For an insight into Wellington as both man and politician during the 1820s, they remain the indispensable source. On the warrior there is little, though Mrs Arbuthnot does record his admitting shedding tears in the aftermath of victory, something which prompted her indignant entry, 'yet this man has been abused & accused of being completely without heart'. To Waterloo specifically there are very few references, the main one occasioned by Wellington's amusement when finding her reading critical accounts of his part in the battle in 1823.[567] Needless to say, her version of Waterloo was his.

Mrs Arbuthnot's journal was not as immediately exploited by writers on Wellington as one might have expected. It was entirely absent from the most successful popular history of the 1950s, Sir Winston Churchill's *A History of the English-Speaking Peoples*. Begun in the 1930s, Churchill returned to his grand project after the war. Volume three, *The Age of Revolution*, covering the years from 1688–1815, appeared in 1957. He was clearly more fascinated by the Emperor than the Duke; his bust of the former is still on display at Chartwell. By contrast, Wellington's Indian wars are reduced to a single sentence in which, 'The [Marathas] thereupon declared war on the British, and after heavy fighting were defeated at Assaye and elsewhere by Wellesley's younger brother, the future Duke of Wellington.' Barely ten pages of text are afforded to the whole of the Peninsular War; to the Waterloo campaign little more than five. In the single page devoted to the battle, he at least gives the Duke credit for being 'in the forefront of danger all day. On his chestnut, Copenhagen, he had galloped everywhere, issuing brusque orders, gruffly encouraging his men [...] Only the power and example of his own personality had kept his motley force together.' He chiefly credits Wellington for having identified the position of Mont St Jean: 'He had noted the advantages of the ridge at Waterloo.' But this was, one feels, only because, 'So had the great Duke of Marlborough a century earlier, when his Dutch allies had prevented him from engaging Marshal Villeroi there.'[568] Sir Winston's real hero was his ancestor, John Churchill.

Churchill's 1965 funeral was the grandest for a British non-royal since Wellington's in 1852. There were striking resonances between the two occasions; even a popular belief that Churchill had wanted his coffin to depart for burial at Bladon from Waterloo station in order that the assembled French dignitaries would be discomfited. The year also marked the 150th anniversary of Waterloo. Given the unscheduled disruption of the 100th and 125th anniversaries, NATO forces in West Germany might well have been forgiven if they had felt some anxiety! Activities in Britain to mark the landmark anniversary were hardly on the grand scale. The closest approximation to an official commemorative event was a seven-week exhibition organised by the army at the Wellington Barracks in the Tower of London. The army also provided £800 for the restoration of the British Waterloo memorial in Evere cemetery, forgotten, covered in ivy, and with everybody denying responsibility for its upkeep. Elsewhere, the 7th Duke hosted a reception at Apsley House for Old Wellingtonians, whilst the 7th Marquis of Anglesey opened an exhibition in a London hotel mounted by the British Model Soldier Society.[569]

Even so, the 150th anniversary year did not pass entirely without incident. Speaking in Koblenz on 20 May, the Queen alluded to Blücher's assisting the British as an example of older ties after fifty years of more recent animosities between the Anglo-Saxon peoples. One suspects that this was a deliberate attempt at diplomatic bridge building with the Germans. It is of a piece with the British press reporting the fact that 50,000 Germans processed to the Waterloo column in Hanover on 18 June as proof of a nostalgia for Hanoverians' past association with Britain 'and pride in the fact that the new Germany was now welcomed back as an ally and comrade in arms on an equal footing'. Frenchmen, however, were taking note. Three days earlier, Lord Kennet had been assured by the government that representatives from the nations of former enemies would not be invited to commemorations of past victories. His Lordship hailed the 'satisfaction with which that answer will be greeted, in view of the fact that the impression had got around that we had invited representatives of the French Government to meet us and celebrate on the battlefield of Waterloo'. Taken together, this was too much. In protest, several French officials would not attend a reception at the British Embassy in Brussels for the Queen's birthday. In tones evocative of its nineteenth-century antecedents, *Le Figaro* declared that it 'was now time for European states to give up commemorating victories over each other in the past'.[570]

More constructively, the 150th anniversary did trigger a spate of new books about Waterloo, notably those by David Howarth, Christopher Hibbert and Jac Weller. Another fine account is to found in Elizabeth Longford's *Wellington: The Years of the Sword*, which appeared in 1969. In writing it, she enjoyed access to family papers not seen by previous biographers. This in particular, in part perhaps because her husband was descended from the 1st Duke's wife, followed hagiographical lines. She thought that her subject admirably fitted the dictum that history should 'help to sustain man's confidence in his destiny'. More important in some ways was her second volume, *Pillar of State* (1972), which not only devoted over 450 pages to Wellington's life after Waterloo but also made a case for him, however reluctantly, as a reformer.[571] Lady Longford's two volumes remain the standard biography.

In the 1992 introduction to her condensed *Wellington*, Lady Longford asserted that there had been no major change in attitudes towards the Duke since her initial biographical endeavours, but that the most significant developments had been ones affecting the better preservation of the battlefield. On the latter point, she was too rosy in her assessment. The Musée Wellington, though enlarged in 1965, and again in 1975, was judged difficult to find, one reason perhaps for relatively poor visitor numbers. Altogether more worrying, the 8th Duke had helped found the Waterloo Committee in 1973, prompted by the news that the Belgian government was proposing to build a motorway through the battlefield, an act of historical vandalism that would have made the construction of the Lion's Mound seem like a minor blemish by comparison. Mercifully, the road was re-routed to the north, leaving the Waterloo Committee to pursue its more general aims of preserving the battlefield, as well as educating the general public about the battle.[572]

Towards the former objective at least, progress has been slow. Even without the motorway, the field was being described in 1973 as 'almost a fairground' made worse, from a Wellingtonian point of view, by the fact that it bore ever-increasing evidence of becoming a shrine to Napoleon. 'The field of Waterloo deserves a better representation,' complained Kenneth Balfour, 'and a British one.' A decade later, matters were even worse. British visitors returned home to reflect upon 'the nasty collection of grubby souvenir shops clustered at the foot of the Lion's Mound'. Whilst Napoleonic kitsch was to be had in abundance, 'there is hardly a sign of the Iron Duke'. To the south, meanwhile, La Belle Alliance had metamorphosed into a discotheque with the name Club Retro![573] Mindful that none of the 1815 commanders had used it for that purpose, the King Baudouin Foundation, in June 1988, launched an international competition for 'creating an international tourist centre of the highest quality', espousing a 'vision of a Waterloo swept clean of the sight and smell of frites stands, the tawdry souvenir shops, the county-fair amusements'. Over 550 entries were received. As was confidently surmised at the time, however, the winning scheme, involving the construction of overlapping walls across the field where the armies stood, needed to surmount so many planning hurdles that it would never come to fruition. Even a lesser project would need to contend with the petty jealousies arising from the fact that the battlefield straddled the four communes of Waterloo, Genappe, Lasne and Braine-l'Alleud. With a misplaced sense of self-importance reminiscent of Herbert Morrison, the mayor of the latter, the largest portion lying within his domain, was apparently sincere in his wish that the battle should be renamed Braine-l'Alleud.[574] For the moment, this new Battle of Waterloo remained in stalemate.

The 175th anniversary of Waterloo in 1990, however, attracted a good deal of attention – in Europe. A five-month programme of events was devised with the usual paradoxical aims of encouraging tourism and galvanising politicians to preserve the site. There were exhibitions at Le Caillou and the Musée Wellington focusing on the lives of ordinary people in 1815, and a light and sound display at the Lion's Mound on 16 June. Celebrations culminated with a re-enactment of the battle the following day. No fewer than 2,000 people from ten countries took part, watched by crowds of 20,000. The most ambitious Waterloo re-enactment to date, this late twentieth century form of commemoration was broadcast live on Belgian television. And to confound those Britons (most), who regard such gatherings as the preserve of cranks and eccentrics – *The Times* mocked the 1988 participants' endeavours 'agreeably sandwiched between breakfast in an Imperial tent and a champagne picnic lunch' – the role of one French general was assumed by Britain's foremost Napoleonic scholar, David Chandler.[575] Chandler also played a key part in saving Siborne's model. In storage at Aldershot from 1962–1975, it was restored to become the centrepiece of the

National Army Museum's 'Road to Waterloo' exhibition, surviving calls for it to be transferred to Apsley House as 'the time has come for the nation to better honour one of its finest generals'. The nation obliged instead with *Nosey*, a 90-minute radio play on Wellington's life, commemorative medals struck by the Royal Mint, and by the British Library's purchasing one version of the Waterloo Despatch from the 8th Duke for £350,000.[576]

Lady Longford's other observation in 1992, that no fundamental change in attitudes towards Wellington had been discernible over the previous twenty years, though essentially correct, required amplification. On Waterloo Day 1983, for example, some of Britain's foremost military historians attended a conference at Apsley House on the Duke, spawning the book *Wellington Commander*. The same year would prove seminal for Wellington studies more generally, for it witnessed the depositing of the bulk of the 1st Duke's papers at the University of Southampton. In 1987 the University co-hosted a major international conference on Wellington's life and times. Some of the first fruits of new research appeared in an important collection of essays, edited by Norman Gash, the following year. Though much personal correspondence was destroyed by the 1st Duke (thereby imparting something of a formal or 'cold' bias to what survives), it was supplemented during his lifetime by Gurwood's efforts to secure copies of originals for inclusion in the *Despatches*. The Wellington archive today contains approximately 100,000 items, making it one of the largest and most important national collections for the period in existence. In tandem with an ongoing programme of digitisation, the painstaking process of conserving some of the more delicate items was scheduled, appropriately, for completion in 2015. For all its fragility, the Duke's archive is in safer hands than his battlefield.[577]

Since 1983, both the concentration and accessibility of the Duke's papers at Southampton has facilitated new work by scholars; for example, examination of hitherto neglected aspects of Wellington's career, such as his Chancellorship of Oxford University and his Lord Lieutenancy of Hampshire.[578] These, in turn, contribute to a better understanding of his character. Taken together with wider historiographical trends over the past generation, the most important general development in Wellington studies is the fuller appreciation of his role in British politics, especially after 1832. Already, during the third quarter of the twentieth century, the work of Professor Norman Gash had demolished the prevailing orthodoxy of British political history after 1832 as a story of inexorable Liberal advance. He replaced it with one that characterised the difficult years to mid-century as the Age of Peel. In this interpretation, Wellington was rescued from the role of reactionary villain and cast in that of able subordinate. A feeling that Gash had overstated the case for Peel, however, has led to Wellington's reputation rising further, so that the relationship between the men can now be viewed as a genuine, if unofficial and sometimes uneasy, partnership. Recently indeed, it has even been suggested that Wellington was the more pragmatic of the two and that his policy of bending to reform when unavoidable – a political version of knowing when to retreat and daring to do it – qualifies him as a contender to be regarded as the true founder of the modern Conservative Party. Gash was heavily involved in establishing the Wellington archive at Southampton. During that period, he revised his own earlier assessment of the Duke. In his entry on Wellington for the 2004 *Oxford Dictionary of National Biography*, he judged him not only Britain's greatest soldier but, for all his personal foibles, a man whose humanity and personality 'left an imprint on his countrymen equalled only by that of Winston Churchill a century after him'.[579]

Whilst the past thirty years have also seen welcome new studies of Wellington and the Peninsular War, the Duke's archive does not contain anything that forces scholars (not that it stops them!) to rewrite the history of the 1815 campaign. As a non-military specialist, Gash simply followed prevailing academic thinking for his *ODNB* entry in describing Waterloo as Wellington's best known, as opposed to his best, battle. It is a verdict with which Wellington would have agreed. He would have been less ready to accept the various criticisms levelled at him in the unrelenting barrage of accounts of the action, which continue to appear. Charles Esdaile, for example, writes of the 'series of extraordinary mistakes' he made prior to the actions of 16 June. The Duke would have denied them, or at the very least dismissed them as counsels of perfection from armchair historians – and probably something far stronger! He would surely also have objected to those accounts that emphasise the shortcomings of his opponents as the main reason why he prevailed, distracting attention, as they do, from the heroics of his own brave soldiers. Whether he would allow the Prussians more credit for their contribution to the campaign, another salient feature of modern accounts, than he was wont to do in his post-Waterloo years, must also be considered extremely doubtful.[580]

For all their caveats, however, modern accounts continue to acknowledge both the personal bravery and tactical nous which Wellington displayed on 18 June. The main dissenting voice is Peter Hofschröer's. His two volumes on the campaign, drawing substantially on Prussian sources largely unfamiliar in Britain, are valuable in correcting the myopia of more narrowly Anglo-centric histories. Where Hofschröer proved tendentious, with what one critic called 'almost missionary zeal', was in his insistence that Wellington was not just slow to react in support of the Prussians on 15 June, but that he subsequently compounded his tardiness by lies, distortion and the destruction of compromising evidence. The Duke's tactics, so Hofschröer argued in a later book, extended to his small-minded victory over Siborne's disposition of the Prussians on his model. Hofschröer's work received endorsement from respected British academics. Unusually, his thesis also made the pages of the national press; there was even a radio play based on the Siborne saga. Hofschröer's most serious charges, however, must be judged, at least by this author, as unproven. His arguments are ingenious but very often circumstantial. To suggest, for example, that Wellington was deliberately spreading disinformation about Waterloo when talking to Stanhope in the 1830s when he did not even know that Stanhope was keeping notes, stretches credibility beyond belief.[581] Why, since he knew she kept a journal, did he not use Mrs Arbuthnot as a conduit? Hofschröer finds Wellington guilty of dishonesty; the only 'crimes', he might be convicted for on the basis of hard evidence, would be the lesser ones of caution and confusion caused by the vagaries of communication in battle.

If nothing else, Hofschröer's books show that Wellington and Waterloo can still stir academic passions. Britain's politicians too, continued to invoke 1815 when taking a subjective view suited them. A fortnight before polling day – 18 June – in the 1970 general election, Julian Amery, the Conservative candidate for Brighton Pavilion, rallied supporters in face of discouraging opinion polls with the thought that Napoleon was presumed to be winning at Waterloo until late in the day. In 1984 Labour MEPs tried to raise a stir by claiming that the bureaucrats of the European Commission wanted to rename Waterloo station. And when the Tory governments of the 1980s started allowing schools to sell off their playing fields, their opponents were quick to remind them what would have happened if, in an earlier age, Eton had sold theirs. Mrs Thatcher herself, on arriving in Downing Street, professed to find her new home dowdy. She introduced portraits of both Nelson and Wellington, telling a BBC documentary that, 'I got more strength into the place [...] This one [...] of Wellington is excellent. You can see the determination, you can see the Iron Duke [...] We were absolutely right to have these two great heroes of British history and people who fought and won crucial battles.' In the days preceding her funeral, in April 2013, it transpired that one of the Iron Lady's favourite books was Elizabeth Longford's biography of the Iron Duke.[582]

Just how far the later-twentieth-century British public fully understood politicians' allusions, or were even aware of the nuances of academic debate, is difficult to judge. Amongst many born in the years immediately after 1945, there existed a presumption that Waterloo is in England; not just south of Brussels. Since Germany, as much as France, moreover, was now regarded as the natural enemy, references to 'Prussia' were surely read, if at all, as a misprint of 'Russia'. For those born a little later, Waterloo was chiefly remembered as the title of the song by Abba which triumphed at the 1974 Eurovision Song Contest. As a source it was unreliable: Wellington is never mentioned and Napoleon did not surrender there. Neither were more high-brow musical presentations necessarily any more accurate. In what might be seen as the long tradition started by Astley's and Vauxhall, military band and classical music spectaculars down to 2015 regularly included Beethoven's *Wellington's Victory* in their programme, oblivious to their error that it was written for Vitoria, not Waterloo. Major Christopher Gilding of the Royal Marines made the same mistake in 1988. He also claimed, as his unsuccessful defence against a charge of speeding on the M5 motorway, that he was listening to the piece on his radio and thereby imagined that he was in a British cavalry charge![583]

Literary and visual representations of 1815 were more likely to impress themselves on the public mind. A notable film depiction, *Waterloo*, was released by Columbia Pictures in 1970, though it played fast and loose with historical accuracy (Lord Hay, for example, dies at Waterloo in the film, not at Quatre Bras), and Christopher Plummer's Wellington is a rather wooden character reduced to spouting some of his many sayings wildly out of context. More solidly based historical novels set in the period found favour with a popular audience, especially Bernard Cornwell's *Sharpe* series, from 1981, which transferred successfully to television (1993–1997). In the latter, however, the Duke, played by Hugh Fraser, was a largely peripheral and benign figure. Far more memorable was Stephen Fry's portrayal in the final episode of the hugely popular *Blackadder the Third*, in 1987. Fry's Wellington was a large, unfeeling martinet who boomed in stentorian tones, was a crack shot and gloried in death – erroneous in every detail. Far fewer watched the excellent three part series on Wellington by Professor Richard Holmes in 2002 or his episode on Waterloo in the series *War Walks*. The Duke nevertheless came fifteenth in the BBC Millenium poll for the greatest Briton, whilst in 2013 Waterloo headed the National Army Museum's online vote for Britain's greatest battle.[584] Both the Duke's and the battle's reputations remained high with the British public.

Why this is so was well illustrated when those behind *Blackadder* were persuaded to reprise their roles for a 1999 film version that premiered in the Millennium Dome as *Blackadder: Back & Forth*. The eponymous hero is sent in a time machine on a series of quests, one of which is to acquire the boots Wellington wore at Waterloo. He lands on and kills the Duke, just as he is about to divulge his battle plans. Hurriedly returning to the present, Blackadder finds Britain part of a French-dominated Europe: the Christmas Day broadcast is about to be made from Versailles by the president. Wellington and Waterloo, in other words, clearly remain, in the popular mind, totemic symbols of British superiority, independence and triumphalism. William Rees-Mogg was being serious when he accused Tony Blair of a lack of historic tact in agreeing to a draft treaty for a European Constitution on Waterloo Day 2004. 'That victory,' he wrote, 'was the culminating point in one of the recurrent British repudiations of European power.'[585]

Europhiles immediately took exception to Rees-Mogg's comments, for they, no less than Eurosceptics, have long since integrated Waterloo into their vision of the past. In 1973, when the Cold War provided additional grist for their mill, Mr J. Macmillan insisted that had the French won in 1815:

> we should by now be enjoying the fruits of a long established united European state of individual nations working together for each other's good. There would not be the present menace of communism if the Russian people had been liberated by the French armies with the principles of Liberty, Equality of opportunity and Brotherhood. We should have been spared the German wars and the rise of Nazism.[586]

Britain had been wholly wrong, he concluded, to ally herself with the decadent monarchies of Europe against Bonaparte in defence of a burgeoning empire and the concomitant evils which this would later bring.

Supposedly more scholarly essays in counter-factualism are hardly less tendentious. G. M. Trevelyan suggested in 1907 that had Napoleon won at Waterloo, a war-weary France would have forced him to make a generous peace with England. Writing ninety years later, an Oxford professor, Norman Stone, speculated that a less generous Emperor would have installed his brothers Lucien and Joseph respectively, as kings of Scotland and England. More nuanced was Alistair Horne in 1996. He was unconvinced that Napoleon was bound to lose at Waterloo. Had he survived to be overwhelmed by the Seventh Coalition at a later date, however, he was adamant in his belief that a victory less dependant on British arms would not have led to a century of peace in Western Europe. But even in defeat, Andrew Roberts suggests, it is Napoleon's rather than Wellington's conception of Europe which more nearly prevails two hundred years later. Roberts further hypothesised that indirectly, by breaking French imperial power, Waterloo ultimately helped pave the way for the rise of the United States in the twentieth century.[587]

The above is important, at least insofar as it helped to inform how Britain would mark the bicentenary of Waterloo. Since Wellington's death, as the current study demonstrates, landmark anniversaries have been essentially low-key. As the bicentenary approached, there were auguries that it too would pass without much official or public notice, in marked contrast to widespread interest in events commemorating Trafalgar 200 in 2005. The premature death of Richard Holmes in 2011 was a serious blow, removing someone who would have been a key driving force. Not least, he was prominently associated with the British arm of Project Hougoumont, a group dedicated to the long overdue restoration of its composite buildings as 'a living memorial' in time for 2015.[588] Neither was confidence inspired by the fact that, in 2013, the members of the Waterloo Association (an enlarged and rebranded version of the 1973 Waterloo Committee and its Friends), stood accused by the editor of its journal of inertia. Almost unbelievably, the National Army Museum housing Siborne's model was closed for refurbishment during 2015. The present author wrote to Boris Johnson, the Mayor of London, in 2012 with the modest proposal that Waterloo Bridge, ostensibly the nation's memorial to the victory and those who fell achieving it, at least carry some plaque recording the fact. He was referred to Transport for London as the relevant body; they did not deign to reply. Central government too made it known that it was not intending allocating significant public funds for any 1815 commemorative events. It is true that it operated in straitened financial times, but its refusal needs to be set alongside the fact that it did see fit to provide £40,000,000 for events to mark the centenary of the start of a war, with no less contestable a legacy, in 2014.[589] Not for the first time with respect to Waterloo, the British government, wanting to appear both politically correct and good Europeans, was averse to doing anything that might be construed by its neighbours as being redolent of national chauvinism. The announcement from the Chancellor of the Exchequer, George Osborne, in his June 2013 Spending Review that a million pounds would be donated towards restoration projects was therefore as welcome as it was unexpected. But his irresistible parliamentary quip in announcing the fact that Waterloo was 'a great victory of coalition forces over a discredited former regime that had impoverished millions' was immediately accompanied by an anxious official from the Foreign Office emphasising that Britain and France were 'the closest military partners in the EU [...] There is therefore no contradiction between our celebrating British military heroism at Waterloo and our close military relationship with France, which has held through two world wars and continues to this day.'[590]

Doubtless mindful in part of the same considerations, the 8th Duke of Wellington wrote that:

> I am often asked whether we should not now, in these days of European unity, forget Waterloo and the battles of the past. My reply is, history cannot be forgotten and we need to be reminded of the bravery of the thousands of men from many nations who fought and died in a few hours on 18th June 1815 and why their gallantry and sacrifice ensured peace in Europe for 50 years.

His words appeared on the website of Waterloo 200, a body independent of government, officially launched at Apsley House in 2009 to plan for the bicentenary. The group's more general aim was to promote a greater understanding of the campaign and period. An '1815 trust' was to be created, geared especially towards young people, whose objective was 'a legacy which takes us all forward into a new European perspective'. Planned national events included a Waterloo dinner, exhibitions at the National Portrait Gallery and British Library, a thanksgiving service at St Paul's and a re-enactment of Major Henry Percy's journey in bringing the Waterloo Despatch to London.[591] The organisation also hoped to encourage local communities to hold their own celebrations, focusing on men known by them to have served in the 1815 campaign. That was a good idea, reflecting, as the present work demonstrates, the reality of the essentially local approach to Waterloo Day commemorations during Wellington's lifetime. Unfortunately, however, it put the onus on local historians to research that information – with no necessary guarantee of success. British bicentenary commemoration consequently risked being both protean and haphazard.

Waterloo 200 also, understandably, sought to harmonise its aims with preparations going forward for the bicentenary in Belgium. The anniversary was better remembered there, partly because it always had been, and partly because there was a growing understanding in mainland Europe during the later twentieth century of what Waterloo meant – or was said to mean. The relative tranquillity of Europe in the century after 1815 seemed attractive juxtaposed with the two global conflicts of the first half of the twentieth century. The 1957 Treaty of Rome, which created the EEC, had clearer echoes, however faint or imaginary, of the earlier period with its Concert of Europe, than the latter. In 1985, Maurice Huisman founded *Waterloo. Relais de L'Histoire*. In doing so, he characterised the battlefield 'as a valuable symbol of the futility of war and the necessity of peace and European unity'. The dramatic end to the divided Europe of the Cold War in 1989–1990, followed by the creation of the European Union in 1994, made the theme of European unity ever more alluring. On the 180th anniversary of the battle in 1995, the mayor of Waterloo, Serge Kubla, declared that he wanted the site to be an expression of the European ideal, not 'an historical or emotional revival of the past'.[592]

The main practical outcome for 2015 was a new visitor centre at Mont St Jean. As late as 2000, Major Graeme Cooper was reflecting on how little still had changed there in the perennially uneven struggle between tourism and commemoration. He was especially infuriated that a go-kart racing circuit had appeared near the foot of the Lion's Mound. 'To mark Europe's transition to peace and to remember those who died,' he pleaded, 'should we not, as Europeans, render the field of Waterloo the same respect as that accorded Gettysburg?' Thankfully, others agreed. The new complex, planned since 2004, and catalysed by the impending bicentenary, became part of a more ambitious scheme to restore the landscape in ways that would allow visitors to gain a better idea of how it appeared in 1815. Sadly, these did not extend to recreating the slope in front of Wellington's line by removing the Lion's Mound. Rather, they involved demolishing buildings in order to give the visitor a more uninterrupted view of it! The construction of large exhibition galleries 5 metres below ground, however, represented a major advance. They included a wall of remembrance, which whilst falling short of listing the names of all known combatants in the battle, did at least list all the regiments who fought in it. A central war memorial to all the British dead was incorporated into the walls of the restored Hougoumont. At last the British Army could be said to have been permanently memorialised on its most famous battlefield.[593]

Ironically, it was a French visitor to the battlefield in 1829 who reflected on the incongruity that, 'Wellington alone disdained to erect column or obelisk to eternalize his glory; iron and marble yield to time, whereas the victory itself will remain his everlasting monument.' Monsieur Saintine would have been amazed to learn that the Duke's role would be marginalised during the commemorative events of 2015. Wellington's countrymen continue to know him best as an item of footwear. At least they have heard of him. Not so, apparently, many of the Japanese or Korean visitors who today number amongst the 250,000 or so annual visitors to Waterloo. The attraction for them is Napoleon. Belgians too, therefore, for commercial as well as cultural and historic reasons, look more fondly on the Emperor than the Duke. The latter lacks the wide appeal of Churchill amongst Europeans as a standard bearer in the cause of freedom. For a generation and more now, Wellington has been the intermittent target of some Belgian deputies who would like to see an end to the annuity paid to him and his descendants since 1817. Whether he would react with indifference, amusement or irritation to these facts is impossible to say: probably all three, depending upon mood and who was asking the question. And yet the Duke, who liked simplicity, provided only days after the battle as good an epitaph on it (as well as a revealing insight into his own character), as any that would be suggested in the following two hundred years: 'It is a bad thing to be always fighting.'[594]

Select Bibliography

The following comprises those titles which I have found the most useful for the present study. Other works used are cited in the notes at the end of each chapter.

Primary Sources

Hartley Library, University of Southampton
Wellington Papers
Broadlands Papers

Parliamentary Debates

Newspapers and Periodicals

Aberdeen Journal
Annual Register
Belfast Newsletter
Birmingham Daily News
Birmingham Daily Post
Blackburn Standard

Bradford Observer
Brighton Patriot
Bristol Mercury
Bury & Norwich Post
Caledonian Mercury
Chartist Circular
Cheshire Observer
Derby Mercury
Dundee Courier
Edinburgh Review
The Era
Essex Standard
The Examiner
Exeter Flying Post
Freeman's Irish Journal
Glasgow Herald
Hampshire Advertiser
Hampshire Chronicle
Hampshire Telegraph
Hull Packet
Illustrated London News
Ipswich Journal
Lancaster Gazette
Leeds Mercury
Leeds Weekly
Leicester Chronicle
Liverpool Mercury
Lloyd's Weekly London Newspaper
The London Dispatch
Manchester Times
Morning Chronicle
Morning Post
Newcastle Courant
North Wales Chronicle
North-Eastern Daily Gazette
Northern Star
Nottinghamshire Guardian
Oxford Journal

Pall Mall Gazette
Political Register
Preston Guardian
Punch
Quarterly Review
Royal Cornwall Gazette
Salford City Reporter
Salisbury and Winchester Journal
Sheffield Independent
The Spectator
The Sphere
The Standard
The Times
Worcester Journal
York Herald

Books

Place of publication is London, unless otherwise stated.

Adkin, Mark, *The Waterloo Campaign: The Complete Guide to History's Most Famous Land Battle* (Aurum Press, 2001).

Albemarle, George Thomas, 6th Earl of, *Fifty Years of My Life*, 2 vols. (Macmillan, 1876).

Aldington, Richard, *Wellington* (Heinemann, 1946).

Andress, David, *The Savage Storm: Britain on the Brink in the Age of Napoleon* (Little Brown, 2012).

Anglesey, Marquis of, *One Leg: The Life and Letters of Henry William Paget* (Jonathan Cape, 1961).

Balen, Malcolm, *A Model Victory* (Harper Collins, 2005).

Bamford, Francis and 7th Duke of Wellington (eds.), *The Journal of Mrs Arbuthnot 1820–1832*, 2 vols. (Macmillan, 1950).

Barbero, Alessandro, *The Battle: A New History of the Battle of Waterloo* (Atlantic Books, 2006).

Barker, Juliet, *The Brontës* (Weidenfeld & Nicolson, 1994).

Batty, Captain Robert, *An Historical Sketch of the Campaign of 1815*, 2nd edition (Rodwell & Martin, 1820).

Becke, A. F., *Napoleon and Waterloo*, new edition (Kegan Paul, 1939).

Bew, John, *Castlereagh: Enlightenment, War and Tyranny* (Quercus, 2011).

Black, Jeremy, *Waterloo* (Icon Books, 2010).

Brett-James, Antony, *The Hundred Days* (Macmillan, 1964).

Bromley, David & Janet, *Wellington's Men Remembered* (Barnsley: Pen & Sword, 2012).

Bryant, Sir Arthur, *The Great Duke* (Collins, 1971).

Byron, Lord, *Childe Harold's Pilgrimage*, Canto the Third (John Murray, 1816).

Chandler, David, *Waterloo: The Hundred Days* (George Philip, 1981).

Chandler, David & Beckett, Ian (eds.), *The Oxford History of the British Army* (Oxford: Oxford University Press, 1994).

Chesney, Charles C., *Waterloo Lectures: The Campaign of 1815* (Longmans, Green & Co., 1868).

Cooper, Thomas, *The Life of Thomas Cooper* (Hodder & Stoughton, 1872).

Cornwell, Bernard, *Sharpe's Waterloo* (Harper Collins, 1990).

Cotton, Edward, *A Voice from Waterloo*, 7th edition (B. Green, 1877).

Creasy, Sir Edward, *Fifteen Decisive Battles of the World* (Richard Bentley, 1867).

Cruttwell, C. R., *Wellington* (Duckworth, 1936).

Curry, Kenneth (ed.), *New Letters of Robert Southey*, 2 vols. (Columbia University Press, 1965).

Dallas, Gregor, *1815: The Roads to Waterloo* (Pimlico, 1996).

David, Saul, *All the King's Men: The British Soldier from the Restoration to Waterloo* (Penguin, 2012).

Davies, Huw J., *Wellington's Wars: The Making of a Military Genius* (Yale University Press, 2012).

De Lancey, Magdalene, *A Week at Waterloo: Letter of a War Widow* (Reportage Press, 2008).

Edgcumbe, Richard (ed.), *The Diary of Frances, Lady Shelley 1767–1817*, 2 vols. (John Murray, 1912–1913).

Elwin, Malcolm (ed.), *The Autobiography and Journals of Benjamin Robert Haydon*, new edition (MacDonald, 1950).

Esdaile, Charles, *The Peninsular War* (Penguin, 2002).

Esdaile, Charles, *Napoleon's Wars: An International History, 1803–1815* (Penguin, 2007).

Fletcher, Ian, *A Desperate Business: Wellington, the British Army and the Waterloo Campaign* (Staplehurst: Spellmount, 2001).

Fortescue, Sir John, *The Campaign of Waterloo*, new edition (Macmillan, 1987).

Foster, R. E., *The Politics of County Power: Wellington and the Hampshire Gentlemen 1820–1852* (Hemel Hampstead: Harvester Press, 1990).

Foster, R. E., *The Duke of Wellington in Hampshire 1817–1852* (Winchester: Hampshire County Council, 2010).

Fraser, Sir William, *Words on Wellington* (John C. Nimmo, 1899).

Frazer, Sir Augustus, *Letters of Colonel Sir Augustus Simon Frazer* (Longmans & Roberts, 1859).

Fuller, J. F. C., *The Decisive Battles of the Western World, and their Influence upon History* (Eyre & Spottiswoode, 1955).

Gash, Norman (ed.), *Wellington: Studies in the Military and Political Career of the First Duke of Wellington* (Manchester: Manchester University Press, 1990).

Gash, Norman, *Wellington Anecdotes: A Critical Survey* (Southampton: Hartley Institute, 1992).

Gaunt, Richard A., *Sir Robert Peel: The Life and Legacy* (I.B. Tauris, 2010).

Gleig, G. R., *The Life of Arthur, Duke of Wellington*, 3rd edition (J.M. Dent, 1864).

Gleig, G. R. *Story of the Battle of Waterloo* (New York: Harper & Brothers, 1875).

Gleig, Mary (ed.), *Reminiscences of the First Duke of Wellington* (New York: Charles Scribner, 1904).

Glover, Gareth (ed.), *Letters from the Battle of Waterloo* (Greenhill Books, 2004).

Glover, Gareth (ed.), *The Waterloo Archive*, 5 vols. (Barnsley: Pen & Sword, 2010–2013).

Glover, Michael, *Wellington as Military Commander* (B.T. Batsford, 1968).

Gourgaud, G., *The Campaign of MDCCCXVIII* (James Ridgway, 1818).

Grierson, H. (ed.), *The Letters of Sir Walter Scott 1815–1817* (Constable, 1933).

Griffith, P. (ed), *Wellington Commander: The Iron Duke's Generalship* (Chichester: Antony Bird, 1986).

Gronow, Rees, *The Reminiscences and Recollections of Captain Gronow* (Nunney: R.S. Surtees Society, 1984).

Guedalla, Philip, *The Duke*, new edition (Hodder & Stoughton, 1974).

Gurwood, J. (ed.), *The Despatches of Field-Marshal the Duke of Wellington, KG, during his various campaigns [...] from 1799 to 1818*, 13 vols. (John Murray, 1837–1839).

Hamilton-Williams, David, *Waterloo: New Perspectives* (Arms & Armour Press, 1993).

Hardy, Thomas, *The Dynasts* (Macmillan, 1910).

Harvey, Robert, *The Mavericks: The Military Commanders who changed the course of History* (Constable, 2008).

Hawker, Peter, *The Diary of Colonel Peter Hawker 1802–1853*, 2 vols. (Greenhill Books, 1988).

Henty, G. A., *One of the 28th: A Tale of Waterloo* (Collins, 1890).

Heyer, Georgette, *An Infamous Army* (Heinemann, 1937).

Hibbert, Christopher, *Waterloo* (New English Library, 1967).

Hibbert, Christopher, *Wellington: A Personal History* (Harper Collins, 1997).

Hill, Joanna, *Wellington's Right Hand: Rowland, Viscount Hill* (Stroud: The History Press, 2011).

Hilton, Boyd, *A Mad, Bad & Dangerous People? England 1783–1846* (Oxford: Clarendon Press, 2006).

Hofschröer, Peter, *1815: The Waterloo Campaign. Wellington, His German Allies and the Battles of Ligny and Quatre Bras* (Greenhill Books, 1998).

Hofschröer, Peter, *1815: The Waterloo Campaign. The German Victory* (Greenhill Books, 1999).

Hofschröer, Peter, *Wellington's Smallest Victory* (Faber & Faber, 2004).

Holmes, Richard, *Redcoat: The British Soldier in the Age of Horse and Musket* (Harper Collins, 2001).

Holmes, Richard, *Wellington* (Harper Collins, 2002).

Horne, Alistair, *How Far From Austerlitz? Napoleon 1805–1815* (Macmillan, 1996).

Horward, Donald D. (ed.), *Napoleonic Military History: A Bibliography* (Greenhill Books, 1986).

Houssaye, Henry, *1815: Waterloo*, 31st edition (Adam & Charles Black, 1900).

Howarth, David, *Waterloo: A Near Run Thing* (Collins, 1968).

Hugo, Victor, *Les Misérables* (Penguin Classic edition, 1982).

James, Lawrence, *The Iron Duke: A Military Biography of Wellington* (Weidenfeld & Nicolson, 1992).

Jennings, Louis J. (ed.), *The Croker Papers*, 3 vols. (John Murray, 1884–1885).

Jupp, Peter, *British Politics on the Eve of Reform. The Duke of Wellington's Administration, 1828–30* (Macmillan, 1998).

Keegan, John, *The Face of Battle* (Jonathan Cape, 1976).

Kennedy, Sir James Shaw, *Notes on the Battle of Waterloo* (John Murray, 1865).

Kincaid, John, *Adventures in the Rifle Brigade* (T. & W. Boone, 1830).

Lambert, Andrew, *Nelson: Britannia's God of War* (Faber & Faber, 2004).

Lambert, Andrew, *The Immortal and the Hero* (Southampton: Hartley Institute, 2005).

Leeke, Reverend William, *The History of Lord Seaton's Regiment*, 2 vols. (Hatchards, 1866).

Longford, Elizabeth, *Wellington: Years of the Sword* (Weidenfeld & Nicolson, 1969).

Longford, Elizabeth, *Wellington: Pillar of State* (Weidenfeld & Nicolson, 1972).

Longford, Elizabeth, *Wellington* (Weidenfeld & Nicolson, 1992).

Lukacs, John, *Historical Consciousness: The Remembered Past* (New Jersey: Transaction Publishers, new edition, 1994).

MacBride, MacKenzie (ed.), *With Napoleon at Waterloo* (Francis Griffiths, 1911).

Mallinson, Allan, *A Close Run Thing* (Bantam Press, 1999).

Mallinson, Allan, *The Making of the British Army* (Bantam Press, 2009).

Maxwell, Sir Herbert, *The Life of Wellington*, 2 vols. (Sampson Low, 1899).

Maxwell, Sir Herbert (ed.), *The Creevey Papers*, 2 vols. (John Murray, 1903).

Maxwell, William Hamilton, *Life of Field Marshal His Grace the Duke of Wellington*, 3 vols. (A.H. Bayly & Co., 1839–1841).

Matthew, H. C. G. and Harrison, Brian, (eds.), *Oxford Dictionary of National Biography*, 61 vols. (Oxford: Oxford University Press, 2004).

Mercer, Cavalié, *Journal of the Waterloo Campaign* (New York: Da Capo Press, 1927).

Müffling, Carl von, *History of the Campaign of the British, Dutch, Hanoverian, and Brunswick Armies etc.* (T. Egerton, 1816).

Muir, Rory, *Britain and the Defeat of Napoleon 1807–1815* (Yale University Press, 1996).

Muir, Rory (ed.), *At Wellington's Right Hand: The Letters of Lieutenant-Colonel Sir Alexander Gordon 1808–1815* (Stroud: The History Press, 2003).

Naylor, John, *Waterloo* (B.T. Batsford, 1960).

Nokes, David, *Jane Austen* (Fourth Estate, 1997).

O' Meara, Barry E., *Napoleon in Exile; or, A Voice from St Helena*, 2 vols. (Philadelphia: Carey & Lea, 1822).

Oman, Charles, *Wellington Army 1809–1814* (Edward Arnold, 1913).

Owen, Edward (ed.), *The Waterloo Papers: 1815 and Beyond* (Tavistock: AQ & DJ Publications, 1998).

Paget, Sir Julian, *Hougoumont: the Key to Victory in Waterloo* (Pen & Sword, 1999).

Parker, C. S., *Sir Robert Peel, from His Private Papers*, 3 vols. (John Murray, 1891).

Pattison, Frederick Hope, *Personal Recollections of the Waterloo Campaign in a Series of Letters to His Grandchildren* (Glasgow: W.G. Blackie, 1873).

Purdy, Richard & Millgate, Michael (eds.), *The Collected Letters of Thomas Hardy*, 7 vols. (Oxford: Clarendon Press, 1978–1988).

Raikes, Thomas, *A Portion of the Journal Kept by Thomas Raikes, Esq, from 1831 to 1847*, 4 vols. (Longman, 1856–1857).

Ramsden, John, *Don't Mention the War: The British and the Germans since 1890* (Little, Brown, 2006).

Reeve, Henry (ed.), *The Greville Memoirs: A Journal of the Reigns of King George IV and William IV*, 3 vols. (Longman, 1874).

Reeve, Henry (ed.), *The Greville Memoirs: Victoria (second part). A Journal of the Reign of Queen Victoria from 1837 to 1852*, 3 vols. (Longman, 1885).

Roberts, Andrew, *Napoleon and Wellington* (Weidenfeld & Nicolson, 2001).

Roberts, Andrew, *Waterloo: Napoleon's Last Gamble* (Harper Collins, 2005).

Roberts, General Lord (Frederick), *The Rise of Wellington* (Sampson Low, Marston & Co., 1895).

Ropes, John Codman, *The Campaign of Waterloo: A Military History* (New York: Charles Scribner, 1893).

Scott, Walter, *Paul's Letters to His Kinsfolk* (Edinburgh: James Ballantyne, 1816).

Scott, Walter, *The Life of Napoleon Buonaparte*, 9 vols., 2nd edition (Edinburgh: James Ballantyne, 1827).

Severn, John, *Architects of Empire: The Duke of Wellington and His Brothers* (Oklahoma: University of Oklahoma Press, 2007).

Siborne, Major-General H. T., *Waterloo Letters*, new edition (Greenhill Books, 1993).

Siborne, William, *History of the War in France and Belgium*, 2 vols. (Constable, 1844).

Sinclair, Sir John, *The Correspondence of the Right Honourable Sir John Sinclair, Bart.*, 2 vols. (Colburn & Richard Bentley, 1831).

Sinnema, Peter W., *The Wake of Wellington: Englishness in 1852* (Athens, Ohio: Ohio University Press, 2006).

Smith, E. A., *Lord Grey 1764–1845* (Oxford: Oxford University Press, 1990).

Smith, E. A., *Wellington and the Arbuthnots* (Stroud: Alan Sutton, 1994).

Snow, Peter, *To War with Wellington: From the Peninsula to Waterloo* (John Murray, 2010).

Strafford, Alice, Countess of (ed.), *Personal Reminiscences of the Duke of Wellington by Francis, 1st Earl of Ellesmere* (John Murray, 1903).

Stanhope, Philip Henry, 5th Earl, *Notes of Conversations with the Duke of Wellington 1831–1851* (John Murray, 1888).

Sweetman, John, *Raglan: From the Peninsula to the Crimea* (Arms & Armour Press, 1993).

Thackeray, William Makepeace, *The Works of William Makepeace Thackeray*, 24 vols. (Smith, Elder & Co., 1879).

Thackeray, William Makepeace, *Vanity Fair* (Penguin Classic edition, 1968).

Thompson, Neville, *Wellington after Waterloo* (Routledge & Kegan Paul, 1986).

Tomalin, Claire, *Thomas Hardy: The Time-Torn Man* (Penguin, 2006).

Uffindell, Andrew and Corum, Michael, *Waterloo: The Battlefield Guide* (Greenhill Books, 2003).

Veve, Thomas Dwight, *The Duke of Wellington and the British Army of Occupation in France, 1815–1818* (Westport: Greenwood Press, 1992).

Weigall, Lady Rose (ed.), *The Correspondence of Lady Burghersh with the Duke of Wellington* (John Murray, 1903).

Weller, Jac, *Wellington at Waterloo* (Longmans, 1967).

Weller, Jac, *On Wellington: The Duke and His Art of War* (Greenhill Books, 1998).

Wellesley, Gerald (later 7th Duke of Wellington) and Steegman, John, *The Iconography of the First Duke of Wellington* (J.M. Dent & Sons, 1935).

Wellesley, Jane, *Wellington: A Journey Through My Family* (Weidenfeld & Nicolson, 2008).

2nd Duke of Wellington (ed.), *Supplementary Despatches and Memoranda of Field-Marshal Arthur Duke of Wellington, KG*, 15 vols. (John Murray, 1858–1872).

Wellington, 7th Duke of (ed.), *The Conversations of the First Duke of Wellington with George William Chad* (Cambridge: St Nicolas Press, 1956).

Wellington, 7th Duke of (ed.), *Wellington and His Friends* (Macmillan, 1965).

Wolffe, John, *Great Deaths: Grieving, Religion, and Nationhood in Victorian and Edwardian Britain* (Oxford: Oxford University Press, 2000).

Wolseley, Field-Marshal Viscount, *The Decline and Fall of Napoleon*, 3rd edition (Samson Low, Marston & Co., 1895).

Woolgar, C. M., *Wellington, His Papers and the Nineteenth-century Revolution in Communication* (Southampton: Hartley Institute, 2009).

Woolgar, C. M. (ed.), *Wellington Studies I* (Southampton: Hartley Institute, 1996).

Woolgar, C. M. (ed.), *Wellington Studies II* (Southampton: Hartley Institute, 1999).

Woolgar, C. M. (ed.), *Wellington Studies III* (Southampton: Hartley Institute, 1999).

Woolgar, C. M. (ed.), *Wellington Studies IV* (Southampton: Hartley Institute, 2008).

Woolgar, C. M. (ed.), *Wellington Studies V* (Southampton: Hartley Institute, 2013).

Zamoyski, Adam, *Rites of Peace: The Fall of Napoleon & the Congress of Vienna* (Harper Press, 2007).

Articles

Foster, R. E., 'Mr Punch and the Iron Duke', *History Today*, May 1984, pp. 36–42.

John Hussey, 'Towards a Better Chronology for the Waterloo Campaign', *War in History*, VII, 2000, pp. 463–480.

Semmel, Stuart, 'Reading the Tangible Past: British Tourism, Collecting and Memory After Waterloo', *Representations*, Winter 2000, pp. 9–37.

Notes

Introduction

1   A. Mallinson, *A Close Run Thing*, pp. 25, 34–5; M. Glover, *Wellington as Military Commander*, pp. 214–5.

2   P. Bew, *Castlereagh*, p. 400; *The Times*, 25 May 1846.

3   R. Southey, 'Poet's Pilgrimage to Waterloo', lines 16–18.

4   J. Fortescue, *The Campaign of Waterloo*, p. 197; *WS*, XII, pp. 155–6, Wellington to Clancarty, 3 December 1817.

5   Bew, *Castlereagh*, p. 400; V. Hugo, *Les Misérables*, p. 310.

6   Broadlands Archives, BR24/11/15, Palmerston to Elizabeth Temple, 29 October 1818. La Haye Sainte and Hougoumont have been variously spelt. For the sake of consistency, except in direct quotations, these are the forms adopted throughout. Likewise 'despatch' for 'dispatch'.

7   A. Uffindell & M. Corum, *On the Fields of Glory*, p. 41; *The Times*, 18 June 1920.

8   R. Gronow, *The Reminiscences and Recollections of Captain Gronow*, p. 184; *Manchester Times*, 27 May 1843.

9   *The Times*, 18 September 1952.

10 *The Times*, 18 February 1958; Sir E. Creasy, *Fifteen Decisive Battles of the World* (45th edition), pp. 354–5, 418–9; Uffindell & Corum, *Fields of Glory*, p. 319.

11 Fraser, p. 185; C. Mercer, *Journal of the Waterloo Campaign*, p. 388; M. MacBride (ed.), *With Napoleon at Waterloo*, pp. 137–8. Dickson died in July 1880.

12 *The Times*, 18 June 1932; W. Thackeray, *The Works of William Makepeace Thackeray*, XVI, pp. 334–5.

13 H. Siborne (ed.), *Waterloo Letters*, pp. 257–8, Dirom to Siborne, 27 February 1835; G. Glover (ed.), *Letters from the Battle of Waterloo*, pp. 65–8, Fricke to Siborne, 16 March 1835.

14 Glover, *Letters*, pp. 335–6, Vivian to Siborne, 19 April 1837; *Glasgow Herald*, 20 June 1866.

15 Creevey, I, pp. 102–3, Wellington to Ferguson, 22 June 1809. Whitbread (1758–1815), scion of the brewing family, Grey's brother-in-law & admirer of Napoleon, would commit suicide three weeks after Waterloo.

16 C. Woolgar, 'Writing the Despatch' in the author's *Wellington Studies II*, pp. 1–25, as also his *Wellington, His Papers and the Nineteenth-Century Revolution in Communication*, p. 10.

17 WP1/478/25, Wellington to Croker, 8 August 1815.

18 *Blackburn Standard*, 16 September 1846; S. Clarke, *1,000 Years of Annoying the French*, pp. 498–9.

19 Irish Nationalist ones too. Few were as vociferous in criticising his fellow Irishman and Waterloo as Daniel O'Connell. See for example *Morning Post*, 1 February 1836 & *The Times*, 18 November 1836.

20 http://news.bbc.co.uk/1/hi/scotland/2714071.stm.

21 Ellesmere, p. 82; Croker, III, p. 126, Wellington to Croker, 16 June 1847.

22 Stanhope, pp. 78, 331; A. Roberts, *Napoleon and Wellington*, pp. 244–6.

23 Ellesmere, pp. 64, note 1, 145–149; C. Greville, *Memoirs 1837–1852*, I, pp. 37–41.

24 Fraser, pp. 21–2.

25 *Belfast Newsletter*, 20 December 1844.

26 *Blackburn Standard*, 18 March 1835.

27 H. Davies, *Wellington's Wars*, pp. viii–x; Stanhope, p. 58.

1. Before Waterloo: Battles for Recognition 1769–1815

28 He was known as Wesley until May 1798, at which point he followed his brother Richard in adopting Wellesley. To reduce the risk of confusing the reader, the latter form is used here. For family background see E. Longford, *Wellington. The Years of the Sword*, chapters 1–3.

29 Ellesmere, p. 202; *The Times*, 11 May 1815.

30 N. Thompson, 'The Uses of Adversity' in N. Gash (ed.), *Wellington*, p. 3.

31 Gronow, *Reminiscences*, pp. 6–7; Longford, *Years of the Sword*, p. 19.

32 *The Times*, 5 October 1852.

33 *Belfast Newsletter*, 3 November 1852.

34 *Belfast Newsletter*, 3 November 1852.

35 Ellesmere, p. 102 note.

36 *The Times*, 5 October 1852.

37 Thompson, 'Uses of Adversity', p. 5.

38 Croker, I, p. 337 note; Ellesmere, pp. 79–80.

39 Stanhope, p. 182.

40 J. Severn, *Architects of Empire*, chapters 3–7.

41 *WS*, I, p. 209, Wellesley to Mornington, 6 April 1799; Shelley, II, pp. 24–6; *The Times*, 29 January 1829; Croker, II, pp. 102–3; S. David, *All the King's Men*, pp. 333–8.

42 *WD*, II, p. 403, Wellesley to Colonel James Stevenson, 19 October 1803.

43 Stanhope, pp. 49, 182; Croker I, p. 354; David, *All the King's Men*, pp. 351–60.

44 Longford, *Years of the Sword*, p. 93; *WD*, I, pp. 339–40, Wellesley to Munro, 1 November 1803.

45 *Morning Chronicle*, 14 October 1808; *The Times*, 7 January 1815.

46 Croker, II, p. 233.

47 *The Times*, 22 August 1806; Severn, *Architects of Empire*, chapter 8.

48 Thompson, 'Uses of Adversity', p. 7.

49   *The Times,* 4 November 1808.

50   *Morning Post*, 8 September 1808.

51   R. Gaunt, 'Wellington in Petticoats' in Woolgar (ed.), *Wellington Studies IV*, p. 140.

52   E. Owen (ed.), *The Waterloo Papers*, pp. 3–5; Severn, *Architects of Empire*, pp. 226–32.

53   *Morning Chronicle*, 14 October 1808; *The Times*, 4 November 1808; Creevey, I, pp. 89–90.

54   *The Times*, 8 & 22 October, 1808.

55   *The Times*, 23 November 1808.

56   *PD*, 1st series, XII, 23 January 1809, cols. 106–13.

57   Croker, I, pp. 32–3.

58   *Bury and Norwich Post*, 16 August 1809.

59   *The Times*, 11 September & 19 October 1809.

60   *The Times*, 27 September & 16 December 1809. An outspoken Radical, Waithman (c.1764–1833) was a turner's son. MP for London 1818–1820 & 1826–1833.

61   *Morning Chronicle*, 14 September 1809.

62   *PD*, 1st series, XV, 26 January 1810, cols. 130–54 & 16 February 1810, cols. 440–67; Croker, I, pp. 342–3.

63   *The Times*, 4 September 1809; Creevey, I, p. 128.

64   *The Times*, 6 January 1812.

65   *The Times*, 26 November 1810.

66   *PD*, 1st series, XIX, 26 April 1811, cols. 762–76; *Morning Post*, 5 July 1811.

67   *Morning Post*, 16 October 1810.

68   *The Times*, 11 January 1811.

69   *Liverpool Mercury*, 20 September & 25 October 1811; *The Times*, 8 January 1812. In later life Burdett (1770–1844) would become a Conservative & father of Wellington's friend Angela Burdett-Coutts.

70   *The Times*, 28 April & 5 May 1812, 10 May 1813; *PD*, 1st series, XXII, 27 April 1812, cols. 1069–77.

71   *The Times*, 13 July, 17 & 19 August 1812.

72   *PD*, 1st series, XXIV, 3 December 1812, cols. 135–46; *Hampshire Telegraph*, 24 August 1812; *Liverpool Mercury*, 2 October 1812; *Royal Cornwall Gazette*, 29 August 1812.

73   *The Times*, 18 & 19 August 1812.

74   *The Times*, 25 November 1812.

75   *Caledonian Mercury*, 8 July 1813.

76   WP1/373/6, Wellington to Bathurst, 2 July 1813.

77   *The Examiner*, 11 July 1813; *The Times*, 5 & 6 July 1813; *Ipswich Journal*, 30 October 1813.

78   *The Times*, 31 July & 9 November 1813, 6 September 1814.

79   For examples, *Morning Post*, 6 September & 9 October 1813.

80   *Bury and Norwich Post*, 29 December, 1813.

81   *The Times*, 4 February 1814; *Morning Post*, 16 February 1814.

82   *Morning Chronicle*, 1 April 1814.

83   *Caledonian Mercury*, 27 June 1814.

84   *PD*, 1st series, XXVII, 24 March 1814, cols. 346–55.

85   Creevey, I, p. 198; Longford, *Years of the Sword*, chapter 18.

86   G. Wellesley & J. Steegman, *The Iconography of the First Duke of Wellington*, p. 12.

87   *York Herald*, 26 June 1813; *Morning Post*, 31 July 1813; *The Times*, 23 February 1814.

88   *The Times*, 24 June 1814.

89   *The Times*, 10 July 1814.
90   C. Woolgar, 'Writing the Despatch', pp. 1–25; *The Times*, 8 July 1813.
91   Liverpool was Secretary for War and the Colonies 1809–1812, Bathurst succeeding him when he became Prime Minister. Wellesley was Foreign Secretary from December 1809 until March 1812 when Castlereagh succeeded him.
92   *PD*, 1st series, XII, 25 January 1809, cols. 145–8; *The Times*, 28 April 1812.
93   *Morning Chronicle*, 17 December 1813; Longford, *Years of the Sword*, p. 330.
94   *The Times*, 9 January 1813; *Morning Chronicle*, 17 December 1813; *PD*, 1st series, XXIV, 3 December 1812, cols. 135–40.
95   *The Times*, 26 April 1814; E. Smith, *Lord Grey*, p. 171.
96   *The Times*, 2 August & 12 October 1814.
97   *Morning Post*, 27 July 1814; *The Times*, 12 April 1814.
98   *The Times*, 16 April 1815.
99   WP1/644/7, letter of 16 April 1820; C. Esdaile, *The Peninsular War*, pp. 499–505.
100 *Morning Chronicle*, 17 December 1813.

2. Waterloo: The Battle of Giants

101 Stanhope, p. 245.
102 *The Times*, 23 November 1814.
103 *WD*, XII, pp. 295–7, Wellington to Clancarty, 10 April 1815.
104 *WD*, XII, pp. 346, 359–62, 438, Wellington to Clancarty, 3 May 1815, Wellington to Stewart, 8 May 1815 & Wellington to Sir H. Wellesley, 2 June 1815.
105 E. Cotton, *A Voice from Waterloo*, pp. 199–201.
106 *WS*, X, pp. 9–10, Torrens to Wellington, 31 March 1815; *WD*, XII, pp. 291–2, Wellington to Bathurst, 6 April 1815; Stanhope, p. 221.
107 *WS*, X, pp. 215–6, Bathurst to Wellington, 2 May 1815.
108 N. Gash, 'Wellington and the Waterloo Campaign' in Woolgar (ed.), *Wellington Studies II*, pp. 216–22.
109 *WD*, XII, p. 290, Wellington to Clancarty, 6 April 1815; Shelley, I, p. 172.
110 Ellesmere, p. 219.
111 *WD*, XII, pp. 449, 462, Wellington to Hardinge, 6 June 1815 & Wellington to Lynedoch, 13 June 1815.
112 *WS*, X, p. 481, Dörnberg to FitzRoy Somerset, 15 June 1815.
113 *WD*, XII, pp. 472–4, Wellington's memorandum of 15 June for De Lancey & Wellington to the Duc de Feltre at 10 p.m. on 15 June; *WS*, X, pp. 509–12, Müffling on Quatre Bras.
114 M. De Lancey, *A Week at Waterloo*, pp. 5–6; *The Times*, 5 & 29 May, 14 June 1815.
115 Gash, 'Wellington and the Waterloo Campaign', pp. 222–4.
116 J. Ropes, *The Campaign of Waterloo*, pp. 373–4.
117 Fortescue, *The Campaign of 1815*, pp. 75–6, 91, 117; Gash, 'Wellington and the Waterloo Campaign', pp. 224–5.
118 See below, p. 189.
119 *The Times*, 22 June 1815.
120 Glover, *Letters*, pp. 203–8, letter of Captain Albertus Cordemann.
121 G. Gourgaud, *The Campaign of MDCCCXV*, pp. 76–7, 85–6, 121–2, 199; Stanhope, p. 109.

122 Stanhope, pp. 109–10.

123 E. Owen (ed.), *Waterloo Papers*, p. 10.

124 Ropes, *Waterloo*, p. 386; *WD*, XII, p. 475, Wellington to Hill, 17 June 1815.

125 Stanhope, pp. 110–11; Gourgaud, *Campaign of MDCCCXV*, p. 81.

126 Pattison, *Personal Recollections*, pp. 20–1; Stanhope, p. 244.

127 *WD*, XII, pp. 476–8, Letters to Sir Charles Stuart, the Duc de Berri & the Governor of Antwerp; *WS*, X, p. 501, Wellington to Lady Frances Webster.

128 *WD*, XII, pp. 476–7, Wellington to the Duc de Berri, 18 June 1815; Fraser, p. 37. This thesis would also explain why, when/because the Battle of Waterloo was in the balance, Wellington dare not summon the force at Hal to Mont St Jean. Leaving them at Hal was neither oversight nor mistake but deliberate calculation.

129 D. Chandler, *Waterloo*, pp. 120–2.

130 Gash, 'Wellington and the Waterloo Campaign', pp. 222–3; Chandler, *Waterloo*, pp. 116–20; Longford, *Years of the Sword*, p. 490.

131 Cotton, *Voice from Waterloo*, p. 37; Owen, *Waterloo Papers*, p. 40.

132 Cotton, *Voice from Waterloo*, p. 37.

133 Ellesmere, p. 182; C. von Müffling, *History of the Campaign*, p. 143; Owen, *Waterloo Papers*, p. 12.

134 Cotton, *Voice from Waterloo*, pp. 32–3; Müffling, *History*, p. 147.

135 Cotton, *Voice from Waterloo*, pp. 42–3; *Morning Post*, 12 July 1845.

136 Stanhope, p. 18.

137 Fortescue, *Campaign of 1815*, pp. 137–9, 147; Gourgaud, *Campaign of MDCCCXV*, p. 89.

138 Fortescue, *Campaign of 1815*, p. 137; *WD*, XII, p. 529, Wellington to Beresford, 2 July 1815.

139 Müffling, *History*, p. 26.

140 Müffling, *History*, pp. 155–6, for the full letter which was widely reproduced.

141 MacBride (ed.), *With Napoleon at Waterloo*, pp. 169–78.

142 J. Weller, *Wellington at Waterloo*, pp. 106–15; Fortescue, *Campaign of 1815*, p. 165; Gourgaud, *The Campaign of MDCCCXV*, p. 102. Ney had attacked the Prussian line without orders at Jena in October 1806, necessitating Napoleon's rescuing him when he became over-extended.

143 Glover, *Letters*, pp. 241–52 for Major Baring's account of his defence of La Haye Sainte.

144 Ellesmere, pp. 208–9; Owen, *Waterloo Papers*, p. 13.

145 *Bradford Observer*, 10 July 1845.

146 Ellesmere, p. 101.

147 Fortescue, *Campaign of 1815*, p. 204; Müffling, *History*, pp. 18–9.

148 M. Adkin, *The Waterloo Companion*, pp. 83–4.

149 Weller, *Wellington at Waterloo*, chapters 11 & 12.

150 *The Times*, 27 June 1815; Owen, *Waterloo Papers*, pp. 42–3. *The Times* of 11 August 1815 carried a letter alleging that the wounded General Duhesme of the Young Guard, offering his surrender, had been cut down by a Brunswicker with the words '"the Duke fell yesterday, and thou shalt also bite the dust." So saying the black hussar cut him down. The fury of the Brunswickers no longer knew any bounds.'

151 P. Hofschröer, *1815. The Waterloo Campaign*, *passim*, especially p. 339. Napoleon abdicated on 22 June; on 3 July the Provisional Government agreed a convention to end hostilities.

152 *The Times*, 18 June 1934; Croker, I, p. 124; *WS*, X, p. 531, Wellington to Lady F. Webster, 19 June 1815.

153 R. Muir, *At Wellington's Right Hand*, pp. 404–9; Stanhope, p. 136.

154 Creevey, I, pp. 236–7; *Morning Post*, 25 September 1852. The letter is not currently in the public domain.

155 Extracts of the letter appeared in the *Morning Post,* 26 June 1815. It was auctioned in 1904. The fullest version is in *The Times*, 18 June 1915.

156 Adkin, *Waterloo Companion*, pp. 73–4; Chandler, *Waterloo*, pp. 171–2. The balance, beyond killed and wounded, is accounted for by c.3,300 who went missing. Half of these were Dutch-Belgians, c.500 Hanoverians. French losses are more problematic, perhaps 30,000 or more.

157 *Morning Post*, 25 September 1852; R. Weigall, *The Correspondence of Lady Burghersh with the Duke of Wellington*, pp. 112–3.

158 *WD*, XII, p. 562, Wellesley to Bathurst, 23 June 1815; Bew, *Castlereagh*, p. 400.

159 Scott, *Paul's Letters*, p. 195; *Morning Post*, 27 June 1815.

3. The Battle of Posterity: Opening Shots 1815–1818

160 *The Times*, 21 June 1815.

161 Stanhope, pp. 122, 172–4.

162 *The Times*, 3 August 1815.

163 *The Times*, 24 April 1811; *Royal Cornish Gazette*, 6 August 1814.

164 *WS*, X, pp. 508–9, Wellington to Sinclair, 8 June 1816; Ellesmere, p. 111; Stanhope, pp. 170–2; Woolgar, *Wellington, His Papers and the Nineteenth-Century Revolution in Communication*, pp. 16–9.

165 *WS*, X, pp. 534–8, letters from Alten and Kempt of 19 June 1815. *WD*, XII, pp. 478–87, for the Waterloo Despatch.

166 A. Zamoyski, *Rites of Passage*, pp. 488–9.

167 *The Times*, 23 June 1815.

168 *WS*, X, pp. 507–8, Wellington to Sinclair, 13 April 1816.

169 R. Harvey, *The Mavericks*, p. 246.

170 Müffling, *History of the Campaign*, p. 158; W. Scott, *Paul's Letters to his Kinsfolk*, p. 195.

171 Gourgaud, *The Campaign of MDCCCXV*, pp. 208–9; *The Times*, 6 October 1815.

172 *Morning Post*, 26 June 1815; *Royal Cornish Gazette*, 1 July 1815.

173 K. Curry (ed.), *New Letters of Robert Southey*, II, pp. 124–7, Southey to Wynn, 15 December 1815; Owen, *Waterloo Papers*, pp. 38–44, Barlow to his father, 7 July 1815; *The Times*, 8 November 1815.

174 *WD*, XII, p. 475, Wellington to Hill, 17 June 1815; *Leeds Mercury*, 5 August 1815.

175 Curry, *Southey*, II, pp. 124–7, Southey to Wynn, 15 December 1815; *WS*, X, pp. 508–9, Wellington to Mudford, 8 June 1815.

176 *WD*, XII, pp. 488–9, Wellington to Aberdeen, 19 June 1815 & Wellington to Beaufort, 19 June 1815; *The Times*, 23 June 1815; *Morning Post*, 26 June 1815.

177 *PD*, 1st series, XXXI, 23 June 1815, cols. 971–6; *The Times*, 24 & 29 June 1815.

178 *The Times*, 29 June 1815.

179 *Morning Chronicle*, 24 August 1815; *Lancaster Gazette*, 28 October 1815. See also *Morning Post*, 27 June 1815, *Liverpool Mercury*, 30 June 1815, *Caledonian Mercury* 3 & 27 July 1815.

180 *The Times*, 3 August 1815; WS, X, pp. 508–9, Wellington to Mudford, 8 June 1815.

181 *The Times*, 6 & 12 December 1815, 15 April & 7 August 1816.

182 *The Times*, 4 June 1816.

183 *The Times*, 3 February 1816.

184 *The Times*, 13 May 1816 & 30 April 1818; *Morning Post*, 18 November 1815 & 5 March 1817.

185 *The Times*, 3 & 6 July 1815, 9 October 1817.

186 *The Times*, 2 August 1816, 14 January & 5 June 1817, 27 November & 2 December 1818; P. Hofschröer, *Wellington's Smallest Victory*, pp. 19–22, 27–9.

187 *The Times*, 21 July 1815; *Morning Chronicle*, 24 August 1815.

188 *The Times*, 6 October 1815; *Caledonian Mercury*, 5 October 1815; *Morning Chronicle*, 15 January 1829; S. Semmel, 'Reading the Tangible Past', *Representations*, 2000, pp. 9, 21.

189 *The Times*, 8 November 1815.

190 *Leeds Mercury*, 9 September 1815.

191 H. Grierson (ed.), *The Letters of Sir Walter Scott*, pp. 78–85.

192 *Morning Chronicle*, 24 August 1815; *Liverpool Mercury*, 22 December 1815; *The Times*, 8 November 1815 & 16 June 1933; Semmel, 'Reading the Tangible Past', pp. 11–2.

193 Semmel, 'Reading the Tangible Past', p. 21; *Morning Post*, 3 October 1818.

194 *The Times*, 10 May 1816; Marquis of Anglesey, *One Leg*, p. 151.

195 *Liverpool Mercury*, 22 December 1815; *Hull Packet*, 5 August 1817.

196 Mercer, *Journal*, p. 189.

197 Scott, *Paul's Letters*, pp. 495–504 was amongst many who reproduced Decoster's testimony.

198 Semmel, 'Reading the Tangible Past', p. 12; Stanhope, p. 84; *The Times*, 18 June 1934.

199 *Morning Chronicle*, 27 June 1815; Semmel, 'Reading the Tangible Past', pp. 19, 28.

200 Owen, *Waterloo Papers*, pp. 35–6, T. Sydenham to B. Sydenham, 11 August 1815; Byron, *Childe Harold's Pilgrimage*, pp. 68–9.

201 Lord Byron, *Childe Harold's Pilgrimage*, p. 67 & *passim*.

202 L. James, *The Iron Duke*, p. 268.

203 *The Times*, 11 December 1817.

204 J. Wellesley, *Wellington*, p. 305; Croker, I, pp. 32–3; Grierson, *Letters*, pp. 91–6.

205 *Morning Chronicle*, 23 February 1816.

206 *Hampshire Telegraph*, 13 November 1815.

207 Grierson, *Letters*, pp. 78–9; Scott, *Paul's Letters*, pp. 171–6.

208 Owen, *Waterloo Papers*, pp. 33–5, T. Sydenham to B. Sydenham, 15 July 1815; *The Times*, 18 June 1934 wrongly ascribes the letter to General Allan. 'Padrone' was a sobriquet Wellington had acquired in the Peninsula.

209 Croker, I, p. 70; C. Parker, *Sir Robert Peel*, I, p. 182; *WD*, XII, pp. 578–9, 617, Wellington to Norcross, 31 July & 24 August 1815.

210 Curry, *Southey*, pp. 124–7, Southey to Wynn, 15 December 1815; *Quarterly Review*, XXVI, July 1815, pp. 448–526.

211 WP1/478/25 & WP1/478/54 for Wellington's letters to Croker of 8 & 17 August 1815. Most writers, probably following Sir Herbert Maxwell, erroneously ascribe the recipient as being Walter Scott.

212 Sir J. Sinclair, *The Correspondence of the Right Honourable Sir John Sinclair*, I, pp. 218–9.

213 *WS*, X, pp. 507–8, letters from Wellington to Sinclair & Mudford of 13 April & 2 May 1816 respectively. Mudford's history was a popular success; Sinclair contented himself with an edition of Müffling's account of the campaign.

214 *WS*, X, pp. 507–9, letters from Wellington to Sinclair & Mudford of 28 April & 8 June 1816.

215 Scott, *Paul's Letters*, pp. 500–1.

216 *The Times*, 29 July 1815; *Derby Mercury*, 16 November 1815.

217 *The Times*, 27 October, 4 & 17 November 1818; Roberts, *Napoleon and Wellington*, pp. 215–9.

218 Gourgaud, *Campaign of MDCCCXV*, pp. 108–9, 122–31.

219 *The Times*, 24 April 1818.

220 Anglesey, *One Leg*, p. 153.

221 *The Times*, 23 June 1815; *Morning Chronicle*, 1 July 1815.

222 *Caledonian Mercury*, 5 October 1815.

223 In 1859 & 1875 respectively. Before then, they lay buried in London.

224 *The Times*, 1 July, 7 August, 8 November 1815 & 16 June 1933; F. Hope Pattison, *Personal Recollections of the Waterloo Campaign*, p. 54.

225 E. de Selincourt (ed.), *The Letters of William and Dorothy Wordsworth*, II, pp. 670–4, D. Wordsworth to C. Clarkson, 28 June 1815.

226 Owen, *Waterloo Papers*, pp. 38–44, Barlow to his father, 7 July 1815. A failure to reflect the popular mood probably explains the ambivalent reception afforded J. M. W. Turner's *The Field of Waterloo* when it was first exhibited in 1818. With dead bodies strewn across the dark foreground, one reviewer preferred to see it as 'an allegorical representation' of war's suffering as opposed to the 'delineation of a particular battle'.

227 *Morning Post*, 3 November 1815.

228 *Morning Post*, 27 June & 12 July 1815, 15 January 1818.

229 *Morning Post*, 8 July & 8 August 1815, 14 October 1816, 12 April 1817; J. Barker, *The Brontës*, pp. 63–4; *WD*, XII, pp. 650–1, Wellington to Rowcroft, 28 September 1815.

230 *The Times*, 2 August 1815.

231 *WD*, XII, p. 636, Wellington to Bathurst, 17 September 1815.

232 *Royal Cornwall Gazette*, 16 October 1817; *The Times*, 15 January & 19 October 1818.

233 J. Austen, *Sanditon*, pp. 335–6.

234 *Morning Post*, 26 October 1815.

235 *PD*, 1st series, XXXI, 29 June 1815, cols. 1048–57. Wynn (1775–1850) generally espoused popular causes before 1832 but later became a moderate Conservative and Father of the House. *WS*, X, p. 554, York to Wellington, 22 June 1815.

236 *The Times*, 26 June & 11 July 1815, 4 May 1816; *Morning Post*, 3 & 29 July 1815.

237 *The Times*, 6 February 1816.

238 *The Times*, 30 May, 3 & 6 June 1817.

239 *The Times*, 19 June 1817. See also 8 June 1816 & 20 June 1817. The same day (18 June 1817), the people of Anglesey and Caernarvonshire dedicated a hundred foot column 'in grateful commemoration of the distinguished military achievements of their countrymen'.

240 *The Times*, 9 January 1816; *Morning Post*, 31 October 1817.

241 *The Times*, 2 December 1817; E. Longford, *Wellington. Pillar of State*, pp. 44–5.

242 R. Foster, 'The Duke of Wellington at Home', *The Historian*, Summer 1985, pp. 8–9. He also acquired Walmer Castle, his favourite home, on becoming Lord Warden of the Cinque Ports in 1829.

243 *The Times*, 12 July 1816 & 19 June 1817.

244 *The Times*, 22 November & 13 December 1815, 17 February 1816; Creevey, I, p. 246.

245 *The Times*, 14 March & 23 December 1818.

246 *The Times*, 5, 28 & 31 December 1818.

4. Heroes and Villains: Wellington, Waterloo and other Battles 1819–1832

247 Fraser, p. 41; *The Times*, 29 September & 6 October 1819, 27 October 1822, 26 February 1827; *Oxford Journal*, 22 December 1827.

248 Arbuthnot, I, pp. 36, 39, 55–6; *Morning Post*, 9 March 1821.

249 Creevey, I, p. 289.

250 In Canto nine of *Don Juan* (1819).

251 *The Times*, 27 July & 30 September 1819; J. Marlow, *The Peterloo Massacre*, pp. 13, 53–4, 84–5, 173–6.

252 R. Foster, *The Politics of County Power*, pp. 108–9; *PD*, 1st series, XLI, 2 Dec 1819, cols. 663–76; Ellesmere, pp. 122–3.

253 *The Times*, 29 August 1820; *Bury and Norwich Post*, 6 December 1820; Thompson, *Wellington after Waterloo*, pp. 33–6.

254 R. Foster, *The Politics of County Power*, p. 109; Creevey, II, p. 6; *PD,* 2nd series, IV, 25 January 1821, cols. 107–15; *The Times*, 19 April 1832.

255 Gaunt, 'Wellington in Petticoats', pp. 158–61; *The Times*, 3 & 7 September 1822.

256 Arbuthnot, I, pp. 116, 121–2; Creevey, II, p. 189; Stanhope, p. 184.

257 *Morning Post*, 15 July 1824; *Morning Chronicle*, 26 October 1825; *Hampshire Telegraph*, 23 December 1822; P. Hawker, *The Diary of Colonel Peter Hawker*, I, pp. 211–2.

258 *Hampshire Telegraph*, 23 December 1822; *Morning Post*, 15 July 1824, *Morning Chronicle*, 26 October 1825; *Hull Packet*, 24 November 1829.

259 *Morning Post*, 21 November 1826.

260 Semmel, 'Reading the Tangible Past', p. 9.

261 *Hampshire Telegraph*, 23 December 1822; *Morning Post*, 15 July 1824; *Hull Packet*, 24 November 1829.

262 I am grateful to Alan Lindsey for this reference. See also *Sheffield Independent*, 17 March 1832.

263 *Morning Chronicle*, 22 November 1825; *Illustrated London News*, 25 September & 27 November 1852. Shakespeare was reputed to have planted a mulberry tree at New Place, Stratford. It was felled in the mid-eighteenth century.

264 *The Times*, 22 September 1822; *The Standard*, 10 June 1830; W. Lovett, *Life and Struggles*, pp. 25–6.

265 *Lancaster Gazette*, 30 January 1819; Chad, p. 7.

266 *Morning Post*, 15 July 1824 & 23 June 1826; *Oxford Journal*, 18 November 1826; Uffindell & Corum, *Fields of Glory*, pp. 32–3.

267 *Morning Chronicle*, 26 October 1825; Arbuthnot, I, p. 413.

268 *Bristol Mercury*, 16 November 1830; Uffindell & Corum, *Fields of Glory*, pp. 33–4; Semmel, 'Reading the Tangible Past', p. 2; *Hull Packet*, 24 November 1829.

269 *Morning Post*, 21 November 1826; *The Times*, 2 August 1819.

270 *Morning Post*, 19 June 1821. Byron's lines are from *Don Juan*.

271 *The Times*, 9 July 1818 & 16 February 1819; *Morning Chronicle*, 29 January 1820; A. Lambert, *Nelson*, chapter 16.

272 *Freeman's Journal*, 30 March 1831.

273 *The Times*, 23 August 1825, 23 April & 3 July 1828; *The Examiner*, 10 June 1821; *Oxford Journal*, 6 July 1822.

274 *Morning Post*, 19 June 1827; *The Times*, 21 May 1828.

275 *Morning Post*, 19 & 20 June 1828; *The Times*, 18 June 1829; J. Flanders, *Consuming Passions*, pp. 317–9.

276 *Glasgow Herald*, 29 December 1820; *Morning Post*, 9 June 1831.

277 *Lancaster Gazette*, 12 June 1819; *Liverpool Mercury*, 24 June 1825; *Morning Chronicle*, 7 February 1821; *Hampshire Telegraph*, 22 June 1829.

278 *Hampshire Telegraph*, 28 June 1819; *Derby Mercury*, 17 August 1825; *Royal Cornwall Gazette*, 28 June 1828.

279 *Aberdeen Journal*, 12 June 1816; *Bury & Norwich Post*, 19 June 1816; *Leeds Mercury*, 24 July 1819.

280 *Morning Post*, 6 October 1825, 24 June 1826 & 25 June 1832.

281 *Morning Post*, 20 June 1825.

282 *The Times*, 19 June 1816; *Hampshire Telegraph*, 19 February 1827. Of the remainder, 189 died in the campaign, 268 had died since and 178 had either resigned or sold out.

283 *The Standard*, 27 June 1829.

284 *Leeds Mercury*, 24 June 1826.

285 *The Times*, 19 June & 12 July 1816; *Morning Post*, 27 June and 4 July 1821.

286 *The Times*, 23 June 1823.

287 Stanhope, p. 14.

288 *Ipswich Journal*, 17 December 1825; *Worcester Journal*, 21 June 1827.

289 *Freeman's Journal*, 26 June 1821; *Morning Post*, 28 June 1822 & 24 September 1828.

290 *Derby Mercury*, 21 March 1821; *Morning Post*, 1 December 1823 & 27 July 1829; *Oxford Journal*, 25 November 1826.

291 WP1/478/25, Wellington to Croker, 8 August 1815; *The Times*, 21 March 1818, 7 September 1819 & 4 February 1829; *Morning Post*, 19 April 1820; *York Herald*, 19 April 1823; *Worcester Journal*, 16 September 1824; *Leicester Chronicle*, 31 March 1827.

292 *Morning Chronicle*, 11 November 1827; *Belfast Newsletter*, 7 May 1830; *The Standard*, 7 November 1830.

293 *Bristol Mercury*, 26 August 1822; *Morning Chronicle*, 19 October 1824; *Morning Post*, 2 June & 14 December 1825.

294 *The Times*, 6 April 1831.

295 *Caledonian Mercury*, 24 June 1819.

296 *Morning Post*, 21 June 1821 & 20 June 1825; *Morning Chronicle*, 19 June 1822 & 7 June 1823.

297 *Morning Post*, 19 June 1829; *Royal Cornwall Gazette*, 25 June 1831.

298 *Morning Post*, 1 January 1821.

299 *Morning Post*, 14 May 1825.

300 *Morning Chronicle*, 3 September 1828.

301 The next five paragraphs draw on C. Greville, *Memoirs 1818–1837,* I, pp. 39–40, 71–2; Chad, pp. 2–7; Shelley, II, p. 33; Arbuthnot, I, pp. 234–5, 361–2; Ellesmere, p. 126; Stanhope, pp. 9, 15.

302 For this controversy see M. Adkin, *The Waterloo Companion*, pp. 415–6.

303 Shelley, II, p. 33; Arbuthnot, I, pp. 234–5, 361–2.

304 B. O'Meara, *Napoleon in Exile*, I, pp. 112–4, 299–301 & II, p. 233.

305 Arbuthnot, I, pp. 234–5; A. Roberts, *Napoleon and Wellington*, pp. 244–7.

306 *Morning Post*, 25 November 1829 & 14 April, 1830; *Liverpool Mercury*, 17 February 1832; *Morning Chronicle*, 15 January 1829.

307 J. Barker, *The Brontës*, p. 160.

308 *The Times*, 27 July 1827.

309 Roberts, *Napoleon and Wellington*, pp. 258, 260–1; W. Scott, *The Life of Napoleon Buonaparte*, VIII, pp. 478–518.

310 *The Times*, 20 July 1819 & 30 July 1821; *Morning Post*, 9 May 1825 & 15 June 1825.

311 S. Jenkins, 'Sir Thomas Lawrence and the Duke of Wellington' in Woolgar (ed.), *Wellington Studies IV*, pp. 126–39.

312 *The Examiner*, 16 June 1822.

313 H. Miles, 'Sir David Wilkie', *ODNB*, LVIII, pp. 965–70. See also *Morning Post*, 4 May 1822.

314 J. Black, *Waterloo*, p. 181; *Morning Chronicle*, 2 January 1819; *The Times*, 16 January 1819; *Morning Post*, 3 April 1819.

315 *Morning Post*, 28 June 1827; *Hull Packet*, 5 July 1831.

316 Creevey, II, pp. 112–3, 121–2; *The Times*, 14 April, 4 & 10 May 1827. It has become conventional to label politicians as either Protestant or Catholic according to where they stood on Catholic Emancipation, the most divisive issue in British politics in the generation after 1800.

317 Arbuthnot, II, pp. 126–7; *Morning Chronicle*, 19 June 1827; *Bury & Norwich Post*, 4 July 1827; Thompson, *Wellington after Waterloo*, pp. 63–4.

318 *The Standard*, 22 June 1827; *PD*, 2nd series, XVII, 18 June 1827, col. 1,317.

319 *The Times*, 1 October 1827; *The Standard*, 29 September 1827.

320 *The Times*, 2 & 9 October 1827; A. Heesom, 'Wellington's friend? Lord Londonderry and the Duke of Wellington' in Woolgar (ed.), *Wellington Studies III*, pp. 1–34.

321 *PD*, 2nd series, XVIII, 29 January 1828, cols. 66–7; *Political Register*, 23 February 1828.

322 K. Bourne (ed.), *The Letters of the third Viscount Palmerston to Laurence and Elizabeth Sulivan*, pp. 212–3; *The Examiner*, 1 June 1828.

323 Thompson, *Wellington after Waterloo*, pp. 82–96; K. Noyce, 'The Duke of Wellington and the Catholic question' in Gash (ed.), *Wellington*, pp. 139–58.

324 *The Standard*, 7 February 1829; *The Times*, 28 March & 19 June 1829.

325 *Leicester Chronicle*, 18 April 1829; *The Standard*, 18 June 1829; *The Times*, 4 March 1830.

326 Thompson, *Wellington after Waterloo*, pp. 91–3.

327 Arbuthnot, II, pp. 269–72.

328 *The Times*, 4 February 1829; *Political Register*, 28 November 1829, 13 March & 28 August 1830; *PD*, 2nd series, XXII, 4 February 1830, cols. 34–41; Thompson, *Wellington after Waterloo*, pp. 98–100.

329 Greville, *Memoirs 1818–1837*, II, p. 53; *PD*, 3rd series, I, 2 November 1830, cols. 44–53; Thompson, *Wellington after Waterloo*, pp. 105–7.

330 Ellesmere, p. 64 & note 1; *The Standard*, 22 November 1830.

331 Arbuthnot, II, p. 251; WP4/1/3/4/26, Wellington to Fleming, 27 May 1831.

332 *The Times*, 5 September & 13 October 1831; Thompson, *Wellington after Waterloo*, pp. 115–9. Wellington's London home had also been attacked on 27 April.

333 *Hampshire Advertiser*, 29 October 1831.

334 *The Times*, 23 May 1832; D. Rowe (ed.), *London Radicalism*, p. 82; Creevey, II, pp. 246–7.

335 *Worcester Journal*, 28 June 1832; *North Wales Chronicle*, 26 June 1832; Fraser, pp. 23–4.

336 J. A. Froude, *Thomas Carlyle*, II, p. 282; *The Times*, 4 June 1832.

337 *Hampshire Chronicle*, 25 June 1832; *The Times*, 15 May & 1 December 1832.

5. Wellington and Waterloo Despatched 1832–1852?

338 *Essex Standard*, 10 May 1839.

339 For overviews see Longford, *Wellington. Pillar of State* and Thompson, *Wellington after Waterloo*.

340 *The Times*, 19 June 1832; Greville, *Memoirs 1818–1837*, II, pp. 372–3.

341 *Morning Post*, 27 June 1832; *The Standard*, 20 June 1833.

342 Greville, *Memoirs 1818–1837*, III, pp. 92, 222–3; Ellesmere, pp. 45, 74; *Morning Chronicle*, 22 October 1834.

343 *Sheffield Independent*, 6 December 1834; Stanhope, p. 62.

344 *Derby Mercury*, 11 February 1835; Glover, *Letters*, p. 94, note 5.

345 *Morning Post*, 4 June 1835 & 15 June 1837; *The Standard*, 2 November 1839; *Glasgow Herald*, 21 June 1844.

346 *The Era*, 13 June 1841; *Morning Post*, 19 June 1841; *The Standard*, 29 July 1841.

347 Greville, *Memoirs 1837–1852*, I, pp. 18–9; A. Kriegel (ed.), *The Holland House Diaries*, p. 259.

348 The evidence of the passing years suggested that he could have qualified that judgement. That he chose not to made it akin to his line on the contribution of the Prussians at Waterloo.

349 Stanhope, p. 160; Greville, *Memoirs 1837–1852*, I, pp. 18–9; *PD*, 3rd series, XLIX, 16 July 1839, cols. 373–5.

350 *Morning Chronicle*, 31 July 1839. R. Foster, *The Politics of County Power*, pp. 29–31.

351 *Bradford Observer*, 13 June 1839; Greville, *Memoirs 1837–1852*, I, pp. 102–3; *Morning Chronicle*, 21 June 1838.

352 Greville, *Memoirs 1837–1852*, I, p. 296.

353 *Morning Chronicle*, 30 June 1838 & 20 November 1839.

354 *Hampshire Advertiser*, 26 December 1835 & 26 August 1837; *Morning Post*, 11 March 1845.

355 *Morning Post*, 5 November 1832; C. Woolgar, 'Wellington's Dispatches' in Woolgar (ed.), *Wellington Studies I*, pp. 189–210.

356 WP2/1/39–40, Gurwood to Wellington, 8 January 1833; WP2/1/60, same to same, 15 January 1833.

357 WP2/36/119, Wellington to Gurwood, 9 December 1835; Chad, *Conversations*, p. 19.

358 *Morning Chronicle*, 25 December 1845; *Chartist Circular*, 22 May 1841. Sir Thomas Munro, the letter's recipient, had earlier published it in 1830.

359 *Blackburn Standard*, 18 March 1835.

360 *The Times*, 6 April 1847; T. Raikes, *Journal*, IV, p. 203.

361 *Freeman's Irish Journal*, 23 November 1838, *Liverpool Mercury*, 23 November 1838 & *Aberdeen Journal*, 5 December 1838.

362 Raikes, *Journal*, IV, p. 203.

363 *Hampshire Advertiser*, 3 July 1847; *The Times*, 17 November 1848.

364 *Morning Post*, 11 March 1845. Maxwell (1791–1850), of Scots-Irish descent, later took holy orders but was deprived for non-residence.

365 *Morning Post*, 8 July 1842 & 27 September 1843; *Aberdeen Journal*, 23 November 1842.

366 Glover, *Letters*, pp. 326–7 & 334–5, for J. Gordon to Somerset, 1 November 1834 & Somerset to Siborne, 7 March 1837. See also M. Balen, *A Model Victory* & P. Hofschröer, *Wellington's Smallest Victory*.

367 *The Standard*, 25 December 1844; *Morning Post*, 5 October 1838; 7th Duke of Wellington (ed.), *Wellington and his Friends*, pp. 133–4, Wellington to Lady Wilton, 23 April 1840.

368 *Morning Post*, 9 July 1844.

369 W. Siborne, *History of the War in France and Belgium in 1815* (5th edition, 1900), preface and pp. 594–9.

370 G. Gleig, *Story of the Battle of Waterloo*, (1875 edition), pp. iii–iv, 252.

371 *Hampshire Advertiser*, 3 July 1847; Siborne, *History of the War in France and Belgium in 1815* (3rd edition, 1848), pp. ix–xxvii.

372 Stanhope, pp. 121, 245; Ellesmere, pp. 98–9; Roberts, *Napoleon and Wellington*, chapters 15–16.

373 Ellesmere, p. 211; Roberts, *Napoleon and Wellington*, pp. 269–71; Glover, *Letters*, p. 80, Cotton to Siborne, 7 September 1845.

374 *The Era*, 29 September 1839; Roberts, *Napoleon and Wellington*, pp. 263–5.

375 *The Times*, 18 February 1840 names Macdonell & Fraser as the beneficiaries. Corporal Graham and Private Lister have also been suggested as part recipients. Wellington also singled out the defence of Hougoumont for special mention at the 1851 Waterloo banquet.

376 WP2/35/1, Gurwood to Wellington, 1 August 1835. Ellesmere, pp. 82–3, 90, 234; Clausewitz's *History of the Campaign* was published posthumously in Prussia in 1835. He was chief of staff to Thielemann's III corps in 1815.

377 WP2/93/17, Wellington to Gurwood, 4 October 1842; Ellesmere, pp. 190–235; Roberts, *Napoleon and Wellington*, pp. 278–9; *Quarterly Review*, September 1842, October 1843 & June 1845.

378 Ellesmere, pp. 185–235. These include some final notes of September 1851.

379 Ellesmere, pp. 192, 210.

380 Fraser, pp. 45–7, 75.

381 M. Slater, *Charles Dickens*, pp. 53, 104; M. De Lancey, *A Week at Waterloo*, pp. 58–62, Dickens to Hall, 16 March 1841. Lady De Lancey was widow of Sir William.

382 C. Dickens, *The Christmas Books*, pp. 135–8.

383 Thackeray, *Works*, XVI, pp. 331–6; *Vanity Fair*, pp. 325, 806.

384 *Vanity Fair*, chapters 26–35, especially pp. 313, 341–5, 384–8.

385 Semmel, 'Reading the Tangible Past', pp. 27–8; Thackeray, *Works*, XVI, p. 336.

386 *Morning Post*, 22 April 1839; Semmel, 'Reading the Tangible past', p. 26; Thackeray, *Works*, XVI, p. 333.

387 *Bristol Mercury*, 23 July 1836; *Morning Post*, 22 April 1839; Cotton, *Voice from Waterloo*, pp. 25, 28.

388 Uffindell & Corum, *Fields of Glory*, pp. 281–9; *Morning Post*, 22 April 1839; Cotton, *Voice from Waterloo*, pp. 25, 28.

389 *Morning Chronicle*, 3 January 1833; *Morning Post*, 22 April 1839; *Belfast Newsletter*, 7 July 1843.

390 B. Elmer, 'Dialogue at Waterloo', *Waterloo Journal*, XVIII, August 1996, pp. 13–6; Wellington, *Iconography*, p. 68; *The London Dispatch*, 6 January 1839.

391 From Wordsworth's sonnet, 'On a Portrait of the Duke of Wellington upon the field of Waterloo', *by Haydon*, lines 1–10.

392 *Aberdeen Journal*, 14 July 1847; *The Times*, 3 July 1849.

393 *Liverpool Mercury*, 2 October 1835; *Hampshire Advertiser*, 20 February 1836; *The Times*, 30 June 1836.

394 *The Times*, 12 June 1843.

395 *Bradford Observer*, 25 September 1845.

396 *Morning Post*, 17 September 1833, 13 September 1838 & 30 June 1843.

397 *The Times*, 5 September 1844.

398 *The Times*, 29 February 1836 & 9 March 1839.

399 *Morning Post*, 30 December 1845.

400 *The Standard*, 13 June 1837; *Caledonian Mercury*, 1 July 1837; *Manchester Times*, 23 September 1837; *The Times*, 8 April 1846 & 2 June 1852.

401 *Worcester Journal*, 21 June 1838.

402 *Manchester Times*, 22 June 1833; *Northern Star*, 7 July 1840; *York Herald*, 30 June 1849.

403 *Leicester Chronicle*, 10 May 1845.

404 *York Herald*, 30 June 1849; N. Edsall, *Richard Cobden*, chapter 17.

405 *Sheffield Independent*, 3 July 1841.

406 *The Examiner*, 14 June 1835; *Hampshire Advertiser*, 23 June 1838; *The Times*, 17 June 1836; *Freeman's Irish Journal*, 19 June 1838. The Waterloo Cup, last run in 2005, fell victim to the 2004 Hunting Act.

407 *The Times*, 3 July 1840 & 22 March 1842; *The Standard*, 2 April 1844.

408 *Morning Post*, 5 November 1846.

409 Thackeray, *Works*, XVI, p. 336; *Essex Standard*, 1 July 1836; *Bristol Mercury*, 20 June 1835; *Morning Post*, 4 October 1840.

410 *Caledonian Mercury*, 7 May 1840; *The Times*, 21 June 1838; *Newcastle Courant*, 21 June 1844. The station became 'Waterloo' in 1886.

411 *Bury and Norwich Post*, 19 November 1834 & 24 June 1840.

412 *Preston Guardian*, 20 June 1846.

413 *The Times*, 14 August 1845; Thackeray, *Works*, p. 335.

414 *Caledonian Mercury*, 5 March 1846; *Lloyd's Weekly London Newspaper*, 29 June 1845; *PD*, 3rd series, LXXXIV, 2 March 1846, cols. 418–19.

415 *Northern Star*, 28 June 1845; Thackeray, *Works*, pp. 335–6.

416 *Morning Post*, 20 June 1836; *Hull Packet*, 26 June 1840; *The Times*, 19 June 1841; *Morning Chronicle*, 20 June 1843.

417 *Morning Post*, 21 June 1837; Greville, *Memoirs 1837–1852*, II, p. 15.

418 *Morning Chronicle*, 19 June 1845.

419 *The Times*, 19 June 1849, 19 June 1850 & 19 June 1852.

420 *Essex Standard*, 28 June 1844.

421 *Derby Mercury*, 2 September 1835; *Morning Post*, 21 June 1837. In 1836, Lady Burghersh commissioned William Salter to immortalise the event in oils. The painting was completed in 1841.

422 *The Times*, 7 December 1840; *The Standard*, 10 October 1844.

423 *The Times*, 18 June 1844 & 19 June 1852.

424 *Morning Post*, 18 June 1841; Ellesmere, p. 89.

425 *Exeter Flying Post*, 7 June 1838; *Morning Chronicle*, 2 August 1838.

426 *Manchester Times*, 22 November 1845; *Essex Standard*, 9 July 1841.

427 *Derby Mercury*, 17 December 1845; *Morning Post*, 29 January 1846; Greville, *Memoirs 1837–1852*, II, pp. 341, 350–1.

428 *Aberdeen Journal*, 21 February 1838; R. Foster, 'Mr Punch and the Iron Duke', *History Today* (May 1984), pp. 36–42.

429 *Lloyd's Weekly London News*, 18 January 1846; Greville, *Memoirs 1837–1852*, I, p. 262.

430 *Dundee Courier*, 7 October 1845; E. Ashley, *The Life of Henry John Temple, Lord Palmerston*, II, pp. 177–8; *Leicester Chronicle*, 12 May 1849.

6. Victorians Remember: Wellington and Waterloo Reassessed 1852–1901

431 Shelley, II, p. 308 ; G. Story, K. Tillotson & N. Burgis (eds.), *The Letters of Charles Dickens*, VI, p. 821, Dickens to Messrs Macmillans, 10–15 Dec 1852.

432 R. Foster, 'Bury the Great Duke' in Woolgar (ed.), *Wellington Studies V*, pp. 299–328.

433 *Dickens*, p. 805, note 1; *Preston Guardian*, 13 November 1852.

434 J. Wolffe, *Great Deaths*, pp. 38–9; Roberts, *Napoleon and Wellington*, pp. 283–7.

435 Thomas Cooper, *The Life of Thomas Cooper*, pp. 330, 333.

436 *Glasgow Herald*, 27 September 1852.

437 *The Examiner*, 23 October 1852; *The Times*, 15 & 16 September 1852; I. Brunskill & A. Sanders (eds.), *Great Victorian Lives*, pp. vii–xiii.

438 *Bristol Mercury*, 28 November 1840; *Hampshire Chronicle*, 25 September 1852; *Salisbury and Winchester Journal*, 18 September 1852.

439 A. Lambert, *The Immortal and the Hero*, p. 18; *The Times*, 10 November 1852.

440 *Dickens*, pp. 764–5, Dickens to Angela Burdett-Coutts, 23 September 1852.

441 P. Hawker, *Diary*, II, p. 349.

442 *The Examiner*, 18 September 1852; *Daily News*, 22 October 1852; *The Times*, 18 September 1852.

443 *The Standard*, 6 November 1852; *Lloyd's Weekly Newspaper*, 25 September & 14 November 1852.

444 *Morning Post*, 18 November 1852; *The Standard*, 21 October 1852.

445 *The Era*, 12 June 1853; *Glasgow Herald*, 13 June 1853; *Manchester Times*, 15 June 1853.

446 *York Herald*, 25 June 1853; *Essex Standard*, 24 June 1853.

447 *Belfast Newsletter*, 21 June 1854 & 19 June 1856; *Morning Post*, 23 June 1855.

448 *The Times*, 9 July 1853, 16 November & 30 December 1854.

449 *Hull Packet*, 29 June 1855; *Cheshire Observer*, 30 June 1855; *PD*, 3rd series, CXXXVIII, 18 June 1855, col. 2,149.

450 Fraser, p. 173.

451 F. Roberts, *The Rise of Wellington*, pp. 175–6, 184; D. Chandler & I. Beckett (eds.), *The Oxford History of the British Army*, chapters 8–9. Sir Garnet Wolseley was supposedly the subject of Gilbert's caricature in the *Pirates of Penzance*.

452 *Morning Post*, 22 June 1858; *Morning Chronicle*, 22 June 1858; *Lloyd's Weekly Newspaper*, 19 June 1859.

453 *Leicester Chronicle*, 22 June 1861; *Worcester Journal*, 21 June 1862; *Bury and Norwich Post*, 23 June 1863; Mercer, *Journal*, pp. 191–3, 397–8.

454 *Preston Guardian*, 25 June 1853, 24 June 1854 & 21 June 1856; *Blackburn Standard*, 27 June 1855.

455 *Preston Guardian*, 19 June 1861.

456 *The Times*, 23 August 1856; http://pmsa.cch.kcl.ac.uk/MR/MR-MCR11.htm.

457 *The Times*, 31 January 1859 & 20 June 1870.

458 Longford, *Years of the Sword*, pp. 16–7; *Nottinghamshire Guardian*, 23 September 1852; *The Times*, 2 February 1857 & 24 June 1885; *Leeds Mercury*, 19 July 1865. *PD*, 3rd series, XXVIII, 12 June 1835, col. 710.

459 *The Standard*, 28 June 1847; *The Times*, 1 May 1863; J. Ramsden, *Don't Mention the War*, p. 17.

460 *North Wales Chronicle*, 20 May 1865; *Liverpool Mercury*, 2 June 1865; *York Herald*, 1 July 1865.

461 *Worcester Journal*, 17 June 1865; *Leeds Weekly*, 25 June 1865; *The Times*, 4 July 1865.

462 *Sheffield and Rotherham Independent*, 20 June 1865; *Leeds Mercury*, 21 June 1865; *Lancaster Gazette*, 24 June 1865.

463 Hope Pattison, *Personal Recollections*, pp. 1–2.

464 *The Times*, 27 June 1865.

465 Hugo, *Les Misérables*, pp. 313–20.

466 *The Times*, 20 June 1864, 18 June 1875, 18 June 1880 & 18 June 1885.

467 *The Times*, 20 June 1887, 26 February & 28 October 1891.

468 *Liverpool Mercury*, 3 June 1867; *Nottinghamshire Guardian*, 22 June 1877.

469 *The Times*, 26 April 1853; *Derby Mercury*, 13 June 1855; *Essex Standard*, 5 May 1857.

470 *Daily News*, 19 June 1867; *The Standard*, 17 June 1870; *The Times*, 20 April 1872. Wellington's friend, Alava, had also been at Trafalgar, albeit on the 'wrong' side!

471 *Birmingham Daily News*, 20 June 1870; *Sheffield and Rotherham Independent*, 19 June 1872; *Leicester Chronicle*, 22 June 1872; *Lancaster Gazette*, 28 June 1873; *Preston Guardian*, 21 June 1879.

472 *The Times*, 15 September 1871 & 15 June 1883, 17 June 1933; *Dundee Courier*, 17 July 1874; *Pall Mall Gazette*, 24 June 1889.

473 *The Times*, 19 June 1880, 14 December 1885 & 6 June 1889.

474 *The Sphere*, 5 January 1901. There are also unsubstantiated claims that Robert Lyons, who died aged 103 in November 1902, was at Waterloo. See *Salford City Reporter*, 22 November 1902. I am grateful to David and Janet Bromley for answering queries on this matter.

475 *The Times*, 18 January 1872 & 11 September 1884.

476 *The Times*, 25 May 1869.

477 P. Usherwood, 'Lady Butler', *ODNB*, IX, pp. 131–2.

478 *The Times*, 17 June 1882, 6 December 1887, 24 March 1888, 25 December 1889 & 27 August 1890.

479 *The Times*, 28 August 1890; Uffindell & Corum, *Fields of Glory*, pp. 261–7.

480 Hugo, *Les Misérables*, pp. 296–7, 316; Semmel, 'Reading the Tangible Past', p. 27.

481 Hugo, *Les Misérables*, pp. 281–2, 316; *Birmingham Daily Post*, 28 June 1870.

482 *Birmingham Daily Post*, 28 June 1870; *The Times*, 16 September 1869; C. Tomalin, *Thomas Hardy*, pp. 158–9. Cotton's family finally sold the hotel and dispersed his incomparable collection at auction in 1909.

483 Fraser, pp. 247–78.

484 Fraser, pp. 250–4; *The Times*, 21 June 1973.

485 *The Times*, 6 December 1881 & 19 June 1890. The Anglo-German Agreements, the chief parts of which involved Britain surrendering Heligoland in exchange for a free hand in Zanzibar, were formally signed on 1 July.

486 *The Times*, 6 December 1881, 12 January 1900 & 19 June 1906; *North-Eastern Daily Gazette*, 18 June 1900.

487 *The Times*, 30 December 1854 & 6 July 1865; Ramsden, *Don't Mention the War*, chapters 1–2.

488 *The Times*, 7 August 1889, 19 June 1890 & 19 June 1895.

489 Sir H. Maxwell, *The Life of Wellington*, II, p. 90; J. Wellesley, *Wellington*, pp. 167–74; Fraser, p. 156.

490 *The Times*, 28 April 1860, 5 & 7 November 1862, 27 June 1865.

491 Hugo, *Les Misérables*, pp. 279–324; Uffindell & Corum, *Fields of Glory*, pp. 194–6.

492 Hugo, *Les Misérables*, pp. 280, 297–8, 302, 311–3.

493 Hugo, *Les Misérables*, especially pp. 286–8, 306, 313–5.

494 Gronow, *Reminiscences*, p. 181; *The Times*, 6 August 1862.

495 M. Gleig (ed.), *Reminiscences of the First Duke of Wellington*, pp. 25–7; Gleig, *Life of Wellington*, second edition, pp. v–vii; third edition, p. viii.

496 Gleig, *Life of Wellington*, second edition, pp. 318–21.

497 M. Foot, 'Sir James Shaw Kennedy', *ODNB*, XXXI, pp. 249–51; J. Shaw Kennedy, *Notes on the Battle of Waterloo*, pp. 152–3, 168–79.

498 J. Falkner, 'Charles Cornwallis Chesney', *ODNB*, XI, p. 325; C. Chesney, *Waterloo Lectures*, pp. v–vi, 3–4, 16, 136–7, 165–7, 209–14; *Bradford Observer*, 10 December 1868.

499 H. Siborne, *Waterloo Letters*, p. xiii.

500 Fraser, pp. 36–7, 202, 275–8, 344.

501 C. Hibbert, 'Charles Cavendish Fulke Greville', XXIII, *ODNB*, pp. 780–2; Arbuthnot, I, pp. 300–1; Greville, *Memoirs 1837–1852*, II, pp. 192–4, 223.

502 Greville, *Memoirs 1818–1830*, I, pp. 39–40; *Memoirs 1830–1837*, II, p. 305; *Memoirs 1837–1852*, I, pp. 135–7.

503 W. Thomas, 'John Wilson Croker', *ODNB*, XIV, pp. 273–8; Croker, III, pp. 270–9; Gleig, *Reminiscences*, pp. 219–21; Raikes, *Journal*, III, p. 43.

504 Croker, I, pp. 337 note, 353–4; II, p. 233; III, pp. 280–1; *The Times*, 5 October 1886.

505 H. Matthew, 'Philip Henry Stanhope', *ODNB*, LII, pp. 149–51; Stanhope, p. v.

506 Stanhope, pp. 70–1, 245.

507 H. Matthew, 'Francis Egerton, first Earl of Ellesmere', *ODNB*, pp. 993–4. He was known as Lord Francis Leveson-Gower until 1833.

508 Ellesmere, pp. 81 note, 104, 106.

509 W. Thomas, 'Thomas Creevey', *ODNB*, XIV, pp. 130–1; *Hampshire Advertiser*, 15 September 1832; Creevey, II, p. 123–4 & chapter 10, especially p. 236.

510 Maxwell, *Life of Wellington*, I, pp. viii–xii; II, chapter 3, especially pp. 88, 91–3.

511 C. Ropes, *The Campaign of Waterloo*, p. iii and chapter 17, especially pp. 343–7.

512 Ropes, *Campaign of Waterloo*, chapter 7.

513 G. Wolseley, *The Decline and Fall of Napoleon*, pp. 135–8, 153–5, 182.

514 Roberts, *Rise of Wellington*, especially pp. 179, 186,188.

515 R. Weigall (ed.), *Correspondence of Lady Burghersh with the Duke of Wellington*, pp. iii–iv, 211–4. Lady Burghersh was daughter of Wellington's brother William.

516 Gleig, *Reminiscences*, preface, p. 343, note and book 3.

517 *The Times*, 21 September 1852, 31 December 1900 & 31 December 1903; R. Aldington, *Wellington*, pp. 1–3.

518 A. Lambert, *Nelson*, chapters 16–17; *The Times*, 29 March & 9 May 1884, 20 August 1885.

519 *The Times*, 14 May 1904.

520 Fraser, pp. 27–9; C. Parker, *Sir Robert Peel*, II, p. 9; Maxwell, *Life of Wellington*, I, p. xi.

521 *The Times*, 13 May 1897.

522 *The Times*, 2 & 18 August 1900, 21 February 1901.

7. Battling into Posterity: Wellington and Waterloo 1901–2015

523 *The Times*, 21 & 23 December 1903.

524 *The Times*, 28 December 1903.

525 H. Houssaye, *Waterloo*, pp. 271–94.

526 Houssaye, *Waterloo*, p. 432, note 33 & p. 433, notes 40 & 41.

527 *The Times*, 24 May 1909.

528 *The Times*, 12 January 1923.

529 *The Times*, 15 January 1906 & 17 June 1915; A. Barbero, *The Battle*, p. 423.

530 *PD*, 5th series, XLII, 22 October 1912, cols. 1,898–1,899.

531 *The Times*, 8 November 1911, 26 January 1912, 19 December 1913 & 23 April 1924.

532 *The Times*, 8 July 1911, 14 May 1912 & 19 June 1914.

533 *The Times*, 21 March, 28 May & 19 June 1914, 26 February 1937.

534 *The Times*, 17, 21 & 26 June 1915.

535 *The Times*, 19 June 1915.

536 *The Times*, 18 June 1815.

537 M. Gilbert, *First World War*, p. 33; G. Sheffield & J. Bourne (eds.), *Douglas Haig. War Diaries and Letters 1914–1918*, p. 59, entry for 19 August 1914.

538 *The Times*, 5 September 1914, 11 & 20 January 1915, 19 June 1933, 25 March 2004.

539 *The Times*, 1 June & 23 November 1915, 9 August 1918; J. Wellesley, *Wellington*, p. 140; Anglesey, *One Leg*, p. 154.

540 *The Times*, 18 June 1815, 10 November 1916 & 9 August 1918.

541 *The Times*, 20 & 26 November 1918, 18 June 1920.

542 *The Times*, 18 May 1921; P. Parker, *The Last Veteran, passim*.

543 *Cambridge Modern History*, IX, pp. 616–45; C. Oman, *Wellington's Army 1809–1814*, chapter 3, especially p. 43; A. Becke, *Napoleon and Waterloo* (1939 edition), p. 235.

544 C. Tomalin, *Thomas Hardy*, pp. 174, 267.

545 Tomalin, *Hardy*, pp. 281–94.

546 J. Fortescue, *The Campaign of Waterloo*, pp. 133–5, 189–90, 203, 209, 212.

547 Shelley, I, pp. 83ff, 102, 171.

548 Arbuthnot, I, pp. xv–xvi.

549 J. & B. Hammond, *The Village Labourer*, p. 302.

550 G. Kitson Clark, *Peel and the Conservative Party*, pp. 255–6; P. Guedalla, *The Duke*, pp. vii–xv.

551 *The Times*, 23 April & 19 June 1924, 27 May 1925.

552 *The Times*, 23 June 1927, 13 February 1930, 19 June 1934 & 2 January 1936.

553 *The Times*, 2 June 1874, 4 April 1910 & 26 August 1936; http://www.waterloo200.org/the-most-illustrious-grey-ensign-charles-ewart-2/#more-889, accessed 26 April 2013. The Eagle was presented to the Royal Scots Greys on Waterloo Day 1956 and is now in Edinburgh Castle.

554 *The Times*, 7 December 1923, 28 March & 27 June 1934; *PD*, 5th series, LXXXIII, 3 March 1934, cols. 777–824.

555 *The Times*, 9 July 1913, 21 February 1922 & 7 May 1923.

556 *The Times*, 29 January 1923, 18 June 1926, 19 March & 7 October 1929, 17 November & 1 December 1934.

557 *The Times*, 13 April 1926.

558 *The Times*, 1 March & 5 September 1930, 23 June 1937.

559 *The Times*, 20 July 1923, 26 February & 12 March 1937.

560 Uffindell & Corum, *Fields of Glory*, p. 33; Wellesley, *Wellington*, pp. 136–41. Proof too, of the twentieth-century's democratisation of death is that his grave is like any other amongst the 1,740 in Salerno War Cemetery.

561 *The Times*, 28 March & 1 October 1940, 16 August 1943; N. Ferguson, *The Ascent of Money*, pp. 78–85.

562 G. M. Trevelyan, *English Social History*, p. 586 note; D. Cannadine, *G. M. Trevelyan*, pp. 169–74.

563 A. Roberts, *Eminent Churchillians*, p. 317. The Duke's name was also appropriated for the Vickers Wellesley, a light bomber, and the company's better known Wellington bomber, which saw service throughout the war.

564 *Nottingham Evening Post*, 16 June & 1 November 1944.

565 B. Montgomery, *The Memoirs of Field-Marshal Montgomery*, pp. 352–3; *The Times*, 14 June 1945. The sword is now at Apsley House.

566 *The Times*, 17 June 1955; Chad, *Conversations*, pp. 3–5; Wellesley, *Wellington*, passim.

567 *Brighton Patriot*, 11 August 1835; Arbuthnot, I, pp. ix–xvi, 140–3.

568 W. Churchill, *A History of the English-Speaking Peoples*, III, pp. 304–8.

569 Foster, 'Thoughts on Wellington's Passing', pp. 319–20; *The Times*, 16 June & 24 September 1964; 20 February, 21 April, 7 May, 18 & 19 June 1965.

570 *PD*, 5th series, CCLXVII, 15 June 1965, cols. 3–4; *The Times*, 21 & 22 May, 26 June 1965, 8 May 1984.

571 E. Longford, *Wellington*, p. 1; R. Gaunt, 'Wellington, Peel and the Conservative Party' in Woolgar (ed.), *Wellington Studies V*, p. 285, note 52.

572 Longford, *Wellington*, pp. 1–9; *The Times*, 19 & 26 June 1975.

573 *The Times*, 14, 18 & 21 June 1973, 9 June 1990.

574 *The Times*, 9 June 1990; C. Moffett, 'Cleaning up the Battlefield', *Waterloo Journal*, XI, December 1989, pp. 22–4.

575 *The Times*, 13 June 1988, 9, 15 & 18 June 1990.

576 *The Times*, 22 January, 18 June, 2 July, 1 September 1990, 16 July 1991; M. Balen, *A Model Victory*, chapter 15. In 1990 one could, as Siborne intended, wander around the entire model. Today, the visitor can stand only behind the Anglo-Allied line, the Prussians barely visible. Wellington might even have approved!

577 C. Woolgar, *Wellington, His Papers and the Nineteenth-Century Revolution in Communication*, passim.

578 C. Woolgar, *Wellington*, p. 34; Gash (ed.), *Wellington*, essays by N. Thompson, G. Finlayson, F. C. Mather & R. Foster.

579 N. Gash, 'Arthur Wellesley, first Duke of Wellington', *ODNB*, LVIII, pp. 1–29, especially pp. 26–7. Gash usefully summarised his earlier position in D. Southgate (ed.), *The Conservative Leadership 1832–1932*, pp. 35–57. For the recent perspective see R. Gaunt, 'Wellington, Peel and the Conservative Party', especially p. 282, note 7.

580 C. Esdaile, *Napoleon's Wars*, pp. 556–9. Amongst others see S. David, *All the King's Men*, chapter 21 & H. Davies, *Wellington's Wars*, chapter 9.

581 *The Times*, 20 & 25 March 2004, 29 October 2005. Hofschröer summarises his case in *Wellington's Smallest Victory*, pp. 141–7. The case for Wellington's integrity is put by J. Hussey, 'Towards a Better Chronology for the Waterloo Campaign', *War in History*, VII, 2000, pp. 463–80.

582 *The Times*, 5 June 1970, 28 September 1984, 31 July 1986, 11 April 2013; BBC 2, *Whitehall*, first broadcast 9 September 2011. Lady Thatcher toned down her comments for her memoirs. See M. Thatcher, *The Downing Street Years*, p. 24.

583 *The Times*, 18 February 1988.

584 J. Cooper, *Great Britons*, p. 8; http://www.nam.ac.uk/exhibitions/online-exhibitions/britains-greatest-battles, accessed 1 May 2013.

585 *The Times*, 21 June 2004.

586 *The Times*, 21 June 1973.

587 *The Spectator*, 23 March 1996; *The Times*, 19 October 1996; Roberts, *Napoleon and Wellington*, p. 298; Roberts, *Waterloo*, pp. 121–2.

588 *The Times*, 18 June 2013; https://en.wikipedia.org/wiki/Trafalgar_200, accessed 1
     May 2013; *The Times*, 8 December 2012. In 2011 Hougoumont's chapel had 'been
     painted a creamy white and now looks like an ice-cream kiosk [...] old signatures
     and smoke stains had been obliterated and the Christ figure varnished'. (Private
     information.) Even more depressing, the Christ figure was stolen in November 2011
     and has not been recovered.
589 I. Fletcher, 'Kings, Car Parks and Silent Members', *Waterloo Journal*, XXXV, Spring
     2013, pp. 4–5; letter from B. Cackett to the author, 11 October 2012; *The Times*, 27
     April 2013.
590 http://www.guardian.co.uk/politics/2013/jun/26/osborne-waterloo-donation-
     restoration-anniversary, accessed 8 July 2013; *Daily Telegraph*, 28 June 2013.
591 http://www.waterloo200.org/, accessed 1 May 2013; Sir E. Webb-Carter, 'Waterloo
     200', *Waterloo Journal*, XXXIV, Summer 2012, pp. 34–5.
592 *The Times*, 19 June 1995.
593 G. Cooper, 'Past and Present', *Waterloo Journal*, XXII, September 2000, pp. 14–22;
     The Times, 11 May 2004 & 29 June 2013. A national memorial at Quatre Bras was
     formally dedicated in June 2002.
594 *Hull Packet*, 24 November 1829; *The Times*, 22 December 1983, 19 January 2000;
     Cooper, 'Past and Present', p. 15; Shelley, I, p. 102.

Index

Alava, Gen Miguel 73, 77, 81, 93, 104, 121
Albemarle, George Keppel, 6th earl of 175
Albert, Prince Consort 159, 162, 163, 165, 167, 172
Aldington, Richard 191, 210
Alison, Sir Archibald 141, 143, 146-7
Almeida 36, 38
Ansdell, Richard 155, 206
Apsley House 15, 31, 101, 118-19, 130-1, 133, 158, 160-1, 188, 198-9, 212, 215, 221
Arbuthnot, Charles 146
Arbuthnot, Harriet 20, 103, 120-2, 126, 129, 185, 204, 211, 217
Arnold, Matthew 179
Assaye 29-30, 33, 186, 211
Astley's circus 38-9, 82, 113, 168, 170, 177, 218
Austen, Jane 98
Badajoz 34-5, 38-9, 44
Barlow, Capt John 59, 69, 78, 96
Bathurst, Henry, 3rd Earl 43-4, 75, 80, 118
Becke, A. F. 202
Bellairs, Rev Henry 176
Bissing, Gen Moritz von 198
Blücher, Marshal Prince Gebhard von 17-18, 47-8, 50-51, 53-6, 67-8, 71, 75-79, 81-2, 108, 120-2, 128, 130, 141, 144-6, 161, 168, 172, 183, 187-9, 194, 198, 201-3, 212
Bonaparte, Jérôme 61, 63
Bonaparte, Napoleon, 14, 18, 23, 30-1, 36, 40-42, 44-6, 47-48, 50-57, 60-61, 63-4, 67-8, 70-1, 72, 74-5, 81-83, 86, 89, 92-95, 107, 120-4, 140-1, 144, 146-8, 156, 165, 167, 169, 173-4, 180-5, 187, 189-90, 195-6, 199, 202, 205, 207, 209-10, 214-15, 217-8, 220, 223
Bowles, Captain 55, 204
Brontë, Charlotte 123, 148
Brontë, Patrick 97, 123
Brougham, Henry 105, 171-2
Brunswick, Friedrich Wilhelm, Duke of 54, 105, 108
Brussels 13, 23, 41, 48, 50-53, 55-57, 60, 72, 83-4, 88-90, 148-9, 177-9, 188, 198, 205, 218
Bryant, Sir Arthur 209
Bülow, Count Friedrich Wilhelm von 67-8, 75-6, 80, 91
Burdett, Sir Francis, 38-40
Burghersh, Priscilla, Lady 74, 190
Bussaco 36-38
Butler, Lady Elizabeth 177, 198
Byron, George Gordon, 6th Baron 87-89, 104, 106, 109, 112, 149, 179
Cambridge, Duke of 178, 181
Cambronne, Gen Pierre 66, 149, 182
Canning, Charles Fox 70
Canning, George 126-7
Cantillon, André 102, 140
Castlereagh, Robert Stewart, Viscount 31, 43-44, 98-9, 104, 127
Chad, G.W. 120-1, 139, 210
Chandler, D.G. 215
Chartism 110, 139, 158, 161, 165
Cheltenham 101, 119
Chesney, Col Charles 184
Chester 114, 119
Children, J.G. 110
Churchill, W.S. 196, 209, 211-12, 216, 223
Clausewitz, Karl von 146
Cobbett, William 31, 33-34, 127, 129
Cobden, Richard 155-6, 161, 171
Colborne, Sir John 66, 76, 169
Conan Doyle, Sir Arthur 177, 207

Cook, Thomas 179

Cooper, Maj Graeme 222

Cooper, John 170-1, 173, 176

Cooper, Sidney 172

Cooper, Thomas 165

Colchester 72, 83

Coleridge, J.T. 92

Coleridge, S.T. 108

Copenhagen (W's horse) 135, 153, 199, 211

Corn Laws 105, 126, 161-2

Cotton, Sgt-Maj Edward 57, 59, 152-3, 178-9.

Creevey, Thomas 36, 70, 106-7, 131, 188-9, 204

Crimean War 168-171, 174, 181, 198

Croker, J.W. 20, 69, 79, 91-93, 117, 186-7, 190, 204

Cruttwell, C.R. 204

d'Erlon, John-Baptiste Drouet, Comte 54, 57, 61-63, 67, 81, 121

De Lancey, Lady Magdalene 148, 184

De Lancey, Col Sir William 43, 52, 70, 76, 177-8

Decoster, Jean 86, 93-4, 107

Derby, Edward Stanley, 14th Earl 161, 191

Dickens, Charles 148, 150, 164-5, 167

Disraeli, Benjamin 141, 166, 182, 191

Duhesme, Count Philippe 68

Dumoulin, Francois 197-8

Edinburgh 19, 83, 112, 131, 134, 155, 160, 201, 206

Egerton, Lord Francis (later 1st Earl of Ellesmere) 20, 146-7, 161, 166, 187-8

Evere 177-8, 205, 212

Ewart, Sgt Charles 62, 154, 205

Flint, Sir Charles 70, 79, 191

Fortescue, Sir John 12, 203

Foy, Gen Maximilien 122, 124

Fraser, Sgt Ralph 145

Fraser, Sir James 179

Fraser, Sir William 15, 21-2, 103, 148-9, 169-70, 179-80, 184-5, 192

Frasnes 53, 189

French, Sir John 198, 200

Gash, Norman 215-16

Gawler, George 135

Genappe 72, 77, 79, 144, 214

George IV 105, 107, 110, 118, 127-9

Glasgow, 113, 135, 160, 162, 166, 168

Gleig, Rev G. R. 143-4, 147-8, 171, 183, 185-6, 190

Gneisenau, Gen August von 54-5, 78, 80, 94, 120, 203

Gordon, Col Sir Alexander 43, 69, 74, 79, 85, 121, 137, 140, 177-8, 208

Gourgaud, Gen Gaspard 54, 94-95, 122, 125

Graham, Cpl James 61, 91

Graham, Sir James 166

Greenwood, Arthur 205-6

Greville, Lady Charlotte 121

Greville, Charles 20, 120-1, 129-30, 134, 136, 162, 185-8

Grey, Charles, 2nd Earl 37, 42, 45, 130-1, 136, 140

Grey, Sir Edward 196

Gronow, Rees 13, 24, 183

Grouchy, Marshal Emmanuel 55, 67-68, 94, 121-2, 182-3, 189

Guedalla, Philip 12, 20, 204-5

Gurwood, Col John 20, 138-40, 144-6, 154, 215

Hal 51, 56-7, 121, 184, 203

Halkett, Maj-Gen Sir Colin 64

Halkett, Lt-Gen Hew 149

Hardinge, Sir Henry 55, 128, 135, 158, 184, 187

Hardy, Thomas 179, 202-3

Hay, Lord James 54, 113, 178, 218

Haydon, B.R. 62, 151-2

Henty, G.A. 177

Hewett, William, 175

Heyer, Georgette 203

Hill, Gen Rowland, 1st Viscount 43, 57, 60

Hillingford, R. A. 177

Hofschröer, Peter 216-217

Holman Hunt, William 150

Holmes, Richard 219, 220

Hopwood, John 177

Hougoumont 13, 59-61, 63, 66-67, 75-76, 81, 85, 88, 91, 96, 107, 118, 121, 145, 150-1, 153, 178-80, 188, 198, 208, 210, 220, 222

Houssaye, Henry 195-6

Hugo, Victor 13, 59, 174, 178-9, 182-4, 197, 203

Hume, Dr John 70, 74, 128

Imperial Guard 57, 63-4, 66, 68, 76, 81, 91, 93-4, 124, 141-3, 149

India 24, 27-31, 35, 39, 139, 159-60, 211

Ipswich 114, 116

Jones, Ann ('Waterloo Tom') 117-8

Junot, Gen John-Andoche 31, 33

Kincaid, Capt John 123

Kingsley, Rev W.T. 199

La Belle Alliance 47, 57, 64, 66, 71, 78-80, 84, 108, 144, 172, 187, 197, 208, 214

La Haye Sainte 59, 63-4, 67, 69, 75, 84-5, 92, 107-8, 110, 121, 144, 179-80, 184

Landseer, Sir Edwin 151, 180

Lawrence, Sir Thomas 22, 42, 124

Le Caillou 60, 180, 214

Leeke, Ensign William 205

Lees, John 105

Ligny 54-55, 67, 76, 120, 144, 188-89, 195

Lion's Mound 110-11, 151-2, 172, 179, 197, 200, 208, 210, 213-14, 222

Liverpool 38-39, 85, 114,123, 152, 156, 175

Liverpool, Robert Banks Jenkinson, 2nd Earl of 38, 43-4, 73, 104, 106, 126

Lobau, Gen Jean, Comte de 57, 67-8, 94

London 27, 35, 39, 40, 42, 45, 62, 72, 74, 82, 97, 98, 99, 101, 103, 106, 112-5, 117, 119, 125, 131-2, 153, 156, 157, 160, 161, 169, 176, 177, 191, 196, 206, 209, 212, 220

Londonderry, 3rd Marquis of (Charles Stewart) 11, 127
Longford, Elizabeth, Countess of 213, 216, 218
Lovett, William 110
Macaulay, T.B. 123, 204-5, 207, 209
Macdonell, Col James 61, 75, 145
Mackworth, Capt Digby 64-66
Maclise, Daniel 172, 201
Macmillan, J. 219
Maitland, Maj-Gen Peregrine 57, 64, 113, 186
Manchester 105, 161, 168, 171, 176, 196
Marlborough, John Churchill, Duke of 37, 73, 212
Marmont, Marshal Auguste 39, 146
Marochetti, Carlo 160
Masséna, André 36-38
Maxwell, Sir Herbert 188-189, 192
Mawell, William Hamilton 141
Mercer, Capt Cavalié 15, 86, 170, 184, 199
Middleditch, William 157
Moon, Edward 197-8
Montgomery, FM, later Viscount B.L. 210
Mornington, Anne, Countess of 23-26, 70-71
Mornington, Garret, 1st Earl of 24, 26
Morrison, Herbert 206, 214
Müffling, Baron Carl von 52, 68, 78, 93
Nelson, Admiral Horatio 11, 31, 34, 99, 161, 166-7, 172, 177, 186, 191, 217
Ney, Marshal Michel 52-55, 63-4, 67, 82, 94, 101
Mont St Jean 11, 23-4, 36, 56-57, 61, 67-8, 80, 85, 87-8, 94, 112, 121, 130, 151-2, 179, 183, 204-5, 208, 210, 212, 222
Murray, Sir George 128
Murray, John 87, 143, 150, 200
Napier, Sir William 22, 138
Napoleon III 163, 173, 179
O'Connell, Daniel 128
O'Meara, Dr Barry 122-23
Oman, Sir Charles 201-2
Orange, Prince William of 50, 52, 83, 110
Osborne, George 221
Oxford 25, 45, 134, 148, 215, 220
Pack, Sir Denis 115
Pakenham, Catherine (later 1st Duchess of Wellington) 26, 30, 213
Palmerston, 3rd Viscount 13, 127, 162-3
Pattison, Frederick Hope 56, 96, 173
Peel, Sir Robert 91, 134-6, 143, 161-2, 187, 191, 205, 216
Peninsular War 11, 20, 24, 30, 31-42, 73, 138, 140, 187, 202, 216
Percy, Maj Hon Henry 73-4, 221
Peterloo 105-6
Pickersgill, Henry 21-22
Picton, Lt-Gen Sir Thomas 43, 53, 57, 61-2, 80-1, 96-7, 108, 113

Plancenoit 57, 67-8, 76, 108, 143
Poole, Ruscombe 135
Ponsonby, Lt-Col Frederick 154
Ponsonby of Shulbrede 206-7
Ponsonby, Maj-Gen Sir William 43, 62, 74, 80, 97, 108, 113
Preston 157, 165, 170-1, 173, 176
Prussians 16-17, 22, 24, 48, 51-6, 60, 67-71, 75-81, 89-96, 108, 120-4, 130-1, 142-4, 149, 151, 159, 168, 172, 181, 183-4, 189, 194-5, 199-204, 216-17
Quatre Bras 13, 52-6, 62, 69, 76, 88, 105, 113, 120, 144, 177-8, 180, 189, 195, 200, 218
Reeve, Henry 166
Richmond, Charles Lennox, 4th Duke of, 204
Richmond, Charles Gordon-Lennox, 5th Duke of 157
Richmond, Charlotte Duchess of 41, 52, 54, 88, 116-17, 145, 149
Roberts, Andrew 220
Roberts, Frederick, 1st Earl 170, 180, 189-191, 198, 203
Ropes, J.C. 189
Rossetti, D.G. 150, 180
Rowan, Sir Charles 116-117
Rudge, Rev 84, 96
Ruskin, John 150
St Helena 94-5, 122, 156
Saintine, Monsieur 108, 111, 223
Salamanca 39-40, 44-5, 113, 115
Scott, G.E. 205
Scott, Giles Gilbert, 206
Scott, John, 83
Scott, Sir Walter 34, 78, 84, 86-7, 89-90, 107, 110, 124, 155, 175
Scots Greys 15, 62, 114, 131, 155, 177, 200
Seringapatam 27
Shaw, Cpl John 62-63, 82, 148, 175
Shaw Kennedy, James, 183-184
Siborne, Maj-Gen Herbert 184
Siborne, Capt William, 16, 141-4, 146-7, 149, 153, 155, 168, 170, 177, 184, 214, 217, 220
Sinclair, Sir John, 59, 92-3
Slade, Sir John 11
Soignes, Forest of, 23, 56-7, 90, 150
Somerset, Lord Fitzroy 43, 64, 79, 95, 140, 142, 170, 187
Soult, Marshal Nicolas 34, 41, 63, 138
Southey, Robert 12, 20, 23, 78-9, 87-89, 91-92, 200-201
Stanhope, Philip Henry, 5th Earl 20, 22, 186-7, 190, 217
Stratfield Saye 20-1, 101, 138, 143, 145, 153, 155, 170-1, 182, 199
Steell, Sir John 160
Stuart, Sir Charles 56, 140

Sutherland, David 117
Sutton, Mr 72, 83
Talavera, 34-5, 89
Tennyson, Alfred, Lord 166-7, 169
Thackeray, William Makepeace 16, 148-51, 156-8, 201
Thatcher, Baroness 217-18
Thiers, Adolphe 20, 182-3
Thompson, James 116, 153
Thorp, George 116
Tipu Sultan 27, 150
Trevelyan G.M. 209, 219
Uxbridge, Henry William Paget, 2nd Earl of, later 1st Marquis of Anglesey 25, 55, 57, 69, 75-6, 80, 85, 95, 107, 116, 129, 137, 147, 151, 157, 159, 163, 167, 174, 179, 186, 200
Vauxhall 45, 113, 156, 218
Victoria, Queen 138, 160-1, 163, 165, 169, 181, 194
Vitoria, 40-1, 43, 45, 52, 113, 115, 125, 218
Vivian, Richard, later Sir Hussey & 1st Baron 17, 39, 57, 64, 178
Waithman, Robert 35, 112
Walmer 138, 144, 164, 187, 191
Walpole, Spencer 166
Waterloo
    Anniversaries of 114, 118, 156, 172-4, 177-8, 182-4, 195-200, 205, 209, 212-15, 220-222
    Banquet 15, 117-18, 126, 131, 158-60
    Battle of, 14, 18, 47, 61-71, 89, 91-94, 129, 141, 209
    Waterloo Bridge, 100, 206, 220
    Cup 156
    Day 15, 17, 97, 104, 113-8, 126, 128, 131, 134-5, 143, 146, 151, 153, 155-158, 160, 168-9, 174-5, 180-1, 187, 192, 205, 207, 215, 219, 221
    Despatch 17, 74-77, 92-93, 119, 121, 124, 188-189, 194, 215, 221
    Empire & 180-1, 192
    Fund 90, 97, 118
    Panoramas & 113-4, 156, 176, 177, 197-198, 210
    St Joseph's Church 85, 107, 151, 178
    Significance of 12-15, 73, 96-7, 109, 111-112, 119, 125-6, 135, 150, 156-7, 173-4, 185, 192, 194-6, 208, 219-222
    Visitors to 78, 83-87, 107-111, 150-1, 178-80, 207-8, 222-3
    Veterans 15-16, 113, 116-18, 124, 129, 142, 149, 153-8, 169-177
WWI & 198-201
WWII & 208-210
Waterlooville 98
Wavre 55-56, 67-69

Webster, Lady Frances 56, 57, 69, 10′
Wellesley, Lady Anne 25
Wellesley, Gerald 25
Wellesley, Henry, later Baron Cowley
Wellesley, Richard Colley, later Marqui 29-31, 34-35, 39, 43, 71, 101, 211
Wellesley, Lord Richard 200
Wellesley, William, later Baron Maryborou 25, 31
Wellington, 1st Duke, Arthur Wellesley
    early life & siblings 24-6;
    in India 27-31;
    Peninsular War & 31-42;
    Waterloo campaign & 48-71;
    Waterloo Despatch & 74-77;
    names Waterloo 78-79;
    in France 1815-1818, 102;
    post-Waterloo unrest & 104-6;
    prime minister 127-130;
    1832 Reform Bill & 130-2;
    1830s Tory revival & 133-137;
    publication of despatches & 138-140;
    last years 161-163;
    death & funeral 164-168;
    Victorian lives & memoirs of 181-192;
    early twentieth assessments of 203-5;
    post 1945 assessments of 209-213, 215-17;
    contemporary assessments of 217-219, 223;
    statues of 19, 99, 100, 113, 129, 135, 160-1, 162, 191, 199;
    on Waterloo 17, 21-22, 81, 90-94, 119-122, 144-147
2nd Duke, Arthur Richard 178, 182
3rd Duke, Henry 190
4th Duke, Arthur 198, 199, 200, 205
6th Duke, Henry 208
7th Duke, Gerald 210-11, 212
8th Duke, Arthur 213, 215, 221
Wellington College 8, 171-2, 180, 199
'Wellington's Elm' 60, 85, 109-110, 121
Wilhelm I of Germany 181
Wilhelm II of Germany 18, 181, 194, 195, 201
Wilkie, Sir David 85, 124-5
William I, King of Netherlands 83, 110, 124
William IV (previously Duke of Clarence) 12, 39, 113, 125, 130, 134, 158
Winchester 104, 114, 204
Wolseley, Garnet, 1st Viscount 189-90
Wordsworth, Dorothy, 96
Wordsworth, William 87-8, 99, 108-9, 152
Wynn, Charles Williams 98, 158, 201
York, Duke of 26-7, 97-8, 100, 115, 126
York 117, 127, 155
Ziethen, Lt-Gen Hans 51, 67-8, 80, 95